I.M. PEI

I.M. PEI

Michael Cannell

MANDARIN OF MODERNISM

Carol Southern Books
New York

For Elisabeth

Text copyright © 1995 by Michael Cannell

Published by Carol Southern Books, a division of Clarkson N. Potter, Inc., Publishers, 201 East 50th Street, New York, New York 10022. Member of the Crown Publishing Group.

Random House, Inc. New York, Toronto, London, Sydney, Auckland

Manufactured in U.S.A.

Design by Susan Carabetta

Library of Congress Cataloging-in-Publication Data

Cannell, Michael T.
  I. M. Pei : mandarin of modernism / by Michael T. Cannell.—1st ed.
    p.   cm.
  Includes index.
    1. Pei, I. M., 1917–   . 2. Chinese-American architects—
Biography.   I. Title.
NA737.P365C36   1995
720′.92—dc20
  [B]   95-13863
                                                          CIP

ISBN 0-517-79972-3

10   9   8   7   6   5   4   3   2   1

First Edition

CONTENTS

ACKNOWLEDGMENTS

Confidentiality prevents me from disclosing some of the three hundred sources contacted in the course of my research. Let me single out a few who were especially helpful: John Price Bell, Fred Fang, Martin Filler, Harold Fredenburgh, Preston Moore and Calvin Tsao. I'm most grateful, as well, to the late William Walton, who answered endless questions and guided me to other valuable sources. He also gave me access to his papers (now housed at the Kennedy Library) and notes written by Jacqueline Onassis.

I am especially grateful to those members of the Pei family who contributed their thoughts and remembrances: Y.K. Pei, Denise Sze, T'ing Pei, Didi Pei, Sandi Pei, Liane Pei Kracklauer and, most of all, Tsuyuan Pei.

A number of people within Pei Cobb Freed & Partners were good enough to speak with me: Henry Cobb, James Freed, Kellogg Wong, Young Bum Lee, Charles Young and Ian Bader. Dale Nagler contributed invaluable guidance, advice and encouragement. Pei's former partner, Eason Leonard, kindly received me at his home in California. The Pei firm's director of communications, Janet Adams, helped to provide photographs for our use, and I particularly thank I. M. Pei himself for his cooperation in making these available.

I am deeply indebted to my agent, Angela Miller, for her friendship and advice throughout this book's complicated gestation. I extend heartfelt thanks, as well, to my editor, Carol Southern, for her editorial guidance, good sense and patience. Thanks also to Eliza Scott for escorting the various parts along, and to Jim Walsh for smoothing rough edges.

I must credit Roger Scholl, who initiated the project, and Jane von Mehren, who added her endorsement. I would also like to thank Cynthia Cannell for her support; Peter B. Cannell for applying his incisive pencil; and Carlo and Jennifer Cannell for housing me on Valparaiso Street during the early months of work.

Crucial research would not have been possible without Joe Tatelbaum, an old friend who gave generously of his time and resources on my behalf. My research associate in Shanghai, Professor Dongsong Zhang, contributed immeasurably. I cannot thank him enough.

I would also like to thank Cheryl Regan at the Library of Congress for her unflagging help in acquiring photographs.

In addition, I would like to acknowledge the research assistance provided by the following: the Avery Library at Columbia University, the Bobst Library at New York University, the New York Public Library, the New York Society Library, the San Francisco Public Library, the Rockefeller Archive, the Kennedy Library, the MIT Museum, the Loeb Library at the Harvard Graduate School of Design and the archive at the National Gallery in Washington, D.C. I am especially indebted to Anne Ritchie of the National Gallery for guiding me through the archive's oral histories, clip files and photographs.

PREFACE

I. M. Pei arouses interest wherever he goes. But for all his ingratiating ways and well-publicized friendships with business leaders, artists and heads of state, the private Pei remains elusive. Like the walled homes of his childhood, his inner precinct defies Western understanding. Even his former partners claim no real closeness. The clues to his enigma lie among the Byzantine politics of Shanghai's segregated society and, deeper still, in the rockeries and trickling waters of ancient gardens.

The architectural community harbors its own uncertainties about Pei. He is their most accomplished living figure, and yet the intelligentsia tend to regard him as an establishment architect hampered by corporate reticence. Like McKim, Mead & White, his firm is large, politically adept and socially connected. He is the laureate of the kind of architecture that expresses symbolic power—the modern equivalent of the cathedral and the courthouse. He excels at the mysterious job of turning talk into concrete, and the consistent quality of his execution sets a punishing standard. Said Paul Goldberger of the *New York Times,* "Pei has a fundamentally commercial outlook, but raised to its highest level of achievement." Unlike his perennial rival, Philip Johnson, who promoted the modern style only to denounce it with equal conviction, Pei maintained his faith in modernism. The China of his childhood taught the value of continuity. So, rather than abandon the maligned style,

Pei humanized it by bringing to it an unexpected subtlety, lyricism and beauty.

This, then, is the portrait of an artist. It is a story of architecture and authority, immigration and assimilation, American exuberance and Chinese control, tough-minded pragmatism and the delicate flourish. It is a tale of East and West.

—Michael Cannell

New York City

March 1995

In architecture the pride of man,

his triumph over gravitation,

his will to power, assume a visible form.

Architecture is a sort of oratory of power.

F. W. Nietzsche

Wheresoever you shall go,

go with all your heart.

Confucius

I

THE BATTLE OF
THE PYRAMID

At 8:00 P.M. on May 10, 1981, election officials in Paris announced a shocker: François Mitterrand would be the new president of France. The prevailing expectation, voiced confidently in bistros and cafés, had favored the incumbent, Valéry Giscard d'Estaing, despite Mitterrand's slight edge in the polls. After twenty-three years of conservative rule, France had come to accept Giscard's rightist coalition as an immutable condition. Besides, Mitterrand's failed campaigns of the past burdened him with the bad odor of a perennial loser.

When news of the upset—the dumb, wondrous fact of it—sank in that spring night, a profane street party erupted, the kind of hooting jubilee that accompanies the triumph of underdogs. Celebrants gargled champagne in the tented courtyard off the Socialist Party's Left Bank headquarters. Honking cars strafed the Champs-Elysées. Bands of teenagers waved red flags and shouted, "Giscard on welfare!" A riotous arm-in-arm crowd carrying red roses, the Socialist emblem, and wine bottles massed on the Place de la Bastille, ancient celebration ground of the working class, where thirty thousand revelers sang the "Marseillaise" in a warm spring rain.

Mitterrand also exploited the city's evocative geography to dramatize the biggest political shift in a generation. After his formal investiture in the

◀ **Vindicated: Pei beside the completed pyramid. For a time, it eclipsed the Eiffel Tower as the defining icon of Paris.**

Elysée Palace, he marched unexpectedly through the cobblestoned Latin Quarter, historic haunt of intellectuals and artists, to the Panthéon, where, as all of France watched on TV, he solemnly mounted the steps in the poignant late-afternoon light while the Orchestre de Paris played Beethoven's "Ode to Joy." Television cameras followed as he laid roses on the tombs of Socialist heroes, his footsteps echoing through the crypt. It was a stirring performance.

Mitterrand enacted socialism's long-deferred reforms in a hurry. In what came to be known as "the quiet revolution," the new president shortened the workweek to thirty-five hours, created a fifth week of paid vacation, increased welfare benefits by a quarter, hired thousands of new government workers, raised the minimum wage by a tenth and, most controversial of all, nationalized key industries and thirty-five banks. Mitterrand's budget also nearly doubled expenditures on the arts—a largesse unmatched in modern times—on the theory that a cultural awakening must accompany economic recovery if France was to realize the New Renaissance he envisioned. "The Socialist enterprise," he asserted, "is first of all a cultural project." He sought nothing less, he said, than the artistic ferment that had accompanied the French and Russian revolutions. Defending the plan before the National Assembly, his flamboyant, mop-haired minister of culture, Jack Lang, argued that the *aesthetics* of living were just as important as the *standard* of living. "Our predecessors' economic failure," he told legislators, "was first and foremost a cultural failure."

Mitterrand prepared for his socialist enlightenment by launching his *grands projets*, a building spree unprecedented in modern France. Over the coming decade he presided over the most far-reaching alteration of the Parisian cityscape since Baron Haussmann sliced wide boulevards through the medieval maze. From the beginning, Mitterrand intended to hire the architect I. M. Pei, a Chinese-American of renowned suavity and charm whose East Building of the National Gallery in Washington, D.C., had opened two years earlier to enormous acclaim. Mitterrand had also been impressed by Pei's proposal for an office complex that would have brought order to a Manhattan-like mess of high-rises in the fringe neighborhood of La Défense at the Western end of the five-mile Louvre-Etoile axis. Pei seemed to have won the La Défense job until, at the last moment, it was awarded to a French architect with the right political connections.

In December 1981, Mitterrand received Pei in the Elysée Palace. The figure who entered the president's ornate study was slender and soft-spoken. His face was mottled with age, but despite his sixty-four years he radiated a restless, ticking alertness and boundless enthusiasm.

Pei is known for his ability to converse with anyone on any topic in a voice that still carries traces of China, and his playful, expressive face lights up at the mention of his wide-ranging interests—French and Chinese cuisine, abstract art, gardening, travel and wine. "He comes," according to his partner Eason Leonard, "with a different set of batteries from the rest of us."

Pei dresses impeccably in conservative suits custom-tailored in Hong Kong. One architecture critic has described his wardrobe as "formal, but not so formal that you'd mistake him for a banker. It has just enough flair to let you know he's creative." His elegant presence is enlivened by a prodigious smile and merry eyes that shine perpetually behind owlish round-rimmed glasses. "He's like the greatest maître d' at the greatest restaurant in the world," said the architect Arthur Rosenblatt, who oversaw much of the expansion of New York's Metropolitan Museum of Art.

Pei imparts unshakable self-assurance and an ambassadorial sense of propriety. He knows how to be gracious without being obsequious. When Mitterrand asked if he would be available for a government commission, Pei politely explained that he no longer participated in competitions at this late stage of his career. As La Défense had demonstrated, the decisions were too often political. "Well," Mitterrand replied, "we are flexible."

A few weeks later, at his first presidential press conference, Mitterrand pledged to "restore the Louvre Museum to its intended purpose" by evicting the Finance Ministry from its palatial quarters in the northern arm, the Richelieu Wing, and converting it to galleries under an ambitious renovation of the museum, which he would rebaptize Le Grand Louvre. It was to be the crown jewel of his *grands projets*.

The Louvre's own curators had repeatedly urged just such an overhaul to rescue the museum from disorder. With its dark blond facade sprawling for half a mile above a fringe of sycamore trees, the Louvre still resembled an imposing palace. But inside its ornate walls lay an institution in shameful decay. As it neared its bicentennial, the Louvre had degenerated into the worst of the West's large museums and a disappointing stop on the compulsory tourist itinerary. Incredibly, only two rest rooms were available to the public. Visitors overran the cafeteria. The guards were notoriously disdainful. Mounds of dust had accumulated on moldings and picture frames in dim galleries. "Your lighting is impossible," Jack Lang told the director after attending his first official opening as minister of culture, "and your floors filthy."

Worst of all, the Louvre was confusing. After searching the perimeter for one of the narrow, poorly marked entrances—one curator said the most frequently asked question was "How do we get in?"—most of the 3.7 million annual visitors wandered among its labyrinthine corridors in search of three-star attractions: the Venus de Milo, the Winged Victory of Samothrace and, of course, the Mona Lisa, who smiled at packed crowds through bullet-proof glass. Less prominent treasures required a marathon walk down dingy, unmarked corridors. Even then, weary art pilgrims might find their treasure locked behind a placard listing its hours as *"très irrégulières."* Too often the Louvre defeated its guests instead of inspiring them.

Parisians considered the Louvre a crucial part of their celebrated cityscape, but they rarely ventured inside. Only one-third of all visitors were

French and a mere one in ten were Parisian. Tourists felt obliged to see it, but they didn't linger. The average visitor stayed only an hour and a half, half as long as they lingered at New York's Metropolitan Museum of Art.

The Louvre had also lapsed into the curatorial equivalent of a Third World country. Most modern museums are divided evenly between galleries and hidden support facilities like storage, administration and restoration labs. The Louvre's ratio was so grossly atilt—galleries occupied fully 90 percent of the building—that curators called it "a theater without a backstage." Under these primitive conditions curators on occasion moved paintings by lowering them out of the windows. And they were forced to use splendid upstairs galleries blessed with high ceilings and enormous windows for storage because the basement lacked temperature and humidity controls. These deficiencies left curators with space to show only about one-tenth of their ill-kept riches. "It was in a pitiful state," one backstage visitor remembered. "I saw Greek statues left in corridors with paint dripped on them. The museum couldn't function."

The Louvre was dysfunctional in part because it had begun as a fortress. King Philippe Auguste had built its first incarnation around 1200 to defend the growing city from marauders. Two hundred years later Charles V encircled the Right Bank with a protective wall and converted the obsolete fort into a château with a fairy-tale silhouette of conical roofs and gilded spires. He dined inside with knights and ladies at banquet tables set with crystal goblets beneath tapestries of hunting scenes. It was variously enlarged and embellished by royal inhabitants as they pursued greater comfort. Napoleon III made the last alteration when he added the Richelieu Wing to house his private apartments and the Ministry of Finance. By Mitterrand's era, the Louvre resembled one of those tribes hidden in the Amazon headwaters, a little pocket of life enshrined in the past. Its bowels, including much of the plumbing, had lain untouched for a hundred years.

The kind of monumental renovation Mitterrand had in mind was customarily awarded by public competition. But with his Socialist Party in control of the National Assembly, Mitterrand was essentially an elected king, and he retained the right to name whomever he liked. Besides, the president fancied himself an aesthete in the tradition of Europe's cultured, art-loving rulers. Before he discovered politics at the Sorbonne, his passions had been Virgil, Erik Satie and Igor Stravinsky. He had written ten books and traveled to Florence to research a biography of the Medici prince Lorenzo the Magnificent. He thus felt qualified to dispense with advisory groups and rely on his own aesthetic judgment.

Mitterrand's inclination to hire Pei was seconded by Emile Biasini, a seasoned civil servant and former minister of culture whom Mitterrand had appointed head of a public agency to oversee the Louvre renovation. Throughout a nine-month tour of the world's leading museums, Biasini made a point of asking curators whom they would hire. Pei's name leaped off every tongue. In early 1982 Biasini asked Pei's friend Zao Wou-ki, a Chinese-born painter living in Paris, to introduce him to Pei. During a meeting arranged at the Hôtel Raphaël, Biasini invited Pei to submit his ideas for the Louvre. Pei politely repeated his aversion to competitions.

It was a brazen stipulation. The Louvre, after all, amounted to a lot more than other monumental commissions awarded Pei late in his career. It was a showcase of unparalleled visibility and one of the most coveted plots in the world—exactly the sort of public platform Pei needed to ensure his standing in posterity. "He must have perceived or feared that if there was a competition, and he lost, it would be humiliating," said the French historian Olivier Bernier. "He may also have perceived that Mitterrand was sufficiently anxious to hire him."

Mitterrand *was* eager. So eager, in fact, that he dispatched Biasini to New York to offer Pei the job outright—the only *grand projet* awarded without competition. Pei at first modestly demurred. "When Mitterrand first asked me to do this project I really didn't believe it," Pei said. "It just seemed incredible that he would come to an American to do a project that is as important as any you can find in France. I told the president I considered it a great honor, but I couldn't accept it outright. I asked him if he'd be willing to give me four months, not to think about it—I'd already decided I wanted to do this—but really to see if I could in fact do it."

Pei told no one about the offer, not even his partners. With his wife, Eileen, as his sole confidante, he made three secret excursions to Paris. He stayed at the Hôtel Crillon on the Place de la Concorde, a short jaunt from the Louvre through the Tuileries Gardens, and rambled for days through the museum and its surrounding streets cogitating on the dilemma at hand: how to graft a contemporary design onto a classical landmark. (Pei says he thinks about design in his native Chinese. The vociferous guardians of French culture would have derived little comfort from the image of an American plotting the Louvre's future in Chinese.)

He studied the works of André Le Nôtre, the greatest of French landscape designers, and traversed the Louvre grounds until a satisfactory solution came to mind. "I would not have accepted it if I hadn't studied the problem for months," he said. "I concluded that it had to be done, and that I would be able to do it." On his fourth visit, Pei presented his concept to Mitterrand and Lang. "I had no pyramids in mind yet, but it was obvious that the center of gravity on the new Louvre had to be the Cour Napoléon." Pei was referring to the gravel courtyard enclosed by the museum's enormous U-shaped wings. When the Ministry of Finance vacated the Richelieu Wing, the Cour Napoléon would become the museum's center point. Pei proposed to put a new entrance in the middle of the courtyard leading to an underground reception hall—if Mitterrand would allow it. *"Très bien,"* Mitterrand said. *"Très bien."*

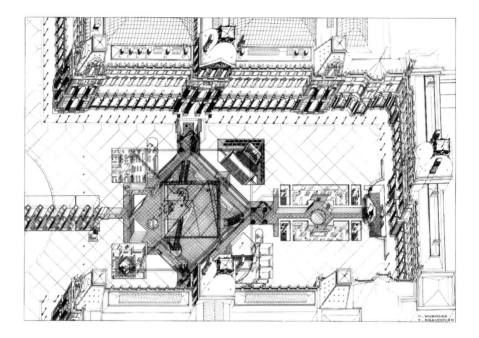

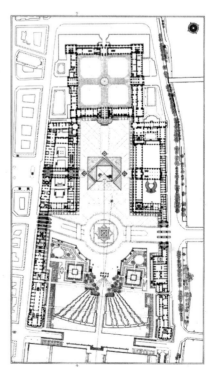

▲

Three corridors disperse from the underground lobby to clearly marked collections housed in three wings. A fourth corridor leads west to a stylish subterranean shopping mall.

▶

When the Ministry of Finance vacated the Richelieu Wing, BOTTOM LEFT, the enclosed courtyard became the museum's centerpoint.

▲

I. M. Pei with François Mitterrand, June
1983. Mitterrand dispensed with the customary public competition and selected Pei
outright. From the beginning, they seemed
a liaison dangereuse.

A riffle of surprise swept through the arrondissements when Mitterrand revealed that he had retained Pei. Despite Pei's prodigious credentials as an institutional image-maker, his appointment provoked buzzes and clucks of disapproval, particularly from French architects, who viewed him as an interloper. "The French were surprised, if not stunned, or even outraged," remembered Pei's son Didi, an associate partner in his father's firm.

In one sense, I. M. Pei *was* a baffling choice. Parisians are famously skeptical of any foreign intrusion, let alone that of a New Yorker poised to rejigger their national treasure-house. That a Socialist government outspokenly critical of American cultural "imperialism" would recruit an American architect for a monumental national commission was too ironic to ignore. Mitterrand's selection was almost guaranteed to invite widespread grousing. From the beginning, Mitterrand and Pei seemed a *liaison dangereuse.*

On the other hand, Mitterrand astutely recognized that Pei's National Gallery addition had caught the American public's fancy by establishing the modern-day museum as a theatrical event for a mass audience, not just a somber repository of art. Pei's airy, open atrium enlivened by escalators and balconies struck some Stateside critics as sadly suitable for the consumer phenomenon that blockbuster art shows had become. But Mitterrand interpreted this trend as a democratization of culture in keeping with his Socialist agenda. He hoped the infusion of American vitality would reanimate the moribund Louvre—and France's lagging position within the art world.

The Paris of Mitterrand's childhood had reigned as the undisputed capital of the arts and the adopted home of Picasso, Léger, Calder and Miró. When the avant-garde mantle passed to New York's abstract expressionists in the 1950s, the world had stopped looking to Paris for exciting new art. By the time Mitterrand took office, the cafés where Fauvists and Cubists had once held forth were catering to foreign tourists. Jack Lang, the would-be architect of France's cultural reawakening, acknowledged that France would have to recapture lost glitter if it hoped to reverse its postwar decline in the visual arts. As a Chinese-American, Pei offered the best of both worlds: he could import his New World flash and efficiency without appearing conspicuously American. His mandarin ancestry somehow inoculated him against French xenophobia. "In this case," Pei said, "I think being a Chinese-American has not hurt. History, you see, is important to the French and I hope that I was able to convince them that I came from a country with a long history and I would not take this problem lightly."

Sequestered in the private eighth-floor studio of his Midtown Manhattan office, Pei and his most trusted aides secretly drafted plans for a five-acre limestone catacomb containing generous storage space, electric carts to transport artworks, a 400-seat auditorium, information booths, conference rooms, a bookstore and a gleaming, luxurious café—all implanted in the Louvre's ancient bowels. From this hub, visitors would move just 100 feet— as opposed to the existing 1,000-foot end-to-end marathon—along underground arteries radiating outward toward clearly marked collections exhibited in the three wings. A fourth passage would lead west to a stylish shopping mall built beneath the Carousel arch. When 165 new rooms opened in November 1993, the revamped Louvre would become the largest museum in the world. An army of curators would rearrange 70,000 artworks over great swaths of history. Many pieces would see the light of day for the first time after languishing for decades in musty storage rooms.

Parisians were mortified to learn that Pei might defile the Cour Napoléon with some sort of glitzy *dropping*. "French critics started to scream, 'What? How can you build there? You're going to destroy one of the most important urban spaces in Paris, if not the world,' " said Didi Pei. In actuality, that area was the Finance Ministry's parking lot by day and a notorious homosexual cruising zone by night—hardly one of the city's proudest outdoor spaces. Its

only distinguishing features were two trash-strewn plots of grass, a few defeated trees and an inconspicuous equestrian statue of Lafayette donated by
the Daughters of the American Revolution.

"The center of gravity of the museum had to be in the Cour Napoléon," Pei
said. "That's where the public had to come. But what do you do when you arrive? Do you enter into an underground space, a kind of subway concourse?
No. You need to be welcomed by some kind of great space. So you've got to
have something of our period. That space must have volume, it must have
light and it must have a surface identification. You have to be able to look at
it and say, 'Ah, this is the entrance.' "

Pei's solution was a 70-foot glass pyramid capable, in theory, of ingesting
15,000 visitors an hour. He based its proportions on the classic Egyptian
pyramid at Giza and surrounded it with a trio of baby "pyramidons" and three
triangular reflecting pools with fountains.

Pei offered his "luminous structure-symbol" as an ingenious way to avoid
upstaging the Louvre. No solid addition imaginable could gracefully blend
with the time-darkened old palace, he reasoned, but a translucent pyramid,
frankly of its own time, would respectfully defer to the heavy presence of the
surrounding building by reflecting its tawny stone. The pyramid is the geometric shape that encloses the greatest area within the smallest possible volume, so it would stand as unobtrusively as possible. It was, Pei assured them,
"a natural solution." There was one more pleasing twist: the ancient form
made of high-tech material would be at once much older and much newer
than the Louvre.

This was not Pei's first pyramid. He had already used a cluster of glass
pyramids to light an underground corridor connecting Washington's National
Gallery with his modern addition. Before that, he had drafted a truncated
glass pyramid for an abortive design for the Kennedy Library in Cambridge,

Massachusetts. "It would be very embarrassing," observed the architectural historian Robert Clark of Princeton, "if the French government found out that what they had was really a warmed-over JFK memorial."

Nonetheless, Pei's pyramid fit the strict geometric spirit of Le Nôtre. It would align with other abstract landmarks—the Arc de Triomphe and the obelisk in the Place de la Concorde—ornamenting the splendid vista that sweeps from the Louvre through the Tuileries and continues up the Champs-Elysées in one unbroken line to the Place de l'Etoile and, by implication, to the setting sun in the west. Moreover, the pyramid appears throughout French history: in seventeenth-century topiaries, in the tip of the obelisk that stands in the Place de la Concorde and in the visionary gateways, factories and crematoriums conjured up by eighteenth-century architects Etienne-Louis Boullée and Claude-Nicolas Ledoux. There is, in fact, a Place des Pyramides just off the Louvre's northern flank.

When Olivier Bernier asked if he had drawn inspiration from Ledoux's un-built designs, Pei looked at him "with great indignation," Bernier recalled, "and he said, 'That had nothing to do with it!' " Pei curiously disavowed any debt to historical precedent. He selected the pyramid, he insisted, by sheer analysis.

It's understandable that Pei might have been a bit touchy. The Louvre is notorious for repelling architects. "Haphazard in appearance," wrote art critic John Russell, "it has in fact been more pondered over, more planned and replanned and schemed-for than almost any other building in Europe." François Mansart produced no fewer than fifteen separate schemes after Louis XIV invited him to redesign the Louvre three hundred years ago. All were rejected. In 1665 the Sun King summoned another preeminent architect, Italy's Giovanni Lorenzo Bernini, to complete the Louvre's east facade. As chief architect of Saint Peter's and the most celebrated sculptor of his time, Bernini was famous enough to attract roadside crowds as his carriage passed en route to Paris. The king welcomed him with fanfare befitting visiting royalty. Some months later a foundation for his undulating Baroque facade was ceremoniously laid. Construction was poised to begin in earnest when the French distaste for Italian excess asserted itself, and after much embarrassed hand-wringing, the Sun King awarded Bernini a pension and a parcel of gifts and sent him back to Italy in a cloud of intrigue and disgrace. Bernini left behind only the memory of a fiasco and a marble statue of Louis XIV on horseback, which the king took with him when he abandoned the Louvre altogether and moved his court to Versailles in 1667. This lesson was not lost on Mitterrand. Anxious to avoid a recurrence, the president made a public promise to Pei: "What happened to Bernini will not happen to you."

Despite Mitterrand's reassurances, a firestorm of protest swept Paris after Pei presented his design to an advisory body called the Commission Supérieure des Monuments Historiques on January 23, 1984. Press accounts reported the delegates' "stupefaction" and "alarm" at seeing a glass pyramid disfiguring the Louvre's semisacred grounds. The commission's former chief architect, Bertrand Monnet, condemned the scheme as "beyond our mental space" and "a gigantic, ruinous gadget."

"One after another they got up and denounced the project," Pei said. "My translator was so unnerved that she started to tremble. She was scarcely able to translate for me when I came to defend my ideas."

After the last delegate had his say, Pei and his bewildered associates retreated to a bistro on the Rue Villedo. "The French can be particularly snotty," observed Anna Mutin, a member of Pei's group. "The questioning was hostile and the words were not always nice. At lunch afterward Pei was puzzled by all the opera. He thought he'd explained the reasons. He concluded that he'd walked into a trap."

▼

Beneath the Cour Napoléon: The pyramid at center designates the museum's entrance. "You have to be able to look at it and say, 'Ah, this is the entrance,' " Pei said. The smaller inverted pyramid to the right marks the shopping arcade.

▲

The Louvre according to I. M. Pei.

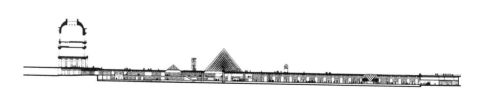

Fortunately for Pei, the commission had no binding authority and Mitterrand bestowed his unqualified approval on the design. "It is a great help," Pei said, "to deal with one man only."

Mitterrand's endorsement did not prevent his countrymen from rolling their eyes at the unsavory prospect of a glitzy carbuncle disfiguring La Belle France's elegant neoclassical countenance. The obscene expectation triggered one of those bouts of public disputation that periodically animate *tout le Paris*. "We found out," remembered Didi Pei, "that it wasn't quite so easy as Mitterrand simply saying yes."

Pei-bashing became a passionate cause célèbre led by a grab bag of historians, politicians and extraneous self-appointed committees. United under the slogans "No pyramid for Paris" and "Hands off the Louvre," the anti-pyramid faction included the museum's own curator of paintings, Bruno Foucart, who compared the pyramid to a tacky diamond, and its director, André Chabaud, who resigned in protest, describing the plans as "unfeasible" and rife with "architectural risks." The conservative writer Jean Dutourd of the prestigious French Academy wrote in a sulfurous editorial that La Pyramide would "reflect the colors of the sky, like the Ewing building in Dallas." The photographer Henri Cartier-Bresson called it funereal and better suited, in his view, to the Père-Lachaise cemetery.

All of France, it seemed, struck up an anti-pyramid chant. Michel Guy, a former minister of culture and founder of an opposition group called the Association for the Renovation of the Louvre, wrote a voluminous criticism comparing the design to "an airport or a drugstore." He urged an alternative scheme that he argued would humanize the Louvre by dividing it into several smaller, more manageable mini-Louvres, each with its own entry. "The key word is 'modesty,'" Guy told an interviewer. "I think that this project is immodest and pretentious."

Not to be left out, everyday Parisians expressed their disapproval by wearing buttons that asked, *"Pourquoi la Pyramide?"* Pei's daughter, Liane, saw women spit at her father's feet as they passed on the street. "My jaw just dropped open," she said, "but he was very poised. His attitude was, Well, grin and bear it. After a particularly ugly interview or press conference he would just chuckle. 'That *was* tough,' he'd say."

The encircling French newspapers gleefully documented each new salvo in what they dubbed "the Battle of the Pyramid," a wry allusion to Napoleon's Egyptian campaign. Predictably outspoken in its distaste for the new Socialist programs, the conservative daily *Le Figaro* vilified Mitterrand's patronage of the pyramid. "The whole layout is absurd," wrote one *Le Figaro* critic, "but what could you expect when the project was conceived in an office in New York?"

Le Canard Enchaîné ran a story under the banner "Mitterramses I and His Pyramid." The *Parisien* called it "The Astonishing Chinese Pyramid." "You rub your eyes," wrote a *Le Monde* commentator. "You think you're dreaming; it seems that you've gone back to the era of castles for sale and Hollywood copies of the temple of Solomon, of Alexander, of Cleopatra. . . . It doesn't seem justified to treat the courtyard of the Louvre like a Disneyland annex or a rebirth of the defunct Luna Park." *Le Figaro* published a survey showing that while 90 percent of Parisians favored the renovation, the same number opposed the pyramid.

The Battle of the Pyramid became more than a spat over the Louvre; it was a philosophical debate over the future of French culture. The French proudly regard themselves as arbiters of taste. In a country where the evening news airs fashion-show footage and top chefs are feted like rock stars, even the uninterested absorb current issues of taste, just as every American at least notices who won a celebrity court trial. In France, issues of taste are unavoidable, and usually political. With characteristic Gallic hauteur, Parisians regarded Pei's alteration to the picturesque fabric of neoclassical Paris as not just an intrusion but a ghastly threat to France's national character, its *Frenchness*.

As the architectural embodiment of the country's past glory and its cultural hub since the Revolution, it carries greater symbolic weight than any comparable American institution. The Louvre's history is, by and large, the history of France. When the Prussians and the English occupied Paris in the wake of Napoleon's defeat at Waterloo, no atrocity perpetrated by the foreign soldiers provoked Frenchmen so much as their attempts to reclaim from the Louvre the artworks plundered during Napoleon's European campaigns. "The evolution of the Louvre is, in fact, an allegory of the evolution of that elusive concept: L'Esprit Français," wrote John Russell. It is an "enormous building which, as much as any in France, justifies the concept of La Gloire."

Entire chapters of French history have unfolded within the Louvre's walls. It was home to eleven kings and the site of courtly masquerades and massacres alike. Louis XIII cruised its Grande Galerie in a petite carriage drawn by two mastiffs. Catherine de Médicis flung massacred Huguenots from its windows. It served variously as fortress, riding academy, prison, market, library, arsenal, treasury and hayloft. It was home to Chardin and other artists and the founding facility of French ballet. Its desecration swelled French hearts with righteous outrage.

Behind much of the anti-pyramid hysteria lurked the xenophobic sentiment that France's cultural independence—particularly from America—depended on safeguarding the country from foreign boorishness. Parisians feared that Pei's glass splinter would reshape the city's profile and open the door for further contemporary vulgarism. They had already seen the ancient Les Halles food market, with its nineteenth-century pavilion and iron umbrellas, replaced by an American-style shopping mall, and they had wit-nessed the encroaching presence of ghastly commercial towers in the fringe neighborhoods of Montparnasse and La Défense. By admitting glass and steel into the very heart of the city, Pei unwittingly fell into the role of For-eign Interloper of Dubious Taste, an ambassador of made-in-America junk culture polluting Europe with mini-American colonies like McDonald's and Hyatt Hotels.

Pei also entered a political power struggle. The ousted Conservatives re-garded the ruling Socialists as a horrid aberration of the natural order, and they latched onto the pyramid as a symbol with which to publicly discredit its presidential patron and steer public sentiment away from his Socialist pro-grams. Pei's pyramid thus became the fulcrum upon which French politics seesawed.

French leaders remained mindful of the visible manifestations of power long after the demise of the monarchy. As rebuilder of postwar France, Charles de Gaulle had beribboned the countryside with highways; in the Beaubourg district, Georges Pompidou had erected the brutalist museum that bears his name; and Valéry Giscard d'Estaing had initiated a new mu-seum of nineteenth-century art in the renovated remains of the old Belle Epoque Orsay railroad station. Although he campaigned as a champion of the common man, Mitterrand proved that he too was susceptible to the van-ity of power. In addition to the Louvre, his so-called *grands projets*—French curators privately called them "the grand monsters"—included a flashy new opera house near the Bastille and an enormous futuristic arch, more than twice the height of the Arc de Triomphe, marking one end of the city's great axis. Although several *grands projets*—including a science and in-dustry park in the outlying area of La Villette, a center for Arab studies and the Musée d'Orsay—were initiated by his predecessor, Mitterrand was happy to take credit for their completion. (He may also have been reluctant to cancel them, lest a Conservative successor retaliate against his Grand Louvre.)

If pressed, most Parisians would have acknowledged the president's time-honored right to leave his mark on the city. But it struck many as unseemly, even hypocritical, for a Socialist to enshrine his presidency with, of all things, a pyramid—the archetypal power symbol. The Mitterrand who, as a presidential candidate, had promised dignity and security for little people, who had assailed Giscard for dividing France into "the exploited and the exploiters," now resembled socialism's own Sun King.

Mitterrand and his aides no doubt invited rancor by high-handedly predicting that, after twenty-three years of right-wing stinginess, France's cultural resources would flourish anew under their enlightened patronage. Nor did they hesitate to posture as the heirs to everything progressive about the French Revolution. Minister of Culture Jack Lang was fond of saying, "Before us darkness, after us light." It was a slogan that rankled ousted cultural officials who had thanklessly upgraded many old arts facilities and built, among other things, the popular Pompidou Center, which, with its extroverted tangle of pop art plumbing, was a rare example of progressive architecture in Paris.

．　．　．　．

Pei withstood the worst trial of his long career with the jaunty disposition for which he is famous. "I never got the impression that he was discouraged or depressed," said Mihai Radu, a junior designer assigned to the project. "He perceived it as part of his job to make people understand his work. He's a very level person. I've never seen I.M. when he wasn't smiling, and he was smiling even then."

"Pei is the consummate diplomat," observed critic Paul Goldberger, "and a brilliant, brilliant master—as many great figures are—of the equally difficult task of appearing perfectly at ease at every moment and being unaffected by the extraordinary pressures that surround him."

Through the nightmarish months of harassment Pei summoned his considerable talents—social, tactical, artistic and diplomatic—and, stepping to the lip of the public stage, put on a bravura public relations performance that rebuffed his many detractors and resurrected his pyramid from the intractable sludge of defeat. "Pei was the perfect man for that job," said architect Philip Johnson. "I would have flunked it. He was the only one who could have worked his way through the mud of French bureaucracy and politics. . . . Pei is, of course, *the* supersalesman. He's the consummate public relations man, except in his case it isn't really PR because he's such a damned natural."

In America, architects have only to win the support of a committee or, in some cases, the whim of a single CEO. As Pei discovered, approval is more complicated in France where, after the Revolution, the state assumed responsibility for maintaining the national heritage. As a result, Pei had to sway government bureaucrats and, by extension, the entire public to whom they answered. "If the Chinese invented bureaucracy, the French have brought it to perfection," Pei told an interviewer. "Yet French bureaucracy at least has one quality: once a decision is made, it is made. It is very difficult to draw back."

Pei campaigned tirelessly to reach that point. He spoke some broken French, but he usually relied on translators as he conversed with any reporter who would listen, made his pitch on any TV show and met with any official to bolster support. He argued, always graciously, that Paris, like all cities, should be free to evolve as a living, growing organism and not be preserved under glass like some French equivalent of colonial Williamsburg. Besides, a modern addition was consistent with the Louvre's history as a composite of overlapping styles. It started out as a circular donjon with moats and towers and ended up, centuries later, as a pastiche of afterthoughts. Why shouldn't our century contribute its own layer? In response to those who called the pyramid intrusive, he explained that it would cover just one-thirtieth of the courtyard. He produced computer-generated graphics demonstrating that its latticework would remain inconspicuous from the Champs-Elysées and the Tuileries. What about the Eiffel Tower and the Pompidou Center? he asked. Did they not also endure periods of ritual outrage before taking their place as a celebrated part of the cityscape? "Nobody would question Einstein about relativity," Pei said, "but everybody has an opinion about architecture. . . . There were times in my career, and the Louvre is one, when even knowing you're right is not enough. All these things you have to take and accept. First of all, you have to be right, and that's not easy, but if you're right and believe in what you're doing, you have to be patient and take all the blows that come and continue to defend."

"He handled himself with great sangfroid," recalled Richard Bernstein, then Paris correspondent for the *New York Times*. "He always spoke about the project with great confidence. When he appeared on television, someone would inevitably accuse him of designing an Egyptian death symbol. He would patiently explain that, no, this was not a death symbol. It was going to be light. It was going to sparkle." Furthermore, Pei stressed that the pyramid was not exclusively Egyptian, but appeared in many cultures, including his native China. He asked France to accept it as a monumental object unencumbered by historical associations.

Pei took on the press and the public single-handedly. When French architects ambushed him in press conferences he answered with surprising force. "He had the skill and the strength and the presence," said designer Christopher Rand, "to put them in their place—to put them to shame."

If Pei did not detooth the critics by force, he did so by ingratiation. "As we sat down in his office he began to give me what I suspect was a scaled-down treatment of the flattery he shows his clients," Olivier Bernier recalled. "It was promptly established that we knew the same people and so forth. It was quite a lengthy song and dance meant to create an atmosphere in which I would feel part of a privileged group, in which I would feel that I was being treated as a friend with whom he was having a pleasant conversation and therefore would not ask difficult questions. Then, in that well-honed technique employed by politicians, he evaded any questions that might be awkward to answer."

Courteous but uncompromising, charming but firm, Pei proved convincing. Others gradually took up his cause. Pierre Boulez, France's premier conductor and an outspoken advocate of avant-garde music, privately lobbied his influential friends. It might, Boulez wrote in the pro-government daily *Le Matin,* "be flattering to a Parisian and even to a Frenchman, that his city, his capital—or at least a certain privileged quarter of it—had achieved the status of immortality, of intangibility." But Paris, he argued, is not "a place finished, completed for eternity." His converts included Claude Pompidou, the widow of the former president who, though her husband was a Conservative, endorsed the project. Pei and his staff also made a private presentation to Catherine Deneuve who, in turn, expressed her support through the press.

Mitterrand himself was Pei's unflagging booster. Like Prince Charles, he was not afraid to speak out on architectural matters. Operating without a formal advisory committee, he personally saw to every major decision and, accompanied by bodyguards, frequently joined Pei at the site, often without prior warning. Visitors to his brocaded Louis XV–style study in the Elysée Palace found themselves encouraged to admire a model of the pyramid.

Meanwhile, Pei's staff launched a publicity blitzkrieg, including sheafs of drawings and a magnificent exhibit in the Tuileries' renovated Orangerie. As originally planned, the exhibit's centerpiece was to have been a massive illuminated model of the pyramid, flown in from New York, but a presidential delegation decided this would send the wrong political message. A revised exhibit dramatically downplayed the pyramid, focusing attention instead on improvements to existing galleries and the history of the Louvre as a composite of buildings, each reflective of its own time.

The tide gradually turned. In February 1984, after a three-day retreat with Pei's design team in the seaside town of Arcachon, the seven chief curators of the Louvre, who rarely agreed on anything, signed a statement of unanimous support. "In the context of the Grand Louvre, it seems to the curators-in-chief," they wrote, "that Mr. Pei's pyramid has not at all the character—as has sometimes been said—of a 'modernist gadget' or at best a gratuitous architectural gesture. It is on the contrary an imaginative concept that fits perfectly into an overall architectural ensemble that for coherence and quality alike has been universally approved and accepted."

To secure his comeback, Pei needed an ally among Mitterrand's opponents, a Conservative who would resist the temptation to denounce the pyramid for political gain. He found that supporter in Mayor Jacques Chirac of Paris, Mitterrand's main political rival and a former prime minister. Pei initially approached Chirac without much optimism. After all, he expected Mitterrand's chief adversary, nicknamed "the Bulldozer" for his abrasive manner, to condemn the design as an example of Socialist disdain for traditional values.

Pei met Chirac at the mayor's office in the Hôtel Matignon and appealed to his knowledge of urban planning. The Louvre stood as a dark, hulking barrier between the Left Bank and the Right. Pei promised to open the Louvre up, to integrate it with the city. Visitors approaching from the Tuileries Gardens, for example, would not have to cross heavy traffic after Pei submerged the Avenue du Général-Lemonnier in a tunnel. Pei would open a covered passage through the middle of the Richelieu Wing so that pedestrians could walk from the Rue de Rivoli to the Cour Napoléon. The fleets of tour buses clogging the surrounding sidewalks would be banished to an underground garage with its own subterranean entrance. "Opening up the Louvre," Pei said, "means opening up Paris." After a private meeting devoted mostly to a discussion of Chirac's recent trip to China, the prime minister told the press that he was "not hostile" to the project. In private, however, Chirac told Pei, "From a city-planning point of view the project is *touché à la perfection.*"

Yet Chirac still harbored doubts about the pyramid itself. Before bestowing his full blessing, he asked Pei to erect a full-scale mock-up on the Cour Napoléon for public inspection. (Chirac's request had a precedent: Napoleon had displayed a cloth-and-beam model of the Arc de Triomphe prior to its construction.) Pei complied by suspending a set of cables from a crane delineating the pyramid's life-size proportions over the courtyard. Sixty thousand curious citizens came around for a sidewalk referendum during the May Day holiday. Those four days were marked by heated sidewalk debate and the occasional fistfight. "We have not come just to look at it," a reporter overheard a mother telling her son, "but to see if it should be there at all."

Chirac came with his entourage and issued his endorsement over the vehement opposition of his advisers. "That was the moment we were under the most severe attack," Pei said. "There was considerable public pressure on Chirac to renounce the project. . . . He looked at it and looked at it and he said, 'Well, it's not too bad.' "

"For us, that was the monumental victory," said Didi Pei. "That was the green light. From then on the project was—as the French say—*irréversible.*"

In the spring of 1985, blue-clad workers excavated behind tall, brightly painted wooden barricades, and half a dozen cranes decorated with red and white flags maneuvered around the site. Men and machines labored under unusual instructions from the architect: build the pyramid first, then excavate around it. Pei wanted to complete the pyramid as quickly as possible to reinforce the impression of inevitability, even though it meant suspending the pyramid in place while precariously digging around its supports. "It was a bit like building the roof before the house," said Didi Pei. "Everyone was extremely nervous."

There was another cause for haste: the bloom had faded from the Socialist rose as Mitterrand's leftist reforms ran afoul of economic realities. France was losing some 100,000 jobs a year while inflation soared out of control. As public confidence ebbed, some prominent French families drove their money across the border to Switzerland. The same month that construction began on the Louvre, Mitterrand scored a 32 percent approval rating, the lowest in the history of the Fifth Republic.

Mitterrand's fall from popular grace threatened the Grand Louvre. If the Conservatives gained control in the parliamentary elections of 1986, they could kill or dramatically modify the plans. And if the pyramid remained unfinished when Mitterrand launched his 1988 reelection bid, he might be forced to bequeath to his successor the honor of snipping the inaugural tricolor ribbon. To ensure that Mitterrand would open his most prized project, the Pei team worked seven days a week practically around the clock in mobile homes parked on the site in order to finish the excavations by the end of April 1986.

The French relish rhetorical violence, but they also love consensus. As Richard Bernstein observed in his book *Fragile Glory*, the continuity of French culture usually prevails over subversion and dissidence. How else to account for the conspicuous absence in France, compared to its neighbors, of skinheads, bikers and other extremists? The country is undivided as well on the question of mandatory military service and nuclear power. In the end, France speaks with one voice.

So when bulldozers rolled across the Cour Napoléon, the Parisian flocking instinct engaged itself and the last of the dissenting voices were hushed. Even the opposition newspapers *Le Figaro* and *Le Quotidien de Paris* fell silent. Why oppose a fait accompli?

"From then on, it was a challenge to make the pyramid what we promised it would be: reflective and translucent," said Didi Pei. In order to show the Louvre's ornately carved facades without the greenish distortion embedded in commercial glass, Pei would have to install a specially composed untinted glass. It also had to be strong enough to resist bombs, stones, bullets and the century's heaviest snowstorm. Saint-Gobain, France's largest glass manufacturer, balked at the order, claiming at first that it could not be done. They found a way, though, after Pei threatened to embarrass them by hiring a German competitor.

Pei further lightened the pyramid's appearance by suspending the 793 panes on a lithe spiderweb of cables inspired by Buckminster Fuller and assembled by Navtec, a Massachusetts naval engineering firm that had devised the rigging for recent America's Cup yachts.

One day, early on, a workman performing preliminary excavation struck something hard with his drill. It was an unexpected bonus: workers had unearthed the remains of an abandoned wall erected by Louis XIV and, beside it, the original twelfth-century turrets and moat of King Philippe Auguste's fortress. A hastily assembled team of archaeologists uncovered the protective walls added two hundred years later by Charles V, and some 25,000 scattered items: plates, pigsties, cattle tracks, tools, helmets and crockery. Everyone agreed the findings deserved to be seen, so Pei added an underground gallery from which to view the rough stone ramparts.

As had been anticipated, the conservatives regained a narrow parliamentary majority in the 1986 election, forcing Mitterrand to take the unprecedented step of appointing his longtime political adversary, Jacques Chirac, as prime minister. With two years remaining in his first term, Mitterrand thus entered into a precarious power-sharing arrangement coyly referred to as *cohabitation*. Chirac wasted no time in dismantling Mitterrand's controls on business and replacing them with supply-side, free-market policies, but the

Conservative resurrection did not threaten Mitterrand's pet project. After all, Chirac had publicly declared his support for the pyramid and his newly appointed finance minister, an aloof big-business advocate named Edouard Balladur, promised to vacate the Richelieu Wing by the end of 1986, as planned. But after less than three months in office Balladur changed his mind: he let it be known through a spokesman that he would not surrender his *beaux quartiers* after all. In fact, he recalled his senior staff from their temporary digs on the Boulevard Saint-Germain and expensively redecorated the Richelieu Wing to accommodate them.

One can understand Balladur's reluctance to leave. With its inlaid antique tables, red velvet chairs and frescoed ceilings populated by horn-blowing cherubs and puffy clouds, these princely chambers, where finance officials had toiled since their own building burned down in 1873, were probably the world's most opulent offices. But there could be no compromising. The Grand Louvre without the Richelieu Wing, Pei said, would be like "an amputee." Besides, a new ministry headquarters was already under construction in Bercy, a gritty neighborhood of abandoned wine warehouses located a short float down the Seine.

With construction workers at his door, the intransigent Balladur argued that his new Bercy address was too far from the city and lacked the prestige his position warranted. Besides, he warned, the national treasury could ill afford to finish the Louvre renovation so soon after paying for the other *grands projets*.

Balladur's appeal for frugality crumbled when it was revealed that his foot-dragging would cost the project an additional $11.6 million and when the press delightedly recounted his imperial trappings, which included white-gloved footmen and antiques borrowed from basement storage rooms. Even the conservative *Le Figaro* urged Balladur to pack up. Under pressure from Chirac, Balladur struck a deal over a private lunch with Pei and Lang: most of the ministry bureaucrats would decamp to Bercy, but his "essential entourage" would remain in the Louvre until suitable quarters could be found in central Paris.

On March 4, 1988, in a ceremony scheduled two months prior to the presidential elections, Mitterrand awarded Pei the Légion d'Honneur inside the finished pyramid. Ironically, the awkward power-sharing arrangement with Chirac helped Mitterrand by allowing him to float serenely above the fray while Chirac tackled the day-to-day headaches. As the 1988 election neared, Mitterrand's prospects brightened. In one of the most remarkable comebacks in modern French politics, the president rescued his popularity and, along with it, his presidency by trading his radical agenda for middle-of-the-road pragmatism. After almost a full term, Mitterrand had acquired the imperial mystique of the *grand homme* despite the fact that he had spent his early career maligning royalist authoritarianism. On election day, Mitterrand retreated, as always, to a small Burgundy inn to await the outcome. When the election results clearly foretold a Mitterrand landslide, the innkeeper entered the dining room with a secret creation: a cake crowned with a tiny replica of Pei's pyramid. It had become the emblem of Mitterrand's political resurrection.

Although the official inauguration was still eight months off, the courtyard and pyramid—the Grand Louvre's fresh new face—had assumed their finished appearance by July 3, 1988, when the *beau monde* lined up two thousand strong along the Rue de Rivoli for a much anticipated preview. The crowd that had filtered in at dusk sat with their backs to the pyramid that evening listening to Pei's advocate, Pierre Boulez, conduct the Orchestre National de France, but rain interrupted the concert. As guests turned to seek shelter, most saw the pyramid illuminated from within for the first time. The museum grounds had always been a spooky pocket of darkness after nightfall. Now the old facades shone under six hundred spotlights, and seven computer-controlled fountains shot floodlit columns of water into the night. The pyramid itself was a crystalline apparition hovering over a formal treeless garden. Critics later compared it to the polished monolith unearthed in *2001: A Space Odyssey,* a prism, a tiara, a gazebo, a diamond, a hologram, a spaceship, a shining spiderweb and a high-tech soufflé.

Pei, the rehabilitated pariah, stood sanctified among a throng of newfound admirers enjoying the rainy denouement. His face lit up like the pyramid as he addressed reporters from beneath a black umbrella. "I've been waiting a long time for this," he told them.

Not everything came off as hoped, however. Critics complained that, because of a bend in the Seine, the pyramid stands slightly off the great Etoile axis. (On the actual point of alignment, just southwest of the pyramid, Pei placed a lead cast of Bernini's seventeenth-century statue of Louis XIV on horseback.) A more persistent misgiving has been the filthy condition of the pyramid's glass walls. Paris is sooty and thickly patrolled by pigeons, as the Pompidou Center's curators discovered when layers of dirt and droppings accumulated on its serpentine ducts. When a plan to clean the pyramid by deploying a robotic scrubber used in nuclear power plants fell through, curators dispatched a team of alpine climbers to rappel down its 52-degree face brandishing sponges and squeegees. The pyramid was not as translucent as expected, but it did reflect the city's famously changeable light in a pleasing way. "The pyramid has the same moods as the sky of Paris," Pei said. "It is like a living organism, and for this reason I think it is a success."

On the whole, the strange plotlines of the pyramid contretemps converged into luxurious gratification for Pei and his presidential patron. On this night all grudges were absolved. Parisians inducted Pei alongside Josephine Baker, Charlie Chaplin and Jerry Lewis in the unlikely fraternity of deified Americans. "It is a story of battles, passionate battles," said museum director Michel Laclotte. "Twice as we came into the courtyard everyone waiting in line recognized Pei and applauded. I believe this warmed his heart. He realized he had won."

"The pyramid started taking over everything, it seemed," recalled Didi Pei. "Even Prince Charles—the bad boy of architectural critics—liked it. Although he told me, 'I wouldn't have done it quite this way.'"

If the French love anything as dearly as culture, it is high technology. Although no longer a first-class power, France has softened its tumble from Napoleonic glory by producing such cutting-edge items as the Concorde, high-speed trains, a computerized telephone information service and the world's most successful nuclear energy program. As France pursued its high-tech future, the pyramid, itself a display of technical virtuosity, had a talismanic effect, reconfirming the country's vision of itself as a forward-looking prestige player in postindustrial Europe. It proved the French were a people still capable of greater contributions than pâté and perfume.

For a time, Pyramid-mania eclipsed the Eiffel Tower as the defining image of Paris. One critic called it "a high media-profile pyramid with a quite famous museum attached." All of Paris descended on the Louvre to admire the city's newest monument, and the entrance line spiraled twice around the Cour Napoléon. A newspaper headline encapsulated the phenomenon as "Louvre: Le Rush."

The sweetest vindication of all was still to come. In October 1989 Pei's most vociferous tormentor, *Le Figaro*, conceded in a headline that "The Pyramid Is Very Beautiful After All," and later invited hundreds of guests to a celebration of the magazine at a fete staged—of all places—inside the pyramid.

2

SHANGHAI AND SUZHOU

Ieoh Ming Pei belonged to the fifteenth generation of a large, prosperous lineage of poets, painters, calligraphers and bankers based in the ancient Yangtze-basin city of Suzhou, a bastion of ornamental gardens and old Chinese crafts like silk, embroidery and scroll painting. Suzhou and its neighboring city were known also for their pleasant lilting dialect and lovely women. "In heaven there is paradise," an old proverb stated. "On earth, Suzhou and Hangzhou."

Barely brushed by Western influence, Suzhou remained a maze of low whitewashed buildings with gray tile roofs and cobblestone streets lined with sycamores where coolies smoked bamboo pipes and women hung laundry on long poles. Over the years, travelers compared it to Florence for its artistic refinement and to Venice for its elaborate canals spanned by humpbacked bridges. Marco Polo described its residents as "merchants and cunning men of all crafts, and also there are wise men called sages, like our philosophers, and great natural physicians who know nature well. Moreover, I tell quite truly there are quite six thousand bridges of stone in this city."

The first Pei arrived in Suzhou during the middle of the Ming dynasty (1368–1644) to practice medicine and sell curative herbs from a marketplace stall erected in the shadow of the Temple of Mystery, a Taoist shrine housing giant deities enveloped by plumes of incense. His descendants developed the

◄ **The Shizilin Garden.**

business into a shop purveying a variety of Chinese medicines—fungi, crushed leaves and ginseng. By the eighteenth century, the Peis had become a great landowning family—"a big household"—that ruled the peasantry.

Ieoh Ming's grandfather, Li-tai Pei, was one of the powerful and learned men at the top of the ruling gentry. Their mandate was to administrate the provinces on behalf of the imperial court. Such positions were awarded by merit rather than by caste. Theoretically, any male could qualify by passing rigorous exams, known as "the ladder to the clouds," on Confucian classics, ancient poetry and dynastic histories. In a land without migration or colonies, these exams were the main path of advancement. In reality, the vast majority were disqualified by illiteracy. With the help of a private tutor, Li-tai passed the highest exams at a young age, but a promising career in the Beijing bureaucracy was cut short by his father's death. At age twenty he returned to Suzhou to manage the family properties. His financial skill earned him responsibility for taxation and administration of the surrounding counties. He helped found the Shanghai Commercial Savings Bank to serve ordinary citizens and encourage local business. An account could be opened with a deposit of about one dollar. The bank prospered, and in 1917 he opened a Suzhou branch and became its manager.

All the while, Li-tai devoted himself to the public works traditionally performed by ruling mandarins. He built roads, headed the fire brigade and founded an orphanage, hospital and kindergarten. One was not a true gentleman without a garden, and Li-tai nurtured a chrysanthemum garden, which he occasionally opened to the public.

Li-tai groomed his sons for banking careers. The third son, Tsuyee, attended a local college run by American missionaries where he met his wife, Lien Kwun, daughter of the empire's top educational official. After graduating in 1911, he briefly worked as an accountant for an iron and coal company. At age twenty-three he joined the Bank of China's accounting department in Peking. The bank later transferred him to Canton, where, on April 26, 1917, Lien Kwun gave birth to Ieoh Ming ("To Inscribe Brightly"), their second child and first son. It was the Year of the Snake, which is said to confer charm and intuition, determination, persistence to the point of excess, a vanity in dress and a reluctance to follow advice. His baby nickname was Canton Darling.

Ieoh Ming entered a world convulsed by civil war. Five years earlier, the child emperor, P'u-yi, the last Son of Heaven, had abdicated the Dragon Throne. China struggled to replace its disintegrating feudal order, which still sanctioned such practices as slavery and foot binding, with a modern society organized around a centralized republic. When Sun Yat-sen's bungling, corrupt government failed to assert itself over the provinces, local warlords seized control and outfitted their own militias by collecting taxes from the peasantry, often at gunpoint. Skirmishes among their private armies despoiled the landscape, destroying roads and bridges and exacerbating an already dire famine. Riots and minor revolutions broke out. Food grew so scarce that rural peasants gnawed on tree bark and parents sold their children for bags of rice. Markets purveyed human flesh.

Ieoh Ming's grandfather, Li-tai, paid the warlords to spare Suzhou. The negotiations filled entire days and nights. He was consumed by the burden of protecting Suzhou, and during this ordeal he contracted an eye disease that eventually blinded him.

One year after Ieoh Ming's birth, Sun Yat-sen's regime demanded cash from the Bank of China's Canton branch to help fund an army capable of pushing northward to extinguish the provincial skirmishes and unify the country under the centralized government. The branch manager resigned under their intimidation, and his post passed to Tsuyee who, in turn, enraged the militia by refusing to meet their demands. Threatened with arrest, he fled south with his wife and two children to Hong Kong, where he reestablished the branch and

◄

The infant Ieoh Ming on his mother's lap. She was a poet, flutist and practicing Buddhist. His sister Yuen Hua is at the right.

▶

Ieoh Ming's father, Tsuyee Pei, belonged to a rising clique of urban elite that tried to replace the Confucian order with a new China of trade, industry and Western customs.

managed its deposits under the safety of British rule. According to family lore, Tsuyee crossed the border disguised as a Western woman.

Hong Kong was a city in which a young banker could feel the pulse of the world beyond China. Frustrated by the scanty capital allotted him by the bank's main office, and by the public's reluctance to trust a new venture, Tsuyee raised his own funds by exploiting the regional differences in exchange rates. Abetted by the city's permissive banking laws, he quickly earned a reputation as a skillful currency trader.

In those days, Britain's powerful Hongkong & Shanghai Bank dominated foreign exchange throughout the Far East. Few dared compete. The Hong Kong branch was managed by A. G. Stephen, a formidable figure known for sprinkling his professional correspondence with quotes from Shakespeare. Stephen noticed the precocious Tsuyee Pei poaching, however insignificantly, on his arbitrage business. "Little boy, are you trying to compete with me?" Tsuyee remembered him asking.

"No. How can I do that?" he responded. "I am just trying to make a little money for the bank."

"Well, I like it," Stephen said approvingly. "Just be careful not to stick your neck out too far."

"From that time on, Stephen became my very great friend," Tsuyee told an American reporter. "Gradually my turnover grew. Money made money."

After extracting government assurances that he would be safe from piracy, Tsuyee returned to his homeland in 1927 to manage the Bank of China's Shanghai branch.

History had conspired to produce in Shanghai a Western city incongruously affixed to the vast Asian continent. Once a malarial riverbank hamlet, it had developed under foreign jurisdiction into the Far East's busiest port and the collision point of East and West. "While Beijing stood for the refined and distilled high culture of the gentry-official-literati," said the Chinese

▲

The Shanghai Bund, a waterfront boulevard
lined with the imposing granite facades of
Western establishments. It was the heart of
a city dominated by foreigners.

scholar Wen-hsin Yeh, "Shanghai was the emporium of the trendy, the gaudy, the decorative, the conspicuous, and the city of the newly rising bourgeoisie." It was a haven of bankers, opium runners, socialites, smugglers, mercenaries, jazz musicians, entrepreneurs, swindlers, colonial snobs and refugees of all description. In 1926, Aldous Huxley called Shanghai "life itself . . . nothing more intensely living can be imagined."

The first sign of the city visible to passengers steaming up the winding Whangpoo River was the Bund, a mile-long waterfront boulevard lined shoulder to shoulder with the imposing granite facades of Western establishments: the Shanghai Club, the Chartered Bank, the British Consulate, Jardine Matheson & Company, the domed Hongkong & Shanghai Bank guarded by two bronze lions and the luxurious Cathay Hotel where Marlene Dietrich stayed in suite 441 and Noel Coward wrote *Private Lives* as he lay bedridden with the flu. "If it hadn't been for the Chinese on the streets and the many Chinese boats cluttering up the river," wrote the Canadian architect Harry Hussey of his 1911 arrival, "I would have had good reasons for believing I had somehow landed in Europe instead of in the largest city in China."

The Bund's waterfront esplanade was a pandemonium of honking Studebakers, barefoot coolies hauling rickshaws, chic Parisian women in high heels, Chinese women in gowns slit to mid-thigh, Englishmen in starched white tropicals on their way to cricket matches, red-turbaned Sikh policemen directing traffic, cruise ship tourists, clanging streetcars and thirsty sailors from every maritime country in the world. The harbor itself was obscured under a bobbing flotilla of gunboats, tramp steamers and high-sterned junks with rust-brown ragamuffin sails and garish eyes painted on port and starboard.

The Bund was the heart of an opulent oasis of Western privilege known variously as the Mistress of the Yangtze Valley, City for Sale, Paradise of Adventurers, City of Sin and Whore of the Orient. Western "taipans" (literally, members of the top class) surrounded themselves with the comforts of home.

They lived in their own self-governed enclaves, known as concessions, where they maintained their own parks, churches, schools, hospitals, police force and even their own private water supply.

Life was a round of well-insulated pleasures for the wealthy taipans. There were racetracks, cricket fields, a Gothic cathedral, a golf course, an orchestra, plush casinos, a social register and amateur productions of Gilbert and Sullivan. The British Country Club even imported sod from Devon. After work, the taipans sipped gin and bitters or English ale at the Shanghai Club's famous Long Bar, stronghold of colonial privilege, and dined on imported roast beef, mutton, and steak-and-kidney pie. There were universities, newspapers, ballet schools, publishing houses and shops stocked to abundance with liquor and cigarettes. Diplomats and merchants escorted wives and mistresses to endless rounds of cocktail parties, dinner dances, prizefights and balls in wardrobes expertly duplicated by Chinese tailors from pictures in European fashion magazines. After dancing in the ballroom of the Majestic Hotel or drinking at any number of White Russian cabarets, they retired to Tudor homes or villas.

Shanghai's economic raison d'être was the mighty Yangtze, a mocha-colored river leading to a vast inland market of rubber, coal, soybeans, oil, flour, cotton, silk, tobacco and opium. Scores of banks opened to service the fortunes amassed on these commodities, legally or otherwise, and the banks generally flourished under Shanghai's relaxed trade laws. While the hinterlands collapsed into medieval squalor, Shanghai grew richer and ever more audacious.

Like that of any boomtown, Shanghai's happy debauchery was accompanied by suffering and hideous overcrowding. To wander off the grand boulevards was to fall through a rabbit hole into a piteous jungle where human excrement accumulated in open drains and families huddled twelve to a room without light or water. Slave traders plucked children off the streets and sold them to factories and brothels. An occupying army of whores—many of whom were the daughters of impoverished White Russians—patrolled dark lanes, and pedestrians stepped over whining legless beggars and the occasional corpse. Shops purveyed scary pictures to dispel evil spirits and caged crickets to attract good luck. Professional letter writers hunched over tiny desks equipped with inkpots, hawkers sold Chinese slippers, cooked noodles and black market silver dollars amid the acrid smell of opium and the click-clack of mah-jongg ivories. "For Shanghai is a maelstrom where all can join the fray," wrote Philippine ambassador Mariano Ezpeleta, "where the rich can grow richer, and the poor can always beg and pray. . . . It is a city of sky-scrapers and mudholes, of luxury liners and jumpy junks, of Constellations and pedicabs, of Cadillacs and bull carts."

Tsuyee Pei and his growing family—Ieoh Ming and his older sister, Yuen Hua, were joined by a second sister, Wei, and two brothers, Yu Kun and Yu Tsung—dwelled comfortably in a two-story Western-style home with a grand garden in the comparative comfort and safety of the French Concession, a well-to-do enclave shaded by poplar trees where much of the city's Chinese gentry resided.

Tsuyee joined a clique of modern-minded bankers and industrialists associated with the wheeling, dealing financier and statesman T. V. Soong, brother of Madame Chiang Kai-shek and scion of one of China's most prominent families. Having come of age during World War I, these so-called national capitalists were painfully aware of China's weakness in comparison to Europe and America. With their generation, China's Confucian image of itself as the Celestial Empire, the Middle Kingdom, gave way to a new China of trade, industry, scientific thought and Western customs. The only way to elevate China from semicolonial status to a position as a self-respecting partner in world affairs, they felt, was to stand up for themselves in areas previously dominated by foreign enterprises, as Tsuyee Pei had done in Hong Kong. One year after Tsuyee arrived in Shanghai, the Bank of China reorganized itself as an insti-

▶

Shanghai at night. Aldous Huxley
called the city "life itself . . . nothing
more intensely living can be imagined."

◀

The Pei home on Ferguson Road. Like much
of Shanghai's Chinese gentry, the Peis
lived in the comparative comfort and safety
of the French Concession.

tution that would handle the republic's international finances. Bank officials made their young currency expert responsible for updating China's antiquated financial system. After observing modern banking practices firsthand on a tour of England and the United States, Tsuyee initiated foreign exchange operations in all commercial ports and opened eighteen new branches around the world. In 1934 he helped draft a monetary reform that replaced China's erratic silver standard with a more manageable paper currency known as *fapi*. When his father's signature appeared on paper bills, Ieoh Ming's classmates kidded him about its resemblance to his own handwriting.

Shanghai was a city incorrigibly obsessed with wealth and style, and its rising class of urban intelligentsia—the foremost writer of the time, Lu Xun, called them "imitation foreign devils"—adopted the mores of British gentlemen. Tsuyee Pei, for example, sported high-collared English-style suits, parted his hair in the Western style, joined clubs and played golf.

Ieoh Ming, too, was enthralled by the glamorous city around him. He and his siblings perched at the window competing to see who could pick the most elegant of the passing cars: "Ford is mine," "Cadillac is mine," "Chevrolet is mine."

Ieoh Ming was enrolled in St. John's Middle School, an exclusive and expensive boarding school run by American Episcopalians—one of many missionary groups dedicated to inculcating elite Chinese youngsters with foreign values. The students wore Western uniforms and competed in tennis and basketball against American students. Except for Chinese history, all subjects were taught in English. They read *The Three Musketeers, A Tale of Two Cities* and the Bible. Their rigorous curriculum culminated each term in three-hour exams administered in an assembly hall. Upon graduation, students received diplomas written in English. "The students were a new sort of being, the product of a Westernized bourgeoisie," said Chinese scholar Fred Wakeman. "They were anglicized and estranged from traditional Chinese society."

Ieoh Ming was an exceptional student. He consistently topped his class in grades and distinguished himself as a precociously poised and persuasive talker. "He was a very confident young man," remembered his brother Yu Kun. "He had a talent for convincing people. He sold his ideas very well from an early age. I always thought he should be a lawyer."

Pei earned top grades without being a bookworm. On the contrary, he was a gregarious participant in after-class activities like tennis and volleyball, and an enthusiastic, if not particularly gifted, singer. On free afternoons he and his friends rode the bus downtown to stroll among the chocolate shops, teahouses, food stalls, department stores and billiard halls. Best of all, there were three elegant movie theaters—the Grand, the Roxy and the Carlton— where the boys faithfully attended Hollywood films that arrived in Shanghai just weeks after their American release.

Tsuyuan, Pei's uncle, who was older by one year and more like a brother, remembers Ieoh Ming gazing intently at him one day and saying, "You look very much like Clark Gable." Ieoh was even able to sing parts of "Tell Me Tonight," the musical theme of a Gable film. American culture was not lost on the boys in Shanghai.

But even youngsters like Ieoh Ming were made to understand how fragile Shanghai was in the face of gathering enmities around the world. In 1931 the Japanese military invaded Manchuria. The Chinese retaliated by boycotting Japanese goods. In Shanghai, 700,000 tons of spurned cargo accumulated in warehouses and on piers. Stores run by Japanese families closed down. Banks refused Japanese tender. On January 18, a mob of coolies roughed up five Japanese priests associated with a Buddhist sect. A Japanese resident, in turn, burned down a Chinese-owned towel factory by throwing blazing newspapers into the weaving room. A week later Japanese warships sailed up the Whangpoo and disgorged thousands of marines, purportedly to protect the city's thirty thousand Japanese nationals from further abuse. Late one

Thursday night, columns of advancing Japanese troops shot out streetlights, ignited buildings and fired on innocent pedestrians. Ieoh Ming's grandfather and his uncle Tsuyuan happened to be en route from Suzhou when martial law was declared. Barricades of sandbags and barbed wire prevented them from entering the safety of the foreign concessions, which the Japanese respected as neutral territory. Fortunately the Shanghai Commercial Savings Bank straddled the border of the French Concession. They were able to reach Tsuyee's home by entering one door and exiting another. Ieoh Ming and his uncle Tsuyuan shared a bed that night. Toward midnight they heard bombardment from Japanese planes and warships as Japanese soldiers clashed with China's Nineteenth Army along the northern edge of the city. The conflict subsided in March after China agreed to pull its troops back and call off the boycott; both governments discreetly called it an "incident." In reality, the Battle of 1932 was the first intimation of a war that would eventually extinguish Shanghai's charmed life.

The foreign residents, many of whom watched the conflagration from balconies and rooftops while sipping cocktails or demitasses, did not believe their world was soon to end. Shanghai's uninhibited social whirl resumed in the Westerners' last bastion of colonial privilege. The taipans partied on in their self-governed enclaves. Having come to Shanghai by way of India, the British in particular perpetuated the colonial atmosphere. Consorting with the natives, they felt, weakened one's moral fiber. To adopt local habits was to "go native," a pitiable fate. A notorious Shanghai story concerns a sign posted in the little Bund Garden outside the British embassy. "No dogs or Chinese allowed," it supposedly warned. In fact, no such sign existed, but it could have, given the prevailing sentiment.

Life was an endless round of well-insulated pleasures for the wealthy taipans. Their relations with Chinese rarely went beyond business. The Shanghai of Matheson and Sassoon, Keswick and Butterfield, Texaco and

Standard Oil, kept its distance from the Shanghai of Soongs and Chens, Changs and Lees. Many taipans were not acquainted with any Chinese at all aside from their houseboys, whom they addressed in a picturesque garble of Chinese and English known as pidgin ("come chop-chop").

Well-to-do Chinese families like the Peis aspired to penetrate concession society, but they remained outsiders in their own city, their noses pressed to the pane. They were barred from the clubs where foreigners swam, played tennis and entertained one another. Ieoh Ming thus grew into adolescent awareness within a milieu charged with the constant pressure to assimilate among the powerful and privileged. It was a restless ambition he would carry throughout his life.

At the same time, however, the Shanghai Chinese harbored a subtle counter-snobbery, for they were equally convinced of their own cultural superiority. For most of the past four thousand years China had the finest standard of living in the world. Long before the European Renaissance, China enjoyed a golden age of refinement, of poetry and subtle paintings, of philosophy and beautiful perfumed women in silk gowns passing under lacquered palace eaves. A fully civilized China had produced silk, a moral code inscribed in Confucian texts, and breakthrough inventions like printing, the mariner's compass and gunpowder, not to mention a sophisticated cuisine (Italy's diet staple developed from the noodles brought home by Marco Polo). Entire libraries had existed in Buddhist monasteries before Europe had its first printed book. More than sixty years before Vasco da Gama rounded the Cape of Good Hope, the Chinese had sailed as far as the Persian Gulf and East Africa. They never colonized or expanded their maritime power because they saw little of interest beyond their borders.

The Confucians divided the world into two spheres: China and the land of the outer barbarians. The Celestial Empire grew insular in the knowledge that it was an island of civilization surrounded by inferior cultures—Japanese, Koreans, Mongols, Turks and Vietnamese. The "foreign devils" who arrived from Europe in search of silk, tea, porcelain and lacquerware only confirmed their view. They dismissed the encroaching Europeans as hairy, big-nosed barbarians burdened with crude morals, a coarse appetite for violence, bulging eyes and unkempt hair.

In the late eighteenth century, having lost its foothold in America, Britain sought another in the Far East. In September of 1792, George III sent Lord George Macartney to Emperor Qianlong's Summer Palace outside Peking to request diplomatic representation and unhampered trade. The Chinese towed Macartney and his party to the palace in a barge with a banner that read, "Red Barbarian Bearing Tribute." The courtiers giggled at the emissaries' powdered wigs and tight-fitting clothes, at their bearded faces and coarse language.

After neglecting to touch his head to the floor nine times in the ritual kowtow prescribed by court etiquette, thereby suggesting that his government was equal to China's, Macartney asked the emperor to open his ports to foreign trade. Qianlong flatly refused. He also scorned the magnificent gifts—telescopes, hunting rifles, cannons, a hot air balloon, and a crystal chandelier—that Macartney offered as examples of Western goods. "We possess all things," Qianlong wrote in a letter to George III. "I set no value on things strange and ingenious and have no use for your country's manufacturers."

Qianlong was vaingloriously convinced that China had already achieved perfection. In reality, it had fallen into a perilous state of complacency. The only way to qualify for imperial service, and hence the only means to achieve power and success, was to master the ancient wisdom enshrined in the Confucian classics, studied at the expense of practical knowledge. Fossilized in a feudal agrarian state, Chinese society made almost no material headway or technological advance for centuries. While its greatest scholars recited codified poetic wisdom in a wistful state of melancholy contentment, the rigorous scientific inquiry of Western thinkers like Bacon, Descartes and Newton led to one invention after another in service to industry, exploration and arms. By the middle of the nineteenth century Great Britain was at the height of its imperial power. China's haughty refusal to join the family of nations provoked the English to subdue the imperial government with devastating naval power based, ironically, on gunpowder and the mariner's compass—both Chinese inventions. A humiliating series of Western incursions culminated in the nineteenth-century Opium Wars, which led in turn to the foreign occupation of Shanghai and four other so-called treaty ports.

Defeat came as a humiliating revelation. China was not the Middle Kingdom after all. "The British victory had turned the Chinese emperor's international status upside down," the Chinese scholar John K. Fairbank once observed. "Instead of being universal ruler at the top of civilization, he became a semicolonial anachronism."

The silk-robed mandarins riding in gilded sedan chairs had, over the centuries, perfected a scornful gaze, which they cast upon the passing peasantry. The Chinese gentry of Pei's childhood inflicted a similar contempt upon the foreigners, whom they secretly regarded as the boorish beneficiaries of a historical accident. The unspoken sentiment was that these crass merchants, with their red faces and protruding eyes, had come only to exploit and amass wealth. They had no appreciation for the gracious way to enter a room or drink a cup of tea. And they displayed a most inelegant habit of pounding the table with their fists when they didn't get their way.

"Throughout the ages, the Chinese have had only two ways of looking at foreigners: up to them as superior beings or down on them as wild animals," Lu Xun wrote in 1911. "They have never been able to treat them as friends, to consider them as people like themselves."

For Chinese youngsters of Pei's station, the trick was to partake of all the superficial Western frippery—the jitterbug and jazz, the movies and fedoras—while maintaining an inward knowledge of China's cultural superiority. "The Chinese had an inferiority complex, but they also had a *superiority* complex," explained Edwin T. Morris, a Far East scholar. "Sometimes they deferred to Westerners and other times they let it be known that their ancestors were dressed in silks and satins while Westerners were walking around in bearskins."

As a result, Ieoh Ming and his classmates, the descendants of the Celestial Empire, led a childhood full of day-to-day paradoxes. Adoration of a Cadillac did not interfere with devotion to Confucian virtues; Bing Crosby cohabited with Buddha. In fact, the Chinese reluctance to pledge exclusive allegiance to a single belief was a source of great frustration to Western missionaries. "It was in keeping with Chinese tradition to live in different worlds," said Chinese historian Wellington Chan. "They moved quite fluidly in and out of different disciplines. In China, there was no one God who gave us everything. There was no original sin. Therefore, there was no one way of interpreting right and wrong." The Middle Kingdom was big enough for many faiths to exist without friction. It was not uncommon for Chinese to light incense for departed ancestors, pray in a Buddhist temple and take communion in a Christian church.

This comfortable duality expressed itself in Shanghai homes, many of which had Western-style entries for foreigners and separate entries with traditional upturned roofs and window latticework for Chinese. The redbrick home of Sun Yat-sen, the meeting place of republican revolutionaries, contained an American Victrola and Dickens volumes beside traditional Chinese furniture. Biographies of Bismarck and Lincoln shared a shelf with ancient Chinese texts.

Ieoh Ming himself passed with ease through starkly different realms. Much of his exposure to traditional Chinese culture came through his learned mother, a flutist, wine maker, chef and practicing Buddhist. Her letters, printed with perfect penmanship, often ended with a poem of her own composition. Seventy years later, a misty-eyed Pei would remember her as the single greatest influence on his life and career. "My father was a banker," he said, "so there was very little rapport between myself and my father when it came to choosing a profession."

As the eldest son, Ieoh Ming alone was allowed to accompany her on retreats to a mountaintop monastery where he sat in silent meditation for long periods. "She could only have me there for about a week because it was a very difficult place for a little boy to be," Pei said. "There was nothing at all to do, no one to play with. At night it was the deepest silence I had ever heard—nothing, nothing at all. Then, just before dawn, there was a strange creaking, groaning sound. It was the shoots of young bamboo, all coming up from the earth at the same time. This was a great gift that my mother had given me, to hear the silence. A few years ago I went to a Buddhist monastery in Japan to try to recapture something of that experience—you can't do it in China anymore, of course—but it just wasn't the same."

When Ieoh Ming was thirteen, his mother became gravely ill with cancer. As the oldest son, he was given the honor of preparing her long-stemmed opium pipe, the customary Chinese sedative. When she died, he prayed for her soul's safe passage into the next life at the traditional funeral held at a Buddhist temple. It was up to him to be strong to set an example for his siblings. "As the oldest son," he said, "I was supposed to understand."

Ieoh Ming was left with a father who, by custom, stood apart from household intimacies. Relations between father and son in traditional Chinese society were based not on Western-style familial affection but on formal expressions of respect outlined in the austere Confucian codes. It was an orderly, sober system, but also repressive. To his children, Tsuyee was an honored figure who rarely shared his feelings or discussed his work. He "was not the sort of man to pat a son on the back, or hug a daughter," Pei said.

After his wife's death, Tsuyee fell into a depression. The bank sent him to Europe for a restorative change of scene. In London he met a much younger woman, Shiyun Jiang, the daughter of a Chinese diplomat stationed abroad. Three years later she married Tsuyee in Paris and moved to Shanghai, on the condition that his four children live separately. When Ieoh Ming left St. John's for weekends and holidays, he and his siblings no longer stayed at his father's comfortable home, but at a series of rented houses in less elegant neighborhoods. These households were maintained by an amah and supervised by his grandfather. On the brink of adolescence, Ieoh Ming had lost not only his mother but his family home as well.

Fortunately, Ieoh Ming's grandfather, Li-tai, helped compensate for the loss with his own presence. If Pei was deprived of his parents he gained through his grandfather a grounding in the fading disciplines of ancient China. Millennia of mandarin culture formed a bedrock to which his developing sense of identity anchored itself.

In China, the Laojia, or ancestral home, goes a long way toward defining the individual. Ieoh Ming occasionally escaped Shanghai's cosmopolitan bustle for the comparative hush of his grandfather's Suzhou home, a sumptuous residence with half a dozen courtyards planted with chrysanthemums and a study where family members read the Chinese classics and practiced calligraphy.

The fifty-mile trip was like plummeting back in time to the picturesque Middle Kingdom, for this walled town dotted with pagodas, temples and honorary gates had changed little since a local chieftain, Prince Ho Lu, built it 2,500 years before, about the time when Confucius and Buddha were alive.

Ieoh Ming's grandfather belonged to the last generation to uphold the Confucian order of Suzhou. He eschewed Western clothes in favor of the long queue and broad-sleeved jackets that symbolized the gentry's status. Ac-

▲ At the center of Suzhou's scholarly life lay
its walled gardens, the most elaborate of
which was the 500-year-old Shizilin, or
Stone Lion Grove. Ieoh Ming played there
among the pavilions and ponds.

▶

A typical Suzhou lane. "In Heaven there
is paradise," an old proverb stated.
"On earth, Suzhou and Hangzhou."

▲

Travelers compared Suzhou to Florence for

its artistic refinement and to Venice for its

elaborate canals.

cording to an old Confucian adage, "Some men labor with their minds, some with their hands. Those who labor with their minds govern others, those who labor with their hands are governed by others."

Li-tai enforced the Confucian codes that emphasized the family as society's fundamental institution. He gathered three hundred relatives at a family temple built on one hundred private acres for seasonal ceremonies of music and fireworks commemorating the ancestral spirits, and he arranged for poor relatives to receive tuition money and bags of rice. In an exercise meant to instill respect for elders, Ieoh Ming was obliged to sit motionless in a rigid straight-backed chair facing Li-tai until the old man moved. Even Li-tai's adult sons feared his summons. When Tsuyuan and Tsuyee returned from a play late one evening they slept in the front hall rather than risk awakening their father.

Li-tai had a particular fondness for Ieoh Ming, and was therefore lenient. He impressed on Ieoh Ming the elaborate code of Confucian virtues that led to noble character: obey one's elders without condition, shun ostentation, never show anger, express oneself calmly and clearly. "He who exercises government by means of virtue," Confucius said, "may be compared to the North Pole star, to which all other stars are attracted." These traits have served Ieoh Ming well throughout his career in America, a country that does not always value such qualities.

Confucian teaching emphasizes that virtuous conduct gives the "superior man" a prestige that translates into influence and allegiance. In Europe, kings ruled by divine birthright, but in China, mandarins earned their authority through moral sensitivity and cultivation. Pei learned at his grandfather's knee that civility must be practiced not just as an end in itself but as a means to power as well.

At the center of Suzhou's genteel scholarly life lay its walled gardens, the most elaborate of which was the Shizilin, or Stone Lion Grove, built in the fourteenth century by the abbot of an adjacent Buddhist monastery. For centuries this sanctuary inspired monks, artists and poets. Its compact acreage contained a Sleeping Cloud Room, a Lotus Flower Hall, a Kiosk Where One Questions the Plum Tree, a Pavilion for Viewing the Mountain, and a Standing in the Snow Reading Room, so named because a student went there to visit a teacher who had fallen asleep and stood patiently in the snow waiting for him to wake up.

The Shizilin's ponds and pavilions fell into disrepair after a quasi-Christian uprising known as the Taiping Rebellion swept through the Yangtze Valley in the 1870s and destroyed parts of Suzhou. The abandoned garden was bought in 1917 and elaborately restored in the opulent Ching style. Ieoh Ming spent many hours there playing hide-and-seek with his cousins and studying the Chinese classics under a tutor's supervision.

It was Ieoh Ming's great-uncle, Runsheng, who bought the abandoned garden in 1917 for 9,900 silver coins. Runsheng came from a poor branch of the Pei clan. As a child he had often lacked food and clothing, but he later parlayed two silver dollars his grandfather gave him into a fortune and became a dyestuffs tycoon. His ownership of the Shizilin lent him a sense of gentility. To own a garden demonstrated a proper appreciation of aesthetic and scholarly matters. It was the rough equivalent of a parvenu acquiring a château from an impoverished aristocrat. Its new inhabitants could renounce the worldly duties outside its walls and devote themselves, as mandarins should, to cultivating bamboo, practicing calligraphy and receiving guests in waterside pavilions.

In a land plagued by internecine conflict, the garden was a refuge of pebble paths rambling among ponds and sweet-smelling shrubs. Through the weary cycles of rebellion and invasion, it remained a tranquil place in which to enjoy a poetic respite, sip tea with friends on moon-viewing terraces and admire the shadow of plum blossoms cast on weathered white walls while children played among lotus flowers and grandparents sunned themselves.

The scholar-official comfortably seated beside trickling waters might ask his servants to bring out his vases, ceramics and scroll paintings for a private viewing. During the sweltering Suzhou summers, families virtually lived within these gardens waiting to catch a restorative breeze.

The garden was more than just a peaceful retreat; it was the medium through which mandarins sought harmony with the universe. While Confucius regulated the affairs of men with rules of conduct, Lao-tzu, the father of Taoism, taught that contentment lay within us all along. "The further one goes," he said, "the less one knows." The garden helped one rediscover the peace inherent in the natural world. By distilling all of the variety of nature to its poetic essence, the garden led the viewer to inward truths.

Unlike European gardens, which flaunt their grandiose symmetry in expansive lawns and manicured hedges sweeping among fountains and marble stairways, Suzhou gardens were obscured behind serpentine paths and miniature mountains. They revealed their inner beauty slowly, tantalizingly over the course of a small episodic journey around the confined acreage. Visitors contemplating the wind soughing through plum trees and water trickling against mossy rocks were meant to feel themselves merge with the natural world and its underlying rhythms of yin and yang, winter and spring, life and death.

The Shizilin garden in particular was famous for its craggy limestone rocks, which had lain for a generation or more at the bottom of a nearby lake where circular currents had scoured them into fantastic shapes. The fourteenth-century artist Ni Tsan had arranged the rocks into grottos and peaks. In her 1939 monograph on Chinese gardens, Dorothy Graham described them as "rocks that seem to have endured since the beginning of time, rocks seared by fierce suns, shaped by sweeping tides, rocks that suggest infinity." The Shizilin, she wrote, was "as remote from actuality as a scene from another planet. . . . Ni Tsan made pictures in imperishable rocks."

In China, rocks were endowed with great metaphysical importance. They were valued for the distinct spirits—the cosmic vapors—inhabiting their forms. The Sung dynasty painter Mei Fei went so far as to adopt a specific rock as his "big brother." Pei remembered the influence of rocks on his own development:

> How such gardens are made, or I should say harvested, is
> very interesting. You see, those rock farmers were, and are,
> artists—and you can go beyond the gardens to the whole
> environment of Suzhou . . . all of it has instilled a lasting
> metaphysical image, if not a direct influence, on the shape of
> my work. The way those rock farmers did things pertains to a
> perception of time, and to a sense of accountability to time.
>
> They usually worked with a porous volcanic rock, and
> they selected the rocks most carefully. Then they chiseled
> them most carefully, just enough to open up that piece of
> rock to the subtle sculptural spirit that the particular farmer
> wanted—yet the rock would still be very raw, not unlike
> the perforations and imperfections implanted by time
> when the farmer found it. Then he would find, also most
> carefully, a spot near the edge of a lake or a stream. And he
> would place the rock, just so, into the water, which, over a
> generation, or sometimes over two or three, would erode
> the shape. The farmer himself, or his son or grandson,
> would later harvest the shape, incorporating it into the
> composition of the garden.
>
> This sense of connection, of continuity, is an extremely
> telling aspect of Chinese culture—the father will sow, the

son will reap—and, in principle, it is a primary impulse in considering the results of any action.

. . . My own development, when I stop to think about it, is very much in that spirit. I have been placed at the edge, or often at the center, of many different lakes and streams. And my buildings, like those of every architect, are always being pulled out of the flow of the water and put back in. Their shapes have hopefully been chosen most carefully, placed most carefully to respond to the functional currents swirling around them. . . . An architect has to try (and I have tried) to participate in such a way that his buildings become congenial, caring and cared-for expressions of that flow. It took me a while to understand this dimension of design—to design in the spirit of that garden of my childhood. And once you build in that spirit—how it humbles you.

When the time came to discuss Ieoh Ming's career, his father advocated banking or medicine. But blood made Ieoh Ming squeamish, and he was all too aware of how difficult his father's profession could be. "I had already sensed that the life of a banker was not ideal," he said. "I had seen from my father's experience that bankers were constantly under pressure. He was not entirely happy."

In fact, for a man who later conducted himself with a preternatural sure-footedness, Ieoh Ming began his career with curious indirection. Like any affluent Chinese teenager, he was caught up in the diversions of Shanghai's bustling downtown boulevards. The architect Louis Kahn, discussing his own childhood, once described a city as "a place where a small boy, as he walks through it, may see something that will tell him what he wants to do his whole life." So it was for Ieoh Ming.

"Next to the billiard hall and motion picture theater was this building under construction," he recalled some forty years later. "They said it was going to be twenty-six stories, and I just couldn't believe it! Imagine, all the buildings around were only five, six, seven, eight stories, and this one was going to be twenty-six stories. So every weekend I would watch it going up."

The object of Pei's fascination was the Park Hotel, which would be the tallest building in the Far East and the culmination of Western glamour. It contained two hundred five luxurious rooms, a spacious air-conditioned dining room and a roof garden with a dizzying view of the racetrack directly below where the taipans raced Mongolian ponies.

The hotel's Czechoslovakian architect, Ladislav Hudec, was an acknowledged master of Shanghai's colonial classicism. But unlike those monuments to Western domination, with their pillars and clock towers preposterously piled above the Whangpoo River, the Park Hotel exhibited the relatively clean lines of a new style evolving a world away. Shortly after the hotel was finished, Ieoh Ming paused as he entered the neighboring Grand Theatre with his uncle Tsuyan. With a few deft strokes, he drew the outline of the building on a piece of paper and held it up for his uncle to see. He was impressed by Ieoh Ming's untrained talent. "That's something!" he said.

"I was fascinated by the idea of a building of that height," Pei remembered. "It was as exciting to me then as the idea of going to the moon is to youngsters today. I decided that was what I wanted to do."

Pei had only the vaguest sense of what his newly chosen career entailed. "I did not know what architecture really was in China," he said. "At that time there was no difference between an architect, a construction man and an engineer." Architecture had never differentiated itself from the artisanship and

▲

As the apotheosis of Western glamour,

the Park Hotel aroused Ieoh Ming's first in-

terest in architecture.

building trades of low social standing. Consequently the design profession did not emerge as a prestigious entity until the arrival of foreign practitioners like Hudec.

Where would Ieoh Ming learn his chosen profession? It was common for the sons of China's gentry to study abroad with the expectation that they would return to help China catch up with the Western world. With his business connections to Shanghai's Scottish and British bankers, Tsuyee advocated an English school. But Ieoh Ming, having fallen under the spell of American movies, defied his father once again. He had been seduced in particular by Bing Crosby's *College Humor,* one of many rousing campus films produced in the 1930s. Not surprisingly, football weekends and spirited cheerleaders appealed to him more than China's strict missionary colleges.

America was an energetic, forward-looking force beckoning from the far side of the world. As he would throughout his life, Pei displayed an eye for the coming thing.

Ieoh Ming took the Oxford exams, as his father requested, but chose instead the University of Pennsylvania. Penn was by far the most popular design school among Chinese students, and by the 1930s, the first wave of graduates had already returned home to compete with well-established foreign architects.

The world would likely never have known I. M. Pei had he remained in China. His talents could scarcely have found expression during the war against Japan and the repressive revolution that followed. How many I. M. Peis, his life begs us to ask, remained in China, never to be heard of?

3

A CHINESE STUDENT
IN CAMBRIDGE

On August 13, 1935, the seventeen-year-old Ieoh Ming Pei rode a small ferry from the Bund to the *President Coolidge*, a comfortable American ocean liner anchored where the Yangtze River emptied into the East China Sea. More than a dozen relatives came aboard to wish him bon voyage. He shared a cabin on the passage with a St. John's friend, J. D. Woo, who was also en route to Penn. They embarked with an unpolished grasp of English and the expectation of returning wiser and more worldly a few years later.

Pei went ashore at Nagasaki the next day and took a train to Tokyo, where he visited Frank Lloyd Wright's Imperial Hotel, one of the most celebrated buildings of the century. The architect himself called it his masterpiece. Pei rejoined the ship in Yokohama and sailed for Hawaii and finally California.

When he arrived with J.D. in San Francisco on August 26, a friend of Tsuyee's, an American banker, met them at the dock and took them to his home. After a few days of sight-seeing, they crossed the United States by train, rolling through the midwestern dust bowl en route to Philadelphia. The two curious boys gained a panoramic view of the country, though America could hardly have resembled the glamorous place Pei had admired through Hollywood's rose-colored aperture. Franklin Roosevelt was midway through his first term as the Depression crept toward low ebb. It was a grim season of breadlines and Hoovervilles. Harry Truman was a freshman senator, and John Steinbeck

◄ **I. M. Pei as a Harvard student.**

had just written *Tortilla Flat.* The rumba was the latest dance. Hopeful young people danced until they dropped in the marathon dance craze.

Pei found Penn's architecture school an inhospitable institution housed in a gloomy Victorian building constructed for the school of dentistry. The curriculum, presided over by a pedantic dean named George Simpson Koyle and the Parisian classicist Paul Cret, ardently subscribed to the nineteenth-century system transplanted from the renowned Ecole des Beaux-Arts in Paris. Students were expected to acquire the rudiments of classical design by laboriously copying plans and by producing elaborate renderings in charcoal or China ink, which they ground themselves. Instructors evaluated and graded their work before the entire class.

All this came as a crushing revelation to Pei. His strength lay in math and science; it had not occurred to him that he would need to be an artist as well. He found himself wandering down unfamiliar hallways plastered with spectacular watercolor renderings of Gothic monasteries and Renaissance palazzi foreshadowed by the slanting light of ancient dusks. Would he be expected to perform such feats himself? "What really determined that this was not the school for me," he said, "was the sight of an enormous drawing at the stair landing. The subject was a lamasary in Tibet. Now, that's my country, and I had no idea how anybody with a name like Fitzgerald could do a lamasary in Tibet. I thought architecture must be something very different from what I imagined."

Socially, Penn languished on the lower rung of the Ivy League, its classrooms filled not with alumni of St. Paul's and Groton, but with their counterparts from the Midwest and from public schools. The architecture school was not above subjecting freshmen—or "niggers," as they were called—to a series of sanctioned hazings. Freshmen had to earn the right to wear smocks in their basement studio by fighting off attacking sophomores in a ritual brawl, known as the smock fight, waged on the school lawn. Raised in a culture that emphasized an appreciation of calligraphy and gardening, Pei must have found this roughneck rite unspeakably coarse. Even more disenchanting, as one of the first big cities north of the Mason-Dixon line, Philadelphia harbored an only slightly suppressed bigotry toward people of color.

Shortly after classes began, Pei and J.D. were visited by friends who were enrolled at the Massachusetts Institute of Technology. In a precocious stroke of pluck, they transferred out of Penn after just two weeks and joined their friends at MIT. Discouraged by what he had seen of Beaux-Arts methodology, Pei arranged to study engineering instead of architecture. By trading the banks of the Schuylkill for the hallowed precincts of Cambridge, Pei gravitated, as he would throughout his life, toward gentility and prestige.

Pei felt more comfortable in Boston. Its banks had commercial ties to China dating back to the late nineteenth century when Yankee clippers had plied the Far East trade routes. (The cargo dumped during the Boston Tea Party came from China.) Pei consequently arrived with introductions to his father's business acquaintances. "So I was able to enter Boston society very early on, long before I managed to speak English," Pei said. "I really had a rather comfortable experience as a foreign student in this country."

MIT also proved more hospitable to foreigners. The school welcomed racial diversity, and Pei found some thirty of his countrymen enrolled, with their own chapter of a national Chinese fraternity called F.F., which served as a network for privileged Chinese students around the country.

MIT's dean, William Emerson, a great-nephew of Ralph Waldo Emerson, took a benevolent interest in promising pupils, and he recognized in Pei's engineering drawings the hand and imagination of a gifted architect. He walked Pei all over Boston pointing out its classical details. "Pei must have been an outstanding student, because he was the only one mentioned at home," said Emerson's stepgrandson, Malcolm Frazier.

Over Thanksgiving dinner at his Brattle Street home, Emerson persuaded Pei to put engineering aside and resume his architectural studies. "He was not only my dean but my guardian as well," Pei recounted. "He treated me very specially. When he said, 'I've seen enough of your work. You will do well,' I took his advice to stay in architecture. But in terms of design, he had little influence on me."

Pei mastered the elaborate technique of Beaux-Arts renderings at MIT's architectural studios, then located in the Rogers Building across the river near Copley Square. In fact, he emerged as something of a studio wonder boy with perennial appearances on the dean's list. Frank Sargent, a classmate who later became governor of Massachusetts, remembered him as a clear stand-out. "I was always careful to sit at the drafting table next to his so I could peer over at his drawings," he said. "It was clear that he was going straight to the top by the way he thought and the way he expressed himself. We all knew this guy had it. . . . He may have been smaller in stature than most of his fellow students, but he soon topped them head and shoulders in every other way."

Pei and his classmates submitted to the drudgery of re-creating the compulsory classical proportions in exquisite detail, but everyone knew this passionless system of superficial pattern-making was doomed to obsolescence. A restless generation afflicted with doubts over Europe's fixed-class system bridled against the academy's obsession with duplicating the corrupt privilege of Victorian status symbols on behalf of a nouveau riche clientele yearning for the false indulgences of aristocracy. Architectural splendor was no longer affordable, nor did it seem appropriate. To design a quaint château or a Tudor mansion amid the misery of the Depression appeared wasteful and exploitive. Restive students inspired by FDR's New Deal wanted to participate in the exhilarating pursuit of new solutions. Philip Johnson and Henry-Russell Hitchcock of the freshly founded Museum of Modern Art in New York had spurred the insurrection some years earlier by exhibiting a new European architecture of undecorated white walls, candidly expressed structure, and mass-produced materials in a show called *The International Style:*

▶

Pei, FRONT ROW, SECOND FROM LEFT, stands with his sophomore classmates. After Dean Emerson persuaded him to resume his architectural studies, he emerged as a studio wunderkind.

Pei's MIT thesis: a mobile theater for the Chinese Ministry of Propaganda.

▼

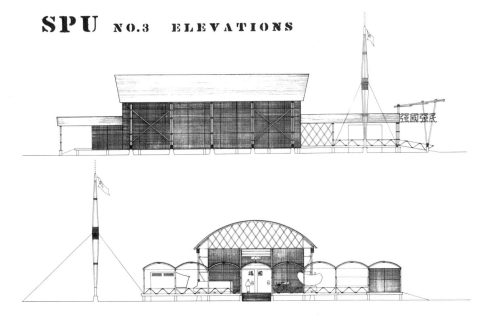

SPU NO.3 ELEVATIONS

Architecture Since 1922. Pei and his classmates carefully followed the chaste new style's development in design magazines received by the school library, their listening post on foreign developments. "Everybody supported the changes occurring in the architectural schools," said Pei's classmate William Hible. "We waited impatiently for the *Architectural Review* to come out every month."

Their search for fresh ideas led them to a Swiss-born celebrity of the Paris art wars named Charles-Edouard Jeanneret who, switching his keen avant-garde sensibility from painting to design, reinvented himself as an architect operating under the nom de plume "Le Corbusier." Mired at their dull drafting tables reconstructing balustrades and ghostly statues, Pei and like-minded students found Le Corbusier a dazzling seducer. "I was not satisfied with Beaux-Arts training," Pei remembered, "nor were many of my contemporaries. So we began to look elsewhere for inspiration. The library was a main source. It was at the library that I learned about Le Corbusier. His books were very much pored over by all the students."

Le Corbusier obliged their restlessness with stirring exhortations for "a fundamentally new aesthetic" in which houses would be "machines for living" and the accumulated styles of history would be tossed on the trash heap. "The styles of Louis XIV, XV, XVI, or Gothic," he wrote in his ringing manifesto, *Vers une Architecture,* "are to architecture what a feather is on a woman's head."

Not everyone embraced Le Corbusier's brash declarations of a new spirit. Frank Lloyd Wright derided him as "a painter and pamphleteer," and a Swiss newspaper warned that his Swiss Pavilion, a stylish slab on stilts, would corrupt the youth who inhabited it. But Le Corbusier gave voice to the collective frustrations of a generation that felt confined by architecture's Old World conventions. These impressionable followers believed he could do no wrong. "There were no teachers to teach us the new architecture," Pei later told

Time, "so we turned to Corbu's books, and these were responsible for half our education."

Le Corbusier's outspoken contempt for antiquity and his harsh utility violated everything Dean Emerson valued. Emerson had attended the Ecole des Beaux-Arts in Paris at the turn of the century and had built hospitals and bunkers for the Red Cross in France during World War I. He faithfully returned to Paris during summer breaks to do research for books on bridges and brickwork—homages to the nineteenth-century France he loved. Nonetheless, Emerson was open-minded enough to invite Le Corbusier to speak at MIT during a lecture tour sponsored by the Museum of Modern Art in New York. In November 1935, Le Corbusier, a cadaverous figure dressed in his usual black suit and thick, owl-eyed glasses, illustrated his irreverent chat with lantern slides and diagrams scribbled on an enormous paper scroll stretched across the stage. This alone was a liberating departure from the formalities of Beaux-Arts presentation. For students who had followed his work from afar, it was as if a god had alighted on Boylston Street. The two days Le Corbusier spent at MIT were "the two most important days in my professional life," Pei said. "He was insolent. He was abusive, but he did everything right as far as I was concerned. We had to be shocked out of our complacency."

The eyes of young architects were also opened by Frank Lloyd Wright, whose low-slung interlocking spaces grounded in the prairie landscape may have reminded Pei of Suzhou. He decided to investigate firsthand. In the summer following his junior year, he somewhat blithely drove his beat-up Chevy to Spring Green, Wisconsin, and showed up, unannounced, at Wright's Taliesin East. "I drove into the compound and stopped, not knowing where to go," he recalled. "Suddenly seven huge Alsatian dogs pounded on my car and barked and yelped at me. They looked ferocious. I felt trapped. Several students just stood there and laughed. I drove away." Pei continued to Los Angeles, where he helped a local firm design a prison.

Wright had avid apprentices gathered around him at Taliesin, but he failed to stir the hearts of a socially conscious generation scouting the horizon for heroes. He seemed to be a relic from another era. "I used to say Frank Lloyd Wright was the greatest architect of the nineteenth century," said Philip Johnson. "None of us regarded him as a major figure. We were wrong, of course. It was a matter of fashion."

Another brief encounter was to change Pei's life. During an excursion to New York in 1938, he went to Grand Central Station to meet a fellow F.F. member. His friend stepped from the train accompanied by a striking Chinese girl named Ai-ling Loo—she later anglicized her name to Eileen—who was en route to Wellesley College, a popular school among well-born Chinese women (its graduates included Madame Chiang Kai-shek). Her father, P.Y. Loo, had, by coincidence, graduated from MIT in 1916 and gone on to become a prominent engineer. Pei offered to drive her to Boston, but she could not accept a ride from a stranger; besides, she already had her train ticket. When Pei later learned that a hurricane had delayed her train in Hartford, he called to tease her—and to ask for a date.

Pei was aware that Harvard's architecture school, located less than a mile from the MIT campus, had emerged as the most progressive alternative for students impatient with Beaux-Arts classicism. While other schools still struggled to detach themselves from the old curriculum, Harvard had already wholeheartedly embraced the new style. Harvard's dean of architecture, a shy, mild-mannered man named Joseph Hudnut, had begun by designing Gothic churches, only to reverse himself and ardently advocate modernism. He used his Harvard bully pulpit to loudly and sarcastically condemn the new neoclassical National Gallery in Washington, D.C., as a "death mask of an ancient culture," the Jefferson Memorial as "an egg on a pantry shelf in a geometric Sahara" and Grant's Tomb as a "ponderous, huge monster." In 1938 he startled the architectural world by offering the school's directorship to Walter Gropius, one of the modern movement's Olympian figures and the founder of Germany's avant-garde Bauhaus, the only established school teaching the new style.

Hudnut's was an auspiciously timed invitation. The Nazis regarded the new architecture polluting their Fatherland as irredeemably infected with socialist sympathies: the Nazi newspaper called Gropius "that elegant salon Bolshevist." The Bauhaus was consequently among the first institutions they closed. Even Gropius's valorous service as a cavalry officer in World War I, for which he received the Iron Cross, did not prevent storm troopers from harassing him at his doorstep. At his wife's urging, Gropius and his family fled to England and then to America, where they were reunited with other Bauhaus refugees—Marcel Breuer, Josef Albers, László Moholy-Nagy and Ludwig Mies van der Rohe. What better place to start from zero, they liked to say, than America, a land of boundless optimism unburdened by history and war?

As the principals of an avant-garde art movement, Gropius and his Bauhaus colleagues had subsisted on minor commissions in their native Germany. Imagine their astonishment, then, when America welcomed them as cultural heroes expelled by Hitler. Thanks to the Museum of Modern Art's assiduous advance promotion, establishment clients awarded the Bauhaus refugees plum commissions, and universities installed them in influential faculty posts. "The White Gods!" Tom Wolfe sarcastically called them in his ardently antimodern book *From Bauhaus to Our House,* "Come from the skies at last!"

Gropius was not a prolific builder like Frank Lloyd Wright, nor was he a rhetorician like Le Corbusier. He filled instead a less visible role as the modern movement's moral backbone—a guiding philosopher and teacher forged in the crucible of European war and destruction. *Architectural Record* published Gropius's pedagogical theories upon his arrival. "More than ever be-

▲

Walter Gropius standing over Pei's desk.

Pei was a slightly skeptical acolyte.

fore," he wrote, "it is in the hands of us architects to help our contemporaries to lead a natural and sensible life instead of paying a heavy tribute to the false gods of make-believe." One month later he received a standing ovation when Dean Emerson introduced him to the Boston Society of Architects. Emerson had to coax the speaker back onstage after his speech to acknowledge the persistent applause.

Pei gleaned some understanding of Harvard's progressive philosophy from a joint MIT-Harvard sketch problem he had participated in. He also came into contact with the neighboring school when a small design magazine called *Task*, produced by Harvard students, published his MIT thesis, a movable pavilion in which the Chinese Ministry of Propaganda could show films and stage plays. "I was aware that something was happening at Harvard," he said, "but Dean Emerson was against the place."

Pei had planned to return home after graduating from MIT in 1940, but his father dissuaded him. Japan's designs on the Asian mainland had only intensified after the Battle of 1932. By 1937, Shanghai was braced for full-scale war. Shortly before 4:30 P.M. on a sweltering hot Saturday in August, five American-made Chinese bombers streaked over Shanghai toward the Japanese cruiser *Idzumo*, flagship of a Japanese fleet menacingly anchored in the Whangpoo. The Chinese hoped to deliver a preemptive strike, but the bombers missed their mark. As they looped back over the city, spectators massed along the Bund watched in disbelief, then horror, as the disabled planes accidentally released four bombs in their direction. Two splashed harmlessly into the Whangpoo. One plunged through the roof of the Palace Hotel. Another caromed off the Cathay Hotel and into the street. Plaster, glass shards and dismembered bodies covered the intersection. The pavement was gooey with dried blood. The seven hundred victims included a neatly decapitated British gentleman in a linen suit. Half an hour later, another errant bomb hit the crowded Great World amusement park, killing five hundred. Later that summer, a shell landed between Shanghai's two main department stores, Wing On and Sincere, during the lunch-hour bustle. "Hundreds of bodies lay in piles," wrote the Associated Press. "It seemed as if the force of the blast had gathered them up and rolled them together. . . . Pools of blood glistened in the streetcar tracks and gutters. Fragments of heads, legs, and arms plastered building fronts. Some were scattered in the street two blocks away."

Until then the taipans, insulated in their grand homes, smugly assumed they were immune from harm, as they had been during the Battle of 1932. But as the Shanghai sky darkened beneath the smoke of daily artillery exchanges, the Japanese encircled the concessions with a barbed-wire fence, and their censors seized the foreign cable offices. The occupying forces pronounced jazz a decadent influence and shut down the dance halls. Some Westerners were evacuated to Hong Kong or Singapore; others were taken to internment camps, where many would die. Meanwhile, the Japanese established gambling and prostitution dens in their deserted homes. "In November the Chinese forces abandoned Shanghai," the American journalist E. O. Hauser wrote. "An army of ninety thousand Japanese pursued them up the Yangtze. . . . The war moved on and Shanghai was left behind. . . . Silence fell upon the city. It was a strange silence after the infernal din of war. . . . The big white office buildings, banks, and hotels were there, along the Bund overlooking the muddy stream below. No one had bothered to destroy them. But behind their windows, life stopped. . . . And there were some who thought that it had been a great and beautiful city, for all its avarice."

The Shanghai of Pei's childhood ended in blood and barbed wire. Pei's stepmother had long since been evacuated to the safety of a Park Avenue apartment in New York with Pei's half sister, Patricia. His father moved with the Bank of China to Chungking, the wartime capital, where he endured repeated air raids. Chiang Kai-shek's Nationalist government and the Communist rebels mounted a united front against the advancing Japanese who by now controlled the railway lines and major cities in the north. Free China could not hold out for long without foreign assistance.

MIT had offered Pei a traveling fellowship upon his graduation in 1940, but Europe was already at war, so Dean Emerson urged him to remain in Cambridge. He took his mentor's advice and accepted a drafting job at Stone & Webster, a Boston-based engineering firm whose wartime contracts included the construction of the first atomic bomb. Pei was driving his Chevy on December 7, 1941, when news of the attack on Pearl Harbor came over the car radio. He was enormously relieved to know that America would be joining the war against Japan.

All the while Pei continued seeing Eileen. They even drove out west together one summer to visit Pei's brother Y.K. at the Colorado School of Mines outside Denver. Although Pei wanted to marry Eileen, she refused until she finished her four years at Wellesley. On June 20, 1942, five days after her graduation, they were wed at the home of the architect William Lawrence Bottomley in New York's River House, a sumptuous apartment building overlooking the East River. The ceremony was performed by Chinese Consul General James Yu.

After a brief honeymoon, the newlyweds returned to Cambridge. Eileen had enrolled in a landscape architecture program at Harvard's Graduate School of Design. Pei had not considered enlisting at Harvard until one of Eileen's professors urged him over dinner one night to enroll in the master's studio taught by Gropius himself. "The next morning," Eileen said, her husband was "off to Dean Hudnut's office." Pei then had to break the news to Dean Emerson who, despite having introduced Gropius at the architectural society meeting, maintained an abiding distaste for him and his strident, inflexible dogma. "When I decided to go to Harvard, Dean Emerson was very unhappy," Pei said. "He felt almost betrayed. He was deeply committed to the Beaux-Arts method of education and genuinely felt that the modern movement was mistaken."

Pei enrolled in the master's program in December 1942. Within a month, however, mindful of the war expanding far beyond the peaceful quadrangles of Cambridge, he deferred his studies and volunteered to serve with a new wartime intelligence agency called the National Defense Research Committee in Princeton, New Jersey. President Roosevelt had created the NDRC in response to a letter from Albert Einstein proposing a permanent liaison between the White House and the physicists conducting secret weapons research. "I would be brought photographs of Japanese towns," Pei said some years later, "and I was supposed to figure out the best way to burn them down. It was awful; I don't even like to think about it."

While not occupied with this work, Pei found time to design. During his stay in Princeton, he won an honorable mention in a design contest sponsored by *Arts & Architecture* magazine for a prefabricated home with modular units linked like the pods of a spaceship. The total cost: $1,060.

While in Princeton, Eileen gave birth to their first child, a son named T'ing Chung. The burdens of motherhood put an end to Eileen's education in landscape design, but with her keen eye and shrewd judgment of character, she remained Pei's closest adviser, his confidante and helpmate. The adult T'ing called her "my father's secret weapon."

In July 1944, Pei's father, Tsuyee, came to the United States to represent China at the United Nations monetary conference at Bretton Woods, New Hampshire. He returned with T. V. Soong in 1945, a few months after the Japanese surrender, to ask the U.S. State Department for a $500 million loan to prop up China's postwar currency. While in New York, Tsuyee was examined by doctors who found an active tubercular spot on his lung. They urged him to stay for sanitarium treatment, but the outbreak of China's civil war demanded his immediate return. While the Allied world celebrated the Pacific victory, Chiang's government and the Communist forces ended their united front against Japan and resumed their struggle for control of China. The Red Army had solidified its guerrilla operations during the war, and it was poised to launch a full-scale offensive. "You must come," commanded a wire from home. "China cannot spare you now."

The same political exigencies that compelled Tsuyee's return also kept his son in the safety of America. "The son of a wealthy man," Confucius said, "does not sit beneath a tottering roof."

Meanwhile, in early 1945, the Peis returned to Cambridge and took a small off-campus apartment with a garden where they grew Chinese snap peas. Pei built a long wooden shelf for the classical records he hoped to take home someday. Early on Saturday morning he would drive through the quiet streets to Boston's flower markets and return laden with colors and scents, reminders of faraway gardens. No doubt he and Eileen could feel the pull of home, like the gravity of a faraway planet. "They missed China; there was a sadness," remembered their friend Chester Nagel. "But there was never any question that they would make the most of being here."

· · · ·

An epochal chapter in American architecture was under way at Harvard's Robinson Hall by the time Pei returned in early 1945. Like other survivors of World War I, disillusioned with the old order, Gropius believed that radical solutions were required if they were to avoid the mistakes of the past. His self-appointed role was to groom second-generation modernists for the heroic task of engineering society's salvation. "There was a great sense of optimism that better architecture would lead to a better world," remembered John Harkness, a contemporary of Pei's. "We were trying to address the basic issues of poverty and housing instead of diddling around with styles or worrying about what costumes to wear to the Beaux-Arts Ball."

With Hudnut's blessing, Gropius expunged the "unassimilated, dead knowledge" of art history from the core curriculum. Students insulated from the corrupting influence of Renaissance and Gothic immersed themselves in the handful of texts elucidating the modern style—Le Corbusier's *Vers une Architecture*, Alfred Roth's *New Architecture*, Sigfried Giedion's *Space, Time and Architecture*, the catalog that accompanied MoMA's International Style exhibit of 1932 and various Bauhaus monographs. "The curriculum was not only ahistoric, it was *anti*historic," said Henry Cobb, a young Bostonian who would later join Pei in private practice. "Gropius believed that students should not study history until they had discovered their own active juices. Everything was embodied in a few books. It was a world in which everything was thought to be possible, and yet our focus was very narrow. That, of course, proved to be our great failing."

While Gropius shaped Harvard's progressive curriculum, a younger Bauhaus expatriate, Marcel Breuer, performed much of the actual instruction. Breuer, who later designed the Whitney Museum in New York, balanced Gropius's intellectual bent with his own easy manner and a facile way of using industrial materials in light, elegant ways. It was Breuer who invented the Wassily chair of leather slung across cantilevered steel tubing, after admiring the graceful form of bicycle handlebars. Much of the familiar bent-steel furniture of today is based on his example. "From Breuer I learned that to understand architecture one must understand life," Pei said. "I also think that Breuer was much more influential than he's been given credit for. A whole generation of architects was influenced by his early work, particularly in the design of houses. When he first came to this country, Breuer was very interested in the use of wood. At that time we had shingles, we had clapboard. But he said, 'Why not use vertical boards and tongue and groove and get completely flat surfaces?' Breuer started all that."

Gropius and Breuer trained an extraordinary corps of precocious talent. In addition to Pei, there was Edward Larrabee Barnes, Henry Cobb, Paul Rudolph, Harry Seidler, and Philip Johnson, who left the Museum of Modern Art to study under Gropius at the relatively advanced age of thirty-four. These acolytes were expected to go forth and occupy frontline positions in modern design. And to a remarkable degree they did.

"It was a very exciting period," Pei recalled. "The school was then full of women and foreigners, aliens like myself, and Philip Johnson, who was a little bit older than the others, so he didn't have to go to war. Plus many, many South Americans. The professors didn't have much work and they were able to concentrate on education. And our relationship with Gropius and Breuer and others was very, very close. We were friends more than just professors and students."

The Peis mixed with easy congeniality. "They were both socially skillful," remembered Constance Breuer, Marcel's widow. "Eileen seemed like the perfect American college girl. She was slim, pretty, active and she spoke with no accent. They fit in perfectly. They always did and they always will."

Gropius had by then built himself a small house beside an apple orchard outside Boston in the genteel village of Lincoln. The Peis house-sat during the summer of 1945 with their baby son, T'ing, while Gropius traveled abroad. The elements showcased in that little white house are so familiar to us now that they barely register: the glass brick, white walls, rooms that flow into one another and the tubular steel chairs. But to Pei and his classmates, who had, up until then, mostly admired modernism in magazines, they came as a revelation—a taste of avant-garde Weimar within walking distance of Walden Pond.

While Gropius conjured up a socialist utopia based on modern worker housing, the professor himself exuded aristocracy. He enthralled the impressionable younger men with the suave manner that led the Bauhaus painter

Paul Klee to nickname him "the Silver Prince." They studied how Gropius held his drink motionless while talking at parties, then downed it in a single gulp. A whole generation of architects, Pei included, affected slicked-back hair and bow ties in imitation of him. "He works until three in the morning, hardly sleeps, and when he looks at you, his eyes are like stars," wrote Bauhaus painter Lyonel Feininger. "I'm sorry for anyone who can't gather strength from him."

Twice a week Gropius circulated through the graduate studio, faithfully stopping at each of the dozen or so drafting tables to offer a critique of the work. Students gathered around as he unsheathed a stubby pencil from his vest pocket to illustrate an idea, twisting his fingers while brooding over the right phrase behind a cloud of tobacco smoke. "When I first came to Harvard," Pei told alumni gathered to celebrate their mentor's eightieth birthday in 1963, "Gropius did not understand my language. Gropius's contribution to the American architectural scene is that he brought us a common language."

In the graduate studio and at occasional Faculty Club dinners, Gropius lavished contempt on the vulgar excesses of Art Deco sunbursts and faux Tudor mansions. He exhorted Pei's contemporaries toward a socially conscious architecture capable of providing low-cost housing constructed of machine-age materials like steel, concrete and glass for a needy world ravaged by depression and war. Only then would the teeming, dark nineteenth-century city give way to light, efficiency and prosperity. "The new architecture," he wrote, "throws open its wall like curtains to admit a plenitude of fresh air, daylight and sunshine. Instead of anchoring buildings ponderously into the ground with massive foundations, it poises them lightly, yet firmly, upon the face of the earth."

Because modernism's founding fathers had already determined that the ideal machine-age building was a stark white cube—"the Harvard box"—Pei and his classmates were most concerned with how to modify the formula to suit the assignment. The unsophisticated "common man" accustomed to the granite embroidery of antiquity might at first resist the sterile prescription of compact kitchens, flat roofs and blank walls, Gropius warned, but he would eventually awaken to see their virtues. "The intellectual groundwork of a new architecture is already established," Gropius promised. "The bench tests of its components have now been completed. There remains the task of imbuing the community with a consciousness of it and its essential rightness."

To study under Gropius was to enlist in a priestly campaign to right the world through design. What young architect could resist such an intoxicating mandate? Pei and his classmates no longer had to cater to a patron's boorish wish list. There would be no more bourgeois imitation villas and custom-tailored châteaux. Their heady, high-minded mission was "to persuade, to educate, and, if necessary, to dictate."

A new egalitarian society would not be built on the puny scale of additions and add-ons. Instead, the graduate studio replaced the organic intricacies of alley and boulevard with entire new master-planned districts. "As students we did many studies in which we would—I shudder to recall—wipe out half of old Boston and examine what it might look like ideally, as if we were the architects for the whole city, starting once again," the architect William Conklin recalled.

None of Gropius's illustrious students would remake downtown America more prolifically than Pei, and yet he did not entirely accept Gropius's eloquently articulated socialist program. "True words are not beautiful," Lao-tzu had warned. "Beautiful words are not true."

Classmates raised on mid-century American optimism might have been naive enough to believe that teamwork and prefabricated materials could save a troubled world, but Pei, as the product of a civilization that had endured millennia of repression and war, viewed architecture's own insurrection with Confucian circumspection. "I was impressionable to the point of being naive, but very curious," Pei later explained. "I think curiosity was an important trait. Because of curiosity I always inquired, and when you inquire, you find different kinds of answers. No, I was not taken in completely by any one dogma."

The Peis were among the first dinner guests invited to the Cambridge home Philip Johnson had built for himself as his thesis project. Having studied the modern masters as a young design curator at the Museum of Modern Art, Johnson arguably had a stronger understanding of the movement than the Harvard faculty he studied under, and he quickly dismissed Gropius as a fine talker but a mediocre architect. The house Johnson built at 9 Ash Street, with its expansive glass wall overlooking a court, was an open declaration of his loyalty to Gropius's longtime rival, Mies van der Rohe, a master of glass-and-steel technology who had succeeded Gropius as head of the Bauhaus. Having lost the Harvard chair to Gropius, Mies, as he was called, became dean of architecture at the Armour (later the Illinois) Institute of Technology in Chicago, birthplace of the steel frame, and was given the enviable assignment of designing its new campus. Johnson would have studied with Mies, but he could not bear to forgo Harvard's cachet for the Midwest of his unhappy upbringing.

Pei and his classmates flocked to Harvard to hear the Gropius gospel, but when it came to design, they, like Johnson, found Mies more inspiring. A big, rough-hewn man partial to expensive cigars and brandy, Mies was a taciturn builder-artist capable of arranging steel I-beam framing and wide sheets of glass into eloquently proportioned masterpieces of austerity. It was Mies who coined the modernist slogans "Less is more" and "God is in the details." Indeed, there was a moral aspect to his classically balanced open spaces that captivated young designers like Pei. At least until the turn of the 1960s, they based their standard language on him.

Pei intended to apply these examples and influences toward a strong, independent China upon his return. It was an ambition he pursued with some reservations, for if modernism became a true International Style, as Gropius predicted, it would constitute a kind of architectural imperialism by replacing China's indigenous styles with Western-bred glass and steel. Pei interrupted Gropius's studio one day to argue that the International Style must not subsume local customs and variation around the world. "I said, 'What about climate? What about history? What about tradition?' He said, 'Very interesting. You can do a project of your own. You have to prove it to me.' "

A few months later Pei presented his thesis before the entire school. It consisted of pen-and-ink drawings and a beautiful balsa wood model of a two-story Shanghai art museum with several pavilions and a stream running through a tea garden. Pei's museum differed by necessity from Western versions, he explained, because Chinese art plays a different role in society:

It was so easy to prove my point in that way. Because at that time . . . the great museums of the world were all designed much like the Louvre or the Metropolitan, with huge walls, very monumental buildings. Of course, that's right because they enshrine public art, Greek and Roman sculptures, enormous tapestries, church art, paintings by Delacroix, Rubens, things of that kind. Enormous things glorifying the Empire, glorifying Napoleon. So it was appropriate that Western art, being so public, have its architecture to match it.

But when you think of Oriental art, you're thinking of something entirely different. It's very private—jade, ivory, porcelain. Even scrolls, regardless of how long, are never extended; they're always put away and only looked at on special occasions. Now, you don't display this kind of art in an enormous Greek or Roman reproduction. So therefore the environment for viewing and exhibiting such art has to be different from our Western museums.

So the design of that museum was quite a topic at that time. Breuer led the discussion; in fact, already at that time it showed Breuer had some misgivings of his own.

Gropius pronounced Pei's thesis "the finest piece of student work I've ever seen."

"It clearly illustrates," Gropius wrote in a blurb accompanying the drawings published in *Progressive Architecture,* "that an able designer can very well hold on to basic traditional features—which he has found are still alive—without sacrificing a progressive conception of design."

After Pei graduated in 1946, Gropius hired him to help his firm, The Architects Collaborative, design a real-life Shanghai project, the Hua Tung Christian University, planned for a 150-acre site on a former airfield west of the city. Pei provided invaluable local information and drafted beautiful renderings of stilt-legged dorms and classroom buildings set among courtyards and ponds. Unfortunately, the growing civil war between Communists and Nationalists forestalled its construction.

Gropius also hired Pei to teach a section of the graduate studio. At twenty-nine, he was among the youngest ever assistant professors, and he engaged his students with casual charm and enthusiasm. His first act was to take his eight or so students and their wives out to see the Lincoln house. "He formed friendships with people quite easily," said Henry Cobb, a student whose forebears were by coincidence sea captains in the China trade. "There was an ex-

◄

Pei, SECOND FROM LEFT, at Harvard. His decision to enlist with a New York developer scandalized Cambridge acquaintances.

▼

In his Harvard thesis, a Shanghai art museum, Pei tried to show that the modern style could accommodate local variation.

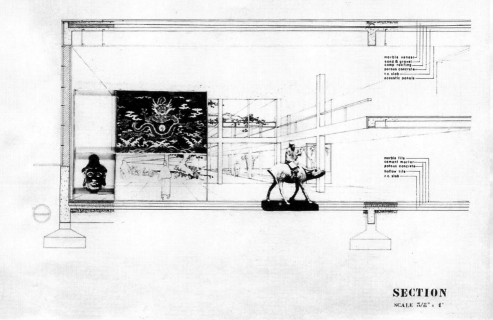

MUSEUM   A STUDY

SECTION
SCALE 3/8" = 1'

oticism that was appealing, especially to a young Bostonian who couldn't wait to get out of Boston."

As an instructor, Pei balanced rigor with informal support. "He was very poor in detail and organization, but he was an inspiring teacher," said Preston Moore who, like Cobb, later joined Pei in private practice. "He immediately understood what you were trying to do and helped you articulate it."

Pei has said that he learned more as a teacher than he did as a student. Most important, teaching gave him an occupation he could abruptly abandon when China stabilized. "I wanted to go home," he said. "I wanted to do something there. Yet I knew it would not be right to go back at that time. Teaching was the only thing I could do, because I couldn't go in and say to someone, 'I'm going to work for you, but I may leave six months from now.' In teaching you can. . . . So it was a struggle with myself when to return, and then it eventually became *should* I return. Teaching bought that time for me. It enabled me to stay here, think about it and wait until political situations settled down."

He and Eileen never bothered to teach little T'ing or their second son, Chien Chung (known as Didi), born in 1946, to speak Chinese on the assumption that they would learn it at home. "When I came to study here I had no intention of staying," Pei told *Time*. "Then I had to stay because of the war. I'm fortunate that I did, but it was difficult for me because my family was in China and I had trouble cutting the ties. I wasn't lonely, but I was homesick. China was very unsettled. My father said, 'Why don't you stay there until things settle down?' "

Pei's prospects of returning diminished when, soon after the Japanese surrender, the war-weary Chinese supported a Communist insurgence that promised to improve their squalid conditions. In March 1946 Tsuyee Pei became governor of the Bank of China and set about stabilizing an economy suffering runaway inflation as the country printed more and more paper money to fund its growing military budget. "I am confident that the situation is well in hand," Tsuyee told an American reporter. "Barring serious political trouble, I think we are on the road to economic recovery."

Despite his outward optimism, Tsuyee must have known that his fiscal policies meant little as Chiang's spiritless Kuomintang army gradually gave way to bands of Communists descending from the hills to claim the strategic coastal cities. In April of 1948 Tsuyee returned to the United States to ask Secretary of State George Marshall for emergency aid. By then it was too late to save Chiang's foundering regime. By the spring of 1949 a dispirited Kuomintang army had lost the will to fight and Chiang's regime had begun to crumble. The generalissimo and his remaining troops evacuated to Taiwan. Tsuyee Pei became a consultant to banks and insurance concerns in Hong Kong and New York.

On May 25, the first units of the onrushing People's Liberation Army crossed the Yangtze and marched unopposed through the Bund and the French Concession where Pei had grown up. The crimson flag of communism was raised over the Bund, marking the end of an era. Within a few months, Mao formally proclaimed the People's Republic of China.

For Pei there would be no homecoming after all. The process of emotionally disowning China that had begun in the movie theaters and classrooms of his childhood continued in the foreign world.

By historical accident, Pei profited from the best of two cultures a world apart. China endowed him with a Confucian perspective and the mystical authority of one grounded in ancient traditions. On the other hand, America released him from what the Chinese writer Lynn Pan called "a past that imprisons the present." His adopted home gave him the chance to think independently, to pursue new opportunities and do what Americans do best: invent the future.

4
WE'RE GOING TO
CHANGE ALL THIS

"The fundamental pedagogical mistake of the academy," Walter Gropius once wrote, "arose from its preoccupation with the idea of individual genius." He encouraged the second-generation modernists training under his aegis to suppress their private ambitions in favor of the egalitarian virtues of brotherly teamwork embodied in his own firm, The Architects Collaborative. Gropius and Breuer themselves built only sparingly, and they expected their acolytes to wait in penurious and anonymous virtue for the chance to build a small suburban home. Then, as now, the breakthrough client was often a mother or some other charitable relative.

I. M. Pei, however, had an instinct for the subtleties of advancement. He was more inclined than his classmates to diverge from the prescribed path in pursuit of a more propitious point of entry. At the age of thirty-one, after two years as a junior professor, he defected from the cloistered confines of academia and attached himself to a new mentor, the flamboyant developer William Zeckendorf—a university unto himself.

Zeckendorf was the kind of irrepressible American Pei had admired in Hollywood movies. He was an oversized bulldog of a man, a caricature of the jowly, big-bellied real-estate operator with a gray homburg cocked atop a bald head and a pungent foot-long cigar clasped in a fleshy fist. He was physically enor-

◄ **William Zeckendorf and Pei at the White House after meeting with President Eisenhower, July 8, 1954.**

mous—around 250 pounds—and larger than life in most other aspects: he was a self-avowed risk addict, a schmooze artist, an insatiable gourmet and a world-champion bon vivant. Postwar New Yorkers knew him as a colorful prince of Midtown, a man often mentioned in the gossip columns, who hobnobbed with financial titans and altered skylines with a phone call.

Life with Big Bill was a nonstop real-estate derby. Despite a proclivity for late-night parties, he prowled to 7:00 A.M. business breakfasts in a black chauffeured limousine—a Chrysler equipped with "WZ-1" vanity plates—yammering with associates held captive in the spacious backseat and placing calls on an early-model car phone. One day a rival developer called the limousine to show off his own car phone. "Hold on," retorted Zeckendorf, a master of one-upmanship, "my other phone is ringing."

Indeed, Zeckendorf had a phone pressed to his ear throughout most of his frenzied ninety-hour workweek. His three secretaries put through as many as thirty-five calls an hour, and it was not unusual for visitors to languish beside his desk while he conducted lengthy negotiations and darkened reams of lined yellow paper with triangular doodles. According to office lore, Zeckendorf once put President Eisenhower on hold to field another call.

Entrepreneurial gamesmanship propelled Zeckendorf more than the money did. He flung himself into flamboyant exploits for the sheer joy of it. He dabbled in shipping, drilled for oil off the coast of Surinam, backed thirty Broadway plays, including *Gentlemen Prefer Blondes,* acquired an entire town in Arizona, a jail in Boise, a railroad in Hoboken and nearly bought the Brooklyn Dodgers.

He gleefully flipped gilt-edged New York properties like baseball cards, holding variously such trophies as the Graybar and Chrysler buildings and the Saint Regis, Astor and Drake hotels. He transacted some of his most inspired deals from the Monte Carlo, a plush Madison Avenue nightclub furnished with chandeliers and overstuffed banquettes. When its proprietors went bust, Zeckendorf took over the management himself rather than lose his private corner table equipped with a telephone. A *New Yorker* cartoon of the time pictured a man admiring the New York skyline with his son. "Someday, my boy," he said, "all of this will belong to Mr. William Zeckendorf."

Zeckendorf was born with many gifts, but he was not born to wealth. The grandson of Arizona pioneers and the son of a shoe manufacturer, he graduated from De Witt Clinton High School in the Bronx and spent three years playing football at New York University before dropping out to collect rent for his uncle's real-estate firm. He got his start in 1925 by filling an undistinguished office building at 32 Broadway with tenants while his uncle vacationed in Europe. He continued to make money throughout the Depression as a journeyman broker and, in 1938, joined Webb & Knapp, a staid Madison Avenue real-estate brokerage and manager of other people's properties, as a $9,000-a-year vice president. A scrappy Long Island Jew hardly fit the profile for a cautious outfit run by blue-blooded graduates of Groton, Harvard and Yale. But Webb & Knapp had grown dangerously quiescent at a time when real estate was heating up; the firm badly needed an injection of new blood and street smarts. "I was familiar with almost every block of property in town," Zeckendorf recalled in his memoir. "I knew or was known to most important brokers and a great many bankers, as well as a number of insurance men. I also brought ebullience and drive. If some of my partners were rich, I was ambitious. Thus, through a combination of background and personality I became the chief enthusiast, contact, an idea man for the organization."

Zeckendorf soon made a name for himself by upgrading Webb & Knapp's old-money resources through a series of spectacular deals facilitated by his uncanny sixth sense for strategic acreage. His facile mind saw through the clutter of numbers to grasp a property's wider potential. "I make grapefruits out of lemons," he liked to say—a credo he later amended to "bananas from peanuts." When the navy called Vincent Astor to reserve duty in 1942, he left his $50 million real-estate holdings in Webb & Knapp's custody. "Well,

▲

William Zeckendorf, the most ambitious de-

veloper of his time.

what do you think of my properties?" Astor asked over martinis at his twenty-room penthouse shortly before shipping out.

"For the most part, Commander, they stink," the thirty-six-year-old Zeckendorf replied. "They are outmoded."

While Astor shepherded convoys across the Atlantic, Zeckendorf, who was too old to be drafted, shrewdly employed the heir's prestigious name to sell his more modest New York holdings to Jewish refugees arriving from Nazi Germany with their life savings. Zeckendorf reinvested the proceeds in stronger properties, which he mortgaged for additional cash that he used, in turn, to buy up more property, not just in New York but around the United States.

After one hundred fifty transactions, Zeckendorf had strengthened Astor's portfolio by some $5 million and tripled its annual earnings. Zeckendorf submitted a bill for $350,000 with a note urging Astor not to pay if he considered the sum exorbitant. Astor instructed aides to send a bouquet along with the check.

When Webb & Knapp's top officers returned from war they found their young buccaneer firmly in charge. By 1947 Zeckendorf was named president, and two years later he owned the firm outright. "At times," wrote *Life*, "Elliot Cross, Henry Sears and John Gould, cautious characters all, give the impression of trailing breathlessly behind him, like tails on a kite, as he soars through the upper air of real-estate finance." *Fortune* predicted that Zeckendorf would likely be the first American to land on the moon.

In fact, Zeckendorf was more than a swashbuckling deal-maker. He was a conceptual thinker, a hard-boiled dreamer restively conjuring up ambitious ventures. His modus operandi was to buy up substandard properties on the wrong side of town and triple their value by redeveloping them according to a new, often radically imaginative idea. "I decided it was time that real estate graduated from the huckstering stage," he told *Newsweek*. "If I'm a maverick or a radical in my business it's because other people work only with money; I employ imagination too."

Some Zeckendorfian schemes verged on science fiction, like the impossible Palace of Progress he envisioned atop New York's Penn Station, which was to house nearly twice as much office space as the Pentagon and a permanent World's Fair. He also planned a $3 billion airport, roughly the size of Central Park, which he hoped to unfurl on top of 144 blocks of ten-story buildings on Manhattan's West Side. When these and other whimsically implausible daydreams failed to progress beyond the drawing board, a skeptical chorus accused Zeckendorf of ballyhooing fantasies simply to garner publicity. He was, in fact, serious enough about the rooftop airport to invest $25,000 in blueprints and drawings, later published in *Life*. Zeckendorf's detractors failed to appreciate that he was by nature a Napoleonic builder. "He is the kind of leader or pioneer who stirs men's minds to greater advances," wrote *Architectural Forum*, "and to new forms and new scales attuned to modern times."

It was with a dreamer's disposition, then, that Zeckendorf surveyed America's decaying cities and rubbed his hands together in anticipation. The Depression had halted new city housing and curtailed the upkeep of nineteenth-century neighborhoods. Conditions deteriorated further during the ensuing war as builders addressed more urgent priorities and hordes of southern blacks and poor rural workers converged on cities to work in wartime plants, spawning new slums.

Meanwhile the Roosevelt administration prepared the way for an outward migration to the leafy suburbs by dangling sunny visions of the "model home" before a public suffering the double deprivation of depression and war. When the lights dimmed at local movie houses, captive audiences watched a series of "Better Housing News Flashes" in which stentorian narrators proclaimed that "home ownership is the basis of a happy and contented life." Advertising promulgated an entire suburban fantasy, extolling the emancipating wonders of new consumer products for the single-family home. Mom would have her washer-dryer. Dad would drive to work in a new Ford. Between 1944 and 1946, young architects published drawings of their dream houses in the *Ladies' Home Journal* and the Museum of Modern Art mounted a show called *Tomorrow's Small House.*

After the war, government mortgages made the American dream of home ownership affordable to the middle class. Families on the cusp of the baby boom abandoned their old mixed-use neighborhoods, with the corner grocery store and the walk-up rental apartment, for long-deferred pleasures awaiting them in the clean suburban expanse widening relentlessly around every city. Developers like William Levitt, father of Levittown, redirected wartime industrial energies directly to the construction of entire suburban towns, and Detroit produced fleets of new cars for a growing network of highways. "For more than five years military necessity had taken priority over consumer goods," wrote Kenneth Jackson in *Crabgrass Frontier,* "and by 1945 almost everyone had a long list of unfilled material wants."

Families that could afford to move were drawn outward by the centrifugal pull of home laundries, central heating, automatic stoves, lawn mowers, garages, cheap land and, most of all, the dream of owning their own private bit of America. By 1950, eighteen of the country's twenty-five largest cities were losing population to the suburbs. The exodus depleted the cities' vital resources and condemned them to decay. There was some talk that the anemic cities might join Stonehenge and the pyramids as relics of a bygone civilization.

William Zeckendorf emerged as a champion of the ailing city long before that stance became fashionable. The enduring meccas of finance and culture—Paris, Rome and New York—remained the finest flowers of civilization, he argued, and the seat of irreplaceable institutions like opera, libraries and churches. "As the flame draws the moth," he wrote in the influential *Yale Review,* "so will the most brilliant beacons of art, finance, commerce, dining and fun gradually absorb and monopolize the most powerful buying element from everywhere."

This line of argument helped Zeckendorf to distinguish himself as an enlightened developer. He also made his case in a series of articles in the *Atlantic* and in a televised debate with Frank Lloyd Wright who saw the city as the "basis for banking and prostitution and very little else." Wright dismissed New York, in particular, as "inhuman," with skyscrapers "growing like weeds."

"I don't agree," Zeckendorf retorted. "I see the city as the expression of man's gregarious nature. And therefore a natural expression. No great civilization has arisen at any time in history . . . that did not come from urban life." After the debate they retired to Zeckendorf's Greenwich estate where their *mano a mano* continued over a succession of drinks. The evening ended abruptly when Wright tumbled down the wine cellar steps in pursuit of more brandy and had to be rushed to the hospital for stitches (after the night's debauchery, he saw no need for an anesthetic). Despite their differences of opinion, Zeckendorf considered Wright a friend. Years later he rescued the architect's 1909 Robie house from demolition and converted it into Webb & Knapp's Chicago office.

Zeckendorf predicted that the great swaths of slums festering in the shadow of Main Street would be rebuilt to fill the needs of a prospering country. The propitiously positioned developer would profit handsomely from the inevitable overhaul, in part because it coincided with the popular acceptance of modern design. As building geared up after the long wartime hiatus, unadorned glass boxes free of stone and expensive detail could be stamped out as efficiently as cars or radios. "The practical appeal of the modernist idiom," the art critic Robert Hughes once observed, "was not its spiritual elevation but its low cost."

Because good design would no longer cost more than bad, Zeckendorf predicted a felicitous rapprochement between architects and developers, who had historically viewed each other with suspicion. In a lecture at the Harvard Graduate School of Design, he predicted that modernism would allow these antithetical groups to share the same goals: "We may well be entering upon a golden era of construction when the merger of the real-estate builder-economist and the artist and designer can be so skillfully integrated that we shall bring forth residential, industrial, and commercial architecture which will stand the important tests of time: economic soundness, and beauty of functionalism."

Zeckendorf was eager to enter into just such a collaboration. But with whom? Webb & Knapp already employed staff architects for incidental improvements like lobby renovations, but the grand projects Zeckendorf anticipated lay beyond their reach. He sought a thoroughly modern in-house architect, a deputy dreamer capable of assembling entire new neighborhoods in the modern idiom.

Zeckendorf solicited advice from Nelson Rockefeller, then chairman of the Museum of Modern Art. "Nelson, don't you think it's about time that the modern Medicis began hiring the modern Michelangelos and da Vincis?" he asked. "I plan to go into a great building program on a national scale, and I'd like to put together an architectural staff that could provide new thinking."

Rockefeller referred him to a veteran museum administrator named John Abbott who had become a bothersome office politician; the rumor was that Rockefeller wanted to get rid of Abbott. Like any developer, Zeckendorf was eager to do Rockefeller a favor, so he hired Abbott as an architectural head-hunter and dispatched him to scout for talented unknowns. "I specified that the man was not to be the scion of a wealthy family, because in architecture they too often turn out to be dilettantes," Zeckendorf later recalled. "Neither did I want him to be a longtime hack in the back of somebody's office, with his spirit already broken."

After consulting Philip Johnson, who by then had returned to New York and resumed his association with MoMA's design department, Abbott produced a dozen suitable candidates, one of whom was I. M. Pei. "When Zeckendorf asked if I would come down and meet with him, I jumped, I literally jumped, because I thought this would be a wonderful opportunity for me to learn about real estate," Pei said. "To be an architect in China, unlike here, you've got to know real estate." The junior professor drove down from Cambridge in the spring of 1948 to find the developer seated behind a pile of papers in a ratty office furnished with photographs of parking garages. An old radio served as a makeshift bar. Strewn about were plans for X City, a self-sufficient development Zeckendorf hoped to build on a forty-foot platform overlooking the East River.

One can scarcely conjure up a more improbable pair than the blustering Jewish developer and the soft-spoken Chinese professor. Unlikely as it sounds, these two men of charm struck up an easy rapport. Wine figured prominently among Zeckendorf's passions—his 20,000-bottle cellar was among the country's largest—and he was delighted to find Pei a fellow connoisseur. Zeckendorf was also devoutly superstitious—he labeled all of his subsidiaries with numbers divisible by thirteen—and he took it as a favorable omen that he, his son, Pei and Pei's father all were born in the Year of the Snake, which occurs every twelve years. The auguries seemed right.

"Pei had never built anything," Zeckendorf wrote, "but when he and his charming wife, Elaine [*sic*], came down for a visit, I could see from his sketches that he was truly talented. I also found him obviously intelligent and very imaginative, as well as a bon vivant and a knowledgeable gourmet. It was a case of instant recognition and liking."

Pei embodied America's imaginary picture of Oriental virtue: he was refined, impeccably groomed and possessed of a dignified reserve. As a Jew accustomed to making his way among Astors and Rockefellers, Zeckendorf was sensitive to the unspoken nuances of ethnicity, and he recognized that a cultivated Chinese designer would make lustrous window dressing for his hardnosed entourage. It was a form of reverse discrimination which benefited Pei throughout his career.

Zeckendorf in turn offered Pei the opportunity to build prodigiously, immediately and on an unprecedented scale with a man who, despite his outward boorishness, clearly wanted to rise above conventional real estate to do great things. "Zeckendorf was already done with the U.N. and X city and all those grandiose projects," Pei said, "at that particular moment that I came to meet him in his office. He was interested in only one thing: mechanical parking. His walls were full of plans for garages that move cars on important frontage. That was my first impression of him. I was taken by his enthusiasm and imagination. I joined him."

"Pei was apprehensive about becoming a captive architect, which might lose him a certain degree of professional freedom," Zeckendorf wrote. "He was also torn between returning to China and remaining here as a teacher, but I set to work and soon persuaded him that the kinds of things we were going to do would be so different and so much better than anyone else in the country was doing that as an architect he could not resist the challenge. Helping me, though I did not know it then, was some advice Pei's father had once given him: that the essence of good architecture was the ability not only to conceive of great buildings but also to tie them effectively to finances and economics."

Zeckendorf had a knack for smoothly swaying others to his will. After six months of persuasive discussion, Pei succumbed to Zeckendorf's overtures. He would leave Harvard's hushed cloister and cast his lot with Webb & Knapp's boisterous office, with its forever ringing phones and Midtown martini lunches. After shaking hands with his new boss, Webb & Knapp's freshly anointed "director of architectural research" emerged onto the unaccustomed bustle of Madison Avenue and decamped to Gallagher's Steak House to celebrate with Eileen and friends.

Back in Cambridge there had been a certain glamour of promise about Pei. News of his defection naturally caused a stir. Harvard's lily-white enclave of bright ideals viewed New York real estate as an unclean game played in the contaminated realm of commerce. To enlist with a big operator like Zeckendorf was considered professionally incorrect; to stray from the true path was to strike one's name from the list of serious architects. "It was a shock that he would go commercial," remembered Philip Johnson. "To be kept by a single developer was a fantastic break in the habits of architecture. It wasn't the accepted way to become an architect, but times were changing. Pei saw that and others did not."

The culture Pei grew up in discouraged the kind of extreme, obstinate posture Gropius struck on behalf of a high moral purpose. Mandarins favored balance, compromise and quiet mediation between extremes. In keeping with the mandarin tendency to work within the system, Pei reasoned that if modern design was ever to amount to more than paper architecture it would have to withstand the market forces of supply and demand as assuredly as it withstood gravity. Architecture was not an art, like painting or poetry, to be practiced in isolation; it had to address itself to power. "Real estate developers," he later told a reporter, "are responsible for the built environment that we see. Rather than hold them in contempt, I thought there was great potential in trying to work from within. One could learn something from them, and I learned a great deal. The way a real estate developer looks at a site is a wonderful lesson for an architect." Besides, Pei was a worldly young man endowed with a sonarlike sensitivity to the nuances of power. China taught the importance of laying one's hands on the right levers, fostering the right connections. For a mandarin stranded in a strange world, Zeckendorf held a stronger allure than Cambridge's genteel bohemianism.

Harvard dispatched Pei in the summer of 1948 with a farewell party held at the Brookline home of Henry Cobb. The move from there to Webb & Knapp was the first of many steps leading incrementally closer to America's power centers. "I.M. started at the top," his associates joked, "and had to work his way up from there." Even as he traveled a corresponding distance away from the insular, self-regarding culture of theory-minded architects, he kept his sensitive antennae attuned to the mood of the moment. He remained a well-informed outrider.

■ ■ ■ ■

In 1948, New York clattered with the noisy urgency of postwar progress. It was, Truman Capote observed, "the most stimulating of all the cities in the world. It's like living inside an electric light bulb." Expensively dressed men marched through the narrow canyons of Wall Street, the world's greatest marketplace. Heaps of competing newspapers crowded newsstands. Television and radio hit their stride. Idlewild Airport opened, the new United Nations broke ground and a subway ride cost a dime. The Dodgers played at Ebbets Field, and ocean liners glided in and out of the city's bustling deep-water harbor. After work, the interlocking realms of finance and culture mingled at the Stork Club or El Morocco, Sardi's or Luchow's, the Waldorf-Astoria or the Biltmore.

New York eclipsed Paris as the art capital of the world as abstract expressionists like Jackson Pollock, Robert Motherwell and Willem de Kooning emerged as the ascendant avant-garde. On Broadway, Henry Fonda starred in *Mr. Roberts,* Tallulah Bankhead in *Private Lives,* Marlon Brando in *A Streetcar Named Desire* and Ethel Merman in *Annie Get Your Gun.* Lena Horne sang at the Copacabana. John Cheever recalled it as a time "when the city of New York was still filled with a river light, when you heard the Benny Goodman quartet from a radio in the corner stationery store, and when almost everybody wore a hat."

In the fall of 1948 Pei installed himself in a bare back-room office at Webb & Knapp furnished with sawhorse desks and windows overlooking Vanderbilt Avenue and the great tidal pageant of commuters passing to and from Grand Central Station. He shared the office, if one could even call it that, with a former reporter named John Price Bell, whom Zeckendorf had plucked from the *World-Telegram*'s City Hall beat to mastermind his public relations. "You always felt Pei's presence," remembered Bell. "The first time I met him, Pei was standing in profile, leaning back against a table, saying nothing. I came in and Zeckendorf introduced us. There was something in the atmosphere which made me feel that this fellow was unique. I've kept that impression until this very day and hour."

If Pei suffered any pangs of dislocation he didn't show it. Webb & Knapp's real-estate lawyers and mortgage mavens remember him as a strikingly poised, engaging young man. He joked with his new colleagues about how Zeckendorf claimed to weigh more than his entire family. Although an unimposing physical presence and considerably younger than the seasoned executives around him, Pei evinced none of the uncertainty of youth. He navigated among Zeckendorf's aides with finesse and watchful calculation. "The important thing is to go about it as confidently as you can," he later said. "You have to say to yourself, 'If I believe something is right, it doesn't matter who I am.' Take your position and have faith in yourself."

Pei's self-assurance was more profound than youthful self-confidence. He seemed to know himself, to know his own mind and the breadth of his abilities. "There was something special about the way he handled himself, even as a young man," said Eason Leonard, the congenial Oklahoma-born architect who joined Pei in the early 1950s. "He came from academia into a hard-nosed real-estate group. It was pretty tough on him. His inexperience could have gotten the whole firm into trouble. He knew the heat was on, but he was diplomatic and bright. He knew the answers. He had not yet built anything, but he still had great confidence."

New York Times columnist William Safire remembered Pei as the brightest mind in the 7:00 A.M. meetings he attended as a young press agent. "Ieoh Ming wouldn't talk until called upon," Safire said, "but when called upon he knew all the answers. He had the same expression on his face as he has now—interested and never nonplussed, excited by the challenge. That of course fit beautifully into the atmosphere of those meetings."

Pei's first assignment was to turn Zeckendorf's conventionally colorless Madison Avenue office into a high modern business boutique capable of amplifying his image as a man in advance of the moment. By way of guidance, Zeckendorf took his young architect to see Metropolitan Life chairman Frederick Ecker's office, which lay beyond a labyrinth of underlings. "This is what I *don't* want," Zeckendorf instructed. "I don't want to be buried away in some inaccessible corner."

Pei responded with a precocious masterpiece of corporate image-making. Borrowing from Mies van der Rohe's Barcelona Pavilion, a founding temple of the International Style, Pei built a sparsely elegant twelfth-floor reception area gazing through plate-glass windows onto a landscaped terrace furnished with an exotic gnarled pine tree and a shiny bronze Gaston Lachaise sculpture Pei had acquired of a bosomy woman dipping her tiny toes into a reflecting pool beside a marble backdrop. Upon stepping from the elevator one sniffed affluence and class and a silky corporate elegance.

Pei enthroned Zeckendorf in his own cylindrical sanctum—its circular shape, Pei said, inspired by Zeckendorf's own profile—planted prominently in the middle of the spacious carpeted reception lounge. Zeckendorf's "igloo" dominated office activity "as effectively," he wrote, "as the lone turret of that famous Civil War ironclad, the *Monitor*, once dominated its own deck and the water for miles around." Negotiators entered Zeckendorf's lair disadvantaged. This was, after all, Big Bill's home court. The igloo was windowless except for eleven domed skylights ringed with colored floodlights, which Zeckendorf manipulated like a Broadway lighting director, bathing prospective buyers in a radiant, optimistic pink and, conversely, plunging sellers into a melancholy twilight blue. The igloo proved so formidable that office wags referred to its canted oak panels as standing coffins for Zeckendorf's competitors. In contrast to the hunting prints and watercolors found in most old-fashioned offices, Pei furnished Zeckendorf's sanctum with a Matisse bronze and a precious Chinese vase. The objets d'art, along with the remarkable pine tree, foreshadowed Pei's lifelong tendency to soften modernism's industrial candor with delicate touches of art and foliage.

If a little gentle persuasion was in order, Zeckendorf led guests a few steps from his door to a tubular stainless-steel elevator and they ascended to a semicircular dining room and lounge parked on the roof like a glass flying saucer. There they sipped cocktails prepared at a bar finished in black satin, or they lunched while admiring Zeckendorf's Midtown domain through a curved window-wall. "It was pure showmanship and a fantastic selling technique," remembered vice president Charles Urstadt. "The elevator looked like a steel rocket. It went just one floor, but it was a slow ride, so it was impressive. People remembered it."

The $500,000 renovation ran considerably over budget, but it more than recouped its cost by establishing Zeckendorf as an architecture patron. He often said he could not have afforded to spend a penny less. Nobody had seen anything quite like it, and half a dozen magazines published admiring stories. "While some may find the Webb & Knapp penthouse details ostentatiously intellectual," observed *Fortune* in its four-page spread, "none can deny that Pei has achieved surroundings coherent with their inhabitants. Moreover, they give its aggressive occupants the advantage of fighting their business games on an impressive, somewhat intimidating home ground."

Pei remained a bright green young architect despite his splashy debut, and doubts lingered over his ability to swing full-scale projects within the budget constraints of speculative real estate. Was he ready for prime time? Pei earned credibility in 1952 with the completion of his first outside job, a modest Atlanta office building leased to Gulf Oil. Its distinction lay not in its design—it may have been the simplest two-story glass box ever assembled— but in its thrift. Pei began with brick, but his sensitivity to local materials led him to Georgia marble. By persuading quarries to supply cheap veneer to promote their product, and by trucking prefabricated pieces from the factory at night, Pei finished the building in just four months at a frugal $7.50 per square foot.

One year later Pei made his planning debut. In a rare suburban foray, Zeckendorf bought the defunct Nassau County airstrip where Charles Lindbergh had taken off for Paris. Webb & Knapp announced they would use it to build Roosevelt Field, the world's largest suburban shopping center. Until then developers had arranged stores in conventional strips. Pei felt they could make more money by consolidating the various ventures around cob-

▲

Pei's first building: an office for Gulf Oil

in Atlanta. It proved that Pei could build

with thrift.

▼ Zeckendorf seated within his circular

sanctum.

◄

Webb & Knapp's penthouse lounge,

an aerie for sipping martinis and

concocting deals.

blestoned plazas with covered walkways, gardens and fountains. That would cost more, but, Pei argued, the pleasing market atmosphere would encourage shoppers to linger. Despite resistance from Macy's, Gimbel's and other retailers accustomed to displaying their own logos, Pei designed all the signs and graphics as well as telephone booths, benches and brick kiosks for the novel amenity of drive-through banking.

Pei demonstrated his resourcefulness just in time. As Zeckendorf had predicted, America was awakening to its urban crisis. The suburban stampede had left in its wake decrepit neighborhoods with cracked sidewalks heaving over the roots of overgrown trees, dusty storefronts and wretched tenement stairways leading to overcrowded apartments. When the decommissioned army turned into an army of homeless families doubling up with relatives, the neglected cities suffered the largest housing shortage in history. By 1946 an estimated 20 to 30 percent of all Americans lived in substandard conditions. Desperate families made do in basements, boxcars and chicken coops. The city of Chicago sold 250 streetcars as makeshift homes, and a newlywed couple lived for two days in a New York department store window in the hope that the publicity would help secure them an apartment. Was this what awaited the sixteen million GIs returning from war? Something clearly had to be done.

Those postwar days were imbued with the conviction that America could right any wrong if it just applied its shoulder to the wheel. The New Deal and the Allied victory had convinced people that government could be trusted to perform beneficent acts. Almost overnight, Washington declared urban renewal a pressing national priority, and a new slogan emerged: "No more slums in ten years." Americans were more inclined to solve the urban problems left in the wake of the Industrial Revolution, Pei said, after having "gone to Italy, Paris, London, Rome, everywhere. And when they came home after the war they went back to places like Kalamazoo or Des Moines, Iowa, and I think they must have felt there was something lacking in their communities, after having seen Rome, Paris and London. It was a good moment."

The era of urban renewal officially began with the passage of a revolutionary bit of legislation known as Title I of the Federal Housing Act of 1949. Until then cities had been permitted to seize only those patches of private property needed to build public works like streets and schools. Title I extended the cities' authority by granting them the power to condemn entire slums, relocate the tenants and sell the bulldozed "renewal area" at a reduced price to a private developer who would rebuild according to city-approved plans. It was a bold departure from previous policy; city fathers now enjoyed a constitutionally dubious mandate to turn confiscated homes over to commercial enterprises for a supposedly higher use.

Urban renewal might have excluded private developers like Zeckendorf had it not been for Senator Robert A. Taft, the era's most influential legislator who, as an upstanding Republican, blocked Congress from launching urban renewal as a New Deal–style social program. On the other hand, Taft was known as a compassionate conservative with a firm belief in government's obligation to provide for all citizens. He approved of Title I as a way of inducing private enterprise to convert run-down neighborhoods with a minimum of government meddling. "If the free enterprise system does not do its best to prevent hardship and poverty," Taft told his congressional colleagues, "it will find itself superseded by a less progressive system which does."

While Zeckendorf welcomed Washington's largesse, he vigorously dismissed its vision of uninspired low-cost housing as "stuffed shirt banking thinking" that would only exchange "new slums for old slums." More than relief from congestion was required to stem the suburban exodus and revive the anemic city. Besides, Zeckendorf was temperamentally averse to any such half measures.

In fact, he was already summoning fantastically ambitious schemes in which he and Pei would replace the industrial city's Gothic gloom and dirt with tomorrow's Babylon. He sang a hymn of gleaming towers above open plazas and boulevards of light and greenery lined with stores and hospitable public gathering places like dance halls, skating rinks, merry-go-rounds, swimming pools and cabarets. Like Baron Haussmann, who remade Paris by slicing wide, tree-lined boulevards through the dark and narrow medieval maze, Zeckendorf understood that urban renewal at its best was about art, not just about engineering. If Title I wouldn't cover the cost, he would finance the work himself by generating projects that were both profitable and beneficial.

Preserving the old city's traditional flavor didn't merit much consideration back then. Current thinking mandated that if the deteriorating downtown area was to be saved, it would first have to be destroyed. "We wouldn't go about it the same way today," Pei later acknowledged, "but at the time there was no doubt in anyone's mind that the way to create better neighborhoods was to make a clean sweep of areas that had decayed and to make a fresh start."

Ironically, Zeckendorf and Pei initially had to scout outside New York for prospective sites because Zeckendorf's dealings on his East Side properties antagonized Robert Moses, New York's all-powerful parks commissioner. During breakfast one morning Zeckendorf read in the *New York Times* that the newly formed United Nations was on the verge of building its permanent headquarters in Philadelphia. It had been operating from a makeshift assembly hall converted from an ice rink at New York's Flushing Meadows, site of the 1939 World's Fair. New York officials invited the U.N. to stay there indefinitely, but dignitaries considered Flushing an undignified address for the paramount international body. In an eleventh-hour bid to keep the U.N. in New York, a prospect that could only enhance his own holdings, Zeckendorf called New York City mayor William O'Dwyer and offered to sell the U.N. seventeen acres on which he had planned to build the enclave of skyscraper hotels and office buildings called X City on a platform raised above the bank of the East River in the East Forties. Four nights later the architect Wallace K. Harrison, entrusted to negotiate on the U.N.'s behalf, marched into the Monte Carlo and unfurled a map across the table where Zeckendorf and his wife were celebrating their sixth wedding anniversary. Zeckendorf agreed to sell the site at whatever price the U.N. wished to pay. A preliminary agreement was signed at 2:00 A.M. over celebratory champagne. Within eight days of Zeckendorf's initial phone call, the U.N. bought the land for $8.5 million donated by John D. Rockefeller. Zeckendorf sacrificed millions that he would have made by developing the land himself, but he gained invaluable publicity—and the right to use the official United Nations rendering on his stock certificates.

The deal also increased the value of Zeckendorf's adjacent holdings. In July 1947 he proposed a monumental boulevard, more than twice the width of Park Avenue, leading from Grand Central Terminal to the U.N. According to his scheme, the city would condemn all property between Forty-sixth and Forty-ninth streets. The proposal ran afoul of Robert Moses, who accused Zeckendorf of angling for a condemnation fee on a portion of the area owned by Webb & Knapp. In the midst of making his case before an unreceptive Board of Estimate, Zeckendorf lost his temper and was asked to leave. "The city fathers made one of the greatest mistakes of their lives when they turned us down," he later said. For years, while Moses snorted at the mention of Zeckendorf, Webb & Knapp had to work its deals elsewhere. Pei thus learned an invaluable lesson: good ideas wither without powerful allies.

Fortunately, the U.N. transaction and other headline-grabbing deals earned Zeckendorf a national reputation as a big operator, and real-estate brokers throughout the hinterlands brought opportunities to his door. Zeckendorf asked them a few incisive questions—In which direction is downtown spreading? Is there a Woolworth's on Main Street? Are your bankers helping new development?—to determine if the property merited further consideration. If so, he summoned Pei for an inspection tour.

The Peis had by then moved into a tiny apartment on the sixth floor of 30 Beekman Place, a building in a fashionable neighborhood owned by Zeckendorf and his wife, Marion, who occupied the nine-room penthouse. "My parents didn't have a lot of money back then," said Pei's son T'ing. "A cheap night out on the town was a visit to Liberty Music where they could listen to records in booths for free." In what became a lifelong ritual, the Peis often spent Saturday sampling the wealth of postwar abstract art exhibited in the Fifty-seventh Street galleries a short walk from their home.

Two years after moving to New York, the Peis had a third son, Sandi. By the time their fourth child, Liane, was born, in 1960, the Peis had moved into a slightly larger two-bedroom apartment on the tenth floor where they removed the radiators and concealed the fireplace behind a pine-board partition. The stereo sat within a white cabinet hung from the wall at an upturned angle— an odd flourish in an otherwise simple, elegant space containing white walls, silk curtains and sisal mats. Pei characteristically warmed the modern edges with a lacy azalea, a scroll painting and a glass bowl filled with ferns and goldfish, admired by Arthur Drexler in a description published in *Interiors:*

> Architect I. M. Pei, regulated only superficially by the
> modern idiom, has assembled the ingredients of his
> living room with a slight backward glance at tradition,
> characteristic of the cultured and gentle, whereby he has
> preferred conversation to television. For this and various
> other reasons the center of the room, spiritually as well as
> physically, is given over to a fishbowl. . . . It seems

anachronistic, and pleasantly old-fashioned, like a doily or a fringed shawl draped over a piano. But when the goldfish suddenly unfold out of the ferns and wave themselves like underwater flags, the bowl and the gray veined marble table on which it stands assume a puzzling and, perhaps, extra-aesthetic significance.

The Peis added a Willem de Kooning painting and a Jacques Lipchitz sculpture. Lipchitz, an older immigrant, was the first of many artists the Peis befriended. Pei must have been reminded of his own Suzhou childhood when Lipchitz recounted how, growing up in a small Lithuanian village, he became so fascinated by the shape of stones that he used to stuff them in his pockets.

Lipchitz was a frequent guest at the Peis' small dinner parties, along with Webb & Knapp colleagues and architectural acquaintances. The Peis learned to travel in many orbits, and over the years their guest list encompassed a wide range of cultural figures—Louise Nevelson, Al Held, Isaac Stern, Arthur Schlesinger, Jr. The evenings were conducted with Pei's inimitable brand of simple elegance. Eileen, pencil-thin, cooked from a repertoire of French, Chinese and American cuisines, and I.M. poured the wine. Pei always seemed to know when a new chef arrived from Hong Kong or Taiwan. He led his friends on occasional forays to Chinatown, personally ordering exotic meals days in advance. "I.M. is a social creature," said Jim Freed, who later became Pei's partner. "He mixed clients, political people and artists at the same tables. He was very good at keeping the discussion going. He has a way of laughing that's contagious. It cuts through thick and thin."

A colony of Harvard architects had by then moved to New York. It included Ed Barnes, Ulrich Franzen, Chester Nagel, Paul Rudolph and their former instructor Marcel Breuer. On Sunday afternoons Pei sometimes at-

▲

I.M. and Eileen, CENTER, seated in Marcel
Breuer's Manhattan home in 1967. The
Japanese sculptor Masayuki Nagare stands
at right. Breuer's wife, Constance, sits at
lower right.

◄

Pei and staff, 1958.

tended an architectural salon convened in the famous glass house Philip Johnson had built as an homage to Mies on his New Canaan, Connecticut, estate. There modernism's leading practitioners—Paul Rudolph, Eero Saarinen, Gordon Bunshaft and others—assembled with samples of their latest work to exchange ideas. Pei is remembered for his silent watchfulness as they discussed the future of the profession. "He never participated in discussions," said Philip Johnson, "but he never missed a trick."

Pei was more inclined to let his hair down with his Chinese friends, many of them old F.F. acquaintances stranded like Pei himself in America. Members from around the country faithfully converged in New York for an annual dinner dance held at a New York hotel. They also went on summer retreats to New Hampshire or Vermont. "Almost without exception they intended to return to China," said T'ing Pei. "It was an uncertain time and they had little contact with their families. Naturally, they formed an expatriate group."

Most well-born Chinese expatriates supported the so-called China Lobby, an array of conservative voices in Congress and the media who angrily blamed President Harry Truman for losing China to communism. *Time* publisher Henry Luce, whose parents were China missionaries, printed a sympathetic portrait of Chiang Kai-shek and his Wellesley-educated wife. *Life* published an article by General MacArthur warning that communism could spread insidiously throughout Asia. It was suggested that communist sympathizers within the State Department, like Owen Lattimore, sabotaged support for Chiang's army. "China asked for a sword," said Senator Styles Bridges of New Hampshire, "and we gave her a dull paring knife."

Educated Chinese living in the United States dared not make known their reservations about Chiang's corrupt and incompetent leadership. "At a time when American foreign policy was dominated by John Foster Dulles and Joe

McCarthy," said one, "to do anything but voice hard-line support for Taiwan was to expose oneself as a traitor."

The Peis did not dwell on the loss of China, as their friends did. They had a rare ability to look beyond that misfortune to the new opportunities awaiting them in their prosperous adopted country. While their friends joined the Republican outrage over Truman's Far East policy, the Peis became lifelong liberal Democrats. Some twenty years later, their son T'ing was approached by a lawyer outside a Manhattan courthouse who remembered giving the Pei boys Adlai Stevenson buttons in a Midtown campaign office. In those days Chinese who supported the Democratic ticket were so rare as to be unforgettable.

．　．　．　．

Pei's residence placed him in hazardous proximity to his tireless boss. Zeckendorf didn't hesitate to call employees, whatever the hour. As neighbors, the Peis were particularly susceptible. "At seven o'clock he would call, and my wife would answer the phone," Pei recalled. " 'Is Ieoh Ming up yet?' he'd ask. 'He's in the shower.' 'Well, tell him to hurry up. I've got some property I want him to see.' And then off we would go, and he would show it to me and say, 'What do you think we can make of that?' "

On other occasions, an intercom affixed to the studio wall would squawk to life with the sound of Zeckendorf's booming voice—"Ieoh Ming!"—and Pei would run down a back corridor to his boss's office.

Their headlong coast-to-coast itinerary is the stuff of real-estate legend—a merchant king and his Chinese sidekick barnstorming the country. Their nationwide campaign generated Title I projects in seven cities, and they submitted proposals in twice that number. In some cases, as in Denver and Montreal, they found sites outside the purview of Title I and assembled their own financing on the theory that good design would pay for itself. Title I's original purpose, to provide low-income housing, was all but lost in the rush to erect new offices, shopping arcades and middle-income housing.

Typically, Zeckendorf sipped a dry martini in Webb & Knapp's battered DC-3 while aides briefed him on their destination. They would circle low over a city so Zeckendorf and Pei could examine it before descending to a reception befitting foreign dignitaries. Indeed, to some provincial hosts the brash New York Jew come from the skies with his Chinese deputy must have seemed positively alien—Cortez in a double-breasted suit. Zeckendorf bantered with reporters who'd been herded to the airport by advance operatives. Then he and Pei were whisked away in a limousine to confer with local bankers and politicians. The central ritual of each stopover was the real-estate tour, often conducted by the mayor himself. As the entourage moved through town, Zeckendorf asked about specific buildings, ducked into shops to chat with proprietors and consulted Pei about elevations and street plans. "We would fly all around the country," Pei said. "Wherever there was a hint of urban renewal, Zeckendorf would sense it and we would go there. The mayors welcomed him. He would tell them exactly what they should do, and they were all spellbound."

These excursions were for Pei a crash course in real estate, and he soon emerged as that rare architect who could speak with authority about real-world details like location and finance. He learned from Zeckendorf how to identify the interested parties and persuade them that Webb & Knapp's design would benefit everyone, including them. It was a skill Pei would use throughout his career. "What the Pei firm has done so impressively," the critic Peter Blake later wrote, "is to persuade the often warring merchants in a capitalist society to do, of their own free will, what is usually done elsewhere, in more severely managed societies, by government fiat."

Pei learned from a master the importance of planning the political strategy along with the design. "All the great cities of the world were built by autocratic forms of government," Pei said. "Look at Paris: it would not have been possible without Napoleon III and Baron Georges-Eugène Haussmann. The popes and dukes were responsible for many of the great cities in Italy. In China there is the imperial city of Peking. But in the U.S. nobody has that kind of absolute authority. So the responsibility for building a city in a coherent fashion rests with the architects."

Zeckendorf made a point of displaying his cultivated Chinese designer everywhere he went. "Zeckendorf loved to show I.M. off," remembered Henry Cobb, Pei's former student who joined him at Webb & Knapp. "If he could have gotten away with dressing I.M. up in an Oriental outfit with a pigtail, I think he would have done it."

With his aristocratic instinct for the understated pitch, and his unshakable self-confidence, it did not take long for Pei to distinguish himself. He was eminently composed and capable of warming boardrooms with his charm. He was a master of the gracious entrance, the witty aside and the self-deprecating word dropped with exquisite timing. All the while his internal Geiger counter detected who in the room held power and who did not.

While his effusive boss was all paunch and spluttered superlatives, the trim, understated Pei proceeded with ingratiating modesty and a Chinese consideration for the need to save face. He penetrated a problem's essence and articulated solutions in practical terms that businessmen understood. He evinced none of the vanity and affectation that afflicted big-name architects. His discourse was mercifully free of pretentious design jargon. He never read from prepared comments or rummaged in his pocket for notes, but spoke spontaneously and with infectious enthusiasm. Part of his genius was his ability to balance the pragmatics of real estate with a delicacy of design. He always managed to convey the impression that his ideas contained something precious. He pitched ambitious ideas without losing his playful Oriental touch. There was an elegance about his presence that was not lost on his audience.

"He shattered their conception of what an architect was," remembered John Price Bell. "He seemed very stable, unflappable, friendly and knowledgeable. He proved himself not so much with his architecture as with the way in which he talked to top executives."

Pei quickly learned that architectural drawings baffled businessmen. For the rest of his career he produced instead beautiful mahogany models crafted in his own model shop. "What makes I.M. and his crew different from other architects," the Boston city planner Ed Logue once observed, "is that they are so articulate and clear-sighted in matters that govern urban redevelopment. . . . They build these detailed scale models of whole sectors of the city, and these models demonstrate to any laymen the implications of a given project—much more clearly than the drawings ever could."

With Pei's invaluable assistance "Mr. Redevelopment," as Zeckendorf came to be called, made deals in some thirty-four states, and for a while Title I was known in Washington as the Zeckendorf Relief Bill because he fathered more projects under its terms than anyone else. "Nearly a billion dollars in Zeckendorf construction projects were under way," Tom Shachtman calculated in *Skyscraper Dreams*. "Now he was a chess grand master: the world was watching him play fifty games at once against as many opponents, and expected him to win them all."

To handle his mounting workload, Pei had recruited a nucleus of bright young Harvard men—Henry Cobb, Don Page and Ulrich Franzen—and rounded the group out with the congenial, organization-minded veteran Eason Leonard. "I took care of the meat and potatoes," Leonard remembered, "while he did the ice cream."

The architectural establishment wondered aloud why anyone would work for a developer, but Pei's confraternity felt only the esprit de corps that animates young men who feel they are breaking new ground. "Pei asked from the outset if we wanted to make money or make good architecture," remembered Don Page, a graphic designer. "We spent *so* many hours on these complicated projects and we weren't paid overtime. We were just concerned about the quality of the work. We worked all the way through many nights, and Pei was always there."

Pei established for his well-dressed young Harvard deputies the atmosphere of an elite group, a think tank, segregated like a discreet men's club from Webb & Knapp's other operations. When Pei hired James Polshek in 1955, he was shown a back office, or "boiler room," where Webb & Knapp's own architects, a lesser caste, performed unglamorous technical tasks.

"If you don't behave," Polshek was told, "you're going in there."

"I looked in," he remembered, "and saw a sea of white shirts and green eyeshades. [The office] was inhabited by elderly architects doing working drawings."

In a little more than a decade Pei's skeletal staff grew into a seventy-five-man office responsible for more than half a billion dollars' worth of construction. "Pei was without doubt the smartest graduate of Harvard," said Philip Johnson. "It was clear he was going to be Mr. Success Boy. He was a convincing speaker, and his designs pleased Zeckendorf as well as other architects. He kept hitting nails on the head."

One day designer Anthony Candido told Pei he was leaving to pursue a painting career. Pei tried to dissuade him by suggesting the grand achievements to come. Looking up Madison Avenue, Pei said, "We are going to change all this."

Ambitious young architects could not have hoped for a more supportive employer. Zeckendorf was keenly interested and encouraged innovation. "He didn't like run-of-the-mill things," remembered Don Page. "He always wanted something new. When Pei presented an idea Zeckendorf would say, 'Has that been done before?'

" 'I don't think so,' [Pei would say].

"He'd say, 'Good, let's do it.' "

Webb & Knapp's vice presidents didn't always give Pei the same encouragement. "The business people in the organization liked I.M. personally," remembered John O'Mara, a vice president, "and they had to doff their caps to him because he was Bill's fair-haired boy, but they were bottom-line types and they threw up their hands at his ideas. Pei took on adversaries with ease. He was not the kind of guy who would get angry in meetings. He kept his cool and kidded them."

The guardians of Webb & Knapp's bottom line watched with mounting concern as Pei and Zeckendorf planned one extravaganza after another. They warned their boss to proceed with caution. "I.M. was a charming, wonderful man and a great architect," said Webb & Knapp treasurer Arthur Phelan. "The problem was that his ideas were so costly. They caused delays, and everything had to be custom-made. I told Bill once that we were running out of money and couldn't afford this. He said, 'We're talking about a man who, in my opinion, will go down in history as one of the greatest figures of our time.' "

5
BROKEN PROMISES

One day a cadaverous, chain-smoking Colorado real-estate broker named B. B. Harding, wearing a wide-brimmed cowboy hat, entered 383 Madison and unfurled a Denver street plan across Zeckendorf's desk. He slid a bony, nicotine-stained finger to Courthouse Square, a two-and-a-half-acre park devoted to lawns and lily ponds, where the old Denver courthouse had once stood. It was a prime plot adjacent to Denver's busiest shopping strip, Harding explained, and the city wanted someone to develop it. He'd almost sold it to Ellsworth Statler for a new hotel, but Statler had died, as had the deal.

After studying Denver for four months, Zeckendorf's staff concluded that it was poised to become the capital of a nascent Rocky Mountain empire. With some thirty federal agencies in residence—more than any other inland city—and elaborate defense facilities planned nearby, Denver, they surmised, would soon become Washington's western annex. Rich oil and uranium deposits had been discovered during the war and a new jet airport was receiving swelling numbers of skiers and tourists.

All of this activity converged on a city sadly bereft of modern office space. City fathers had passed an ordinance in 1908 barring construction above twelve stories in order to preserve the mountain views. They need not have bothered. When the silver boom fizzled out in 1893, Denver regressed into a low-rise town snoozing at the foot of the Rockies. Its somnolent downtown

ι **Place Ville Marie under construction.**

consisted of crumbling Civil War–era brick buildings no taller than five or six stories masked by cheap Victorian storefronts—a tumbledown ward that might have seemed quaint if it hadn't been so ugly. Not a single office building or hotel had gone up since the Depression. "Denver, like so many other cities, was decentralizing so rapidly that its dry-rotted core had begun to fall in on itself," Zeckendorf observed.

In June 1945, Zeckendorf bought Courthouse Square for $818,600 and announced his intention to build a complex comparable to Rockefeller Center as soon as wartime shortages abated.

Pei and Zeckendorf were not universally welcomed as harbingers of progress. Like other provincial cities into which they would insinuate themselves, Denver was an insular community controlled by a tight-knit circle of old families—the Denver Country Club was sometimes called the Denver Cousins' Club—who had controlled local doings among themselves for generations. Having suffered the vicissitudes of boom and bust, this old guard viewed progress with gloomy caution. Why bet on the future? They preferred to sleepwalk through their comfortable routine while their dividends multiplied. In fact, the aging patriarchs on Seventeenth Street, the so-called Wall Street of the West, actively discouraged growth with tightfisted money policies. According to a local joke, the Denver chamber of commerce existed to keep new business *out.*

Zeckendorf abhorred stultified thinking. He vowed to shake up "Rip Van Winkle City," as he called it, with or without local support. "Even the fact that nothing vital had happened to Denver real estate in forty years had its positive side: holding down the lid for such a long time meant that there was a demand waiting to be tapped," he wrote. "All we had to do was get into that town and *make* something happen."

When the Seventeenth Street gentry heard that out-of-towners—not to mention a New York Jew and a "Chinaman," as Pei was often called—were encroaching on their private domain, a force field of resistance materialized. They filed lawsuits contending that the city could not sell the park without submitting the proposal to popular vote. A syndicate of local real-estate agents offered a counterbid. The *Denver Post* lashed out at Zeckendorf with sarcastic editorials entitled "Dreams of Glory" and "A Good Square Deal."

Zeckendorf persisted, relying largely on B. B. Harding and a local lawyer to work the city's back channels and represent him at the endless hearings and appeals. Having worked for the New York *World-Telegram*, Webb & Knapp's public relations operative, John Price Bell, found a sympathetic reception at its Scripps-Howard affiliate, the *Rocky Mountain News*, which countered the *Post* tit for tat.

Zeckendorf himself went to great lengths to court the local press. He attended the *Denver Post*'s annual Frontier Days retreat, for example, wearing a red vest and his grandfather's Colt .45 pistols slung around his ample waist. Flying back to New York, he happened to sit beside a Denver radio announcer on his way to cover a nudist wedding. Zeckendorf joined him on a whim—although he did manage to keep his cowboy outfit on. Press photographers spotted him in his conspicuous costume standing beside the notorious stripper Gypsy Rose Lee. New York newspapers had published the picture by the time he returned to Manhattan for a meeting at J. P. Morgan's executive offices. A mortified Zeckendorf pleaded with Bell to buy every copy off the newsstands.

While the Courthouse Square plan ground slowly through the courts, Zeckendorf built a speculative office building and shopping complex called Mile High Center two blocks to the north, across from the lavish Brown Palace Hotel, an onyx and cast-iron edifice where Buffalo Bill Cody had once lived. In their first important collaboration, Pei and Zeckendorf aspired to build an integrated cluster of spectacular buildings arranged around an office tower—an infusion of elegance in the heart of the Victorian brick pile—

that would quicken the urban pulse and lure people downtown for shopping, dining and entertainment.

Pei persuaded Zeckendorf to defy real-estate convention by banishing the garish ground-floor shops, with their cluttered windows, to a basement concourse. "What will we have?" he asked. "As tenants we'll get a drugstore and a brassiere shop and other little stores. They will cheapen the building. . . . By adding just five cents to the rental of each square foot of space in those twenty-three floors, you will more than make up for the loss of revenue on the ground floor. And because this will be such a beautiful building, you will be able to get your premium rent."

Pei also broke from convention by drawing his glass-and-aluminum building back from the street so that it occupied less than a quarter of the two-acre site, and by elevating it on stilts, as Mies advocated, allowing pedestrians to stroll unobstructed through an open lobby of understated elegance and a courtyard animated by flower beds, fountains and a refrigerated reflecting pool stocked with mountain trout, where piped-in music played until midnight. It was among the first of endless commercial facilities in the country to provide an open precinct in which the public could linger among fountains and trees, and the first inkling of a career-long penchant for handsome open spaces. To Pei, the spaces between the buildings were as important as the solids themselves. To those who questioned his generous allotment of public space, Pei cited the Chinese philosopher Lao-tzu: "The essence of the vessel is in its emptiness."

Mile High Center demonstrated the extent to which Pei dutifully subscribed throughout these early years to the Miesian glass-and-steel formula established most conspicuously by Mies's celebrated Lakeshore Drive apartments in Chicago, and by a 1947 exhibition of his work at New York's Museum of Modern Art. In a 1983 interview, Pei's associate, Henry Cobb, explained the sway Mies exerted over the Pei studio:

The early work of our firm in the 1950s came quite directly from the Miesian ethic. I use the word "ethic" rather than "aesthetic" because Mies's belief system had—or at least we interpreted it as having—a very significant moral dimension. This was both its strength and its limitation. Within this belief system, there was a right and a wrong way of making things, and that notion of right and wrong permeated the entire enterprise of architecture, from its broadest conception at the scale of urban planning to its ultimate materialization in the smallest detail.

In retrospect, it seems an irony of history that this rigorously moral attitude toward architecture should have been adopted by so many American architects as the lodestone for practice in an era now viewed as having been pragmatic to the point of expediency. Be that as it may, in our early work for William Zeckendorf, Miesian notions of order clearly constituted the essential design strategy for dealing with tough real-world development problems.

Although borrowed straight from the Mies van der Rohe recipe book for a steel frame filled in with glass, Mile High Center's office building was nonetheless a local revelation when it opened in 1955. Zeckendorf promoted it as the most progressive building between San Francisco and Chicago. Newspapers called it a skyscraper, though it stood just twenty stories. Denverites themselves dubbed it "the New York building," and Zeckendorf charged New York rents: six dollars per square foot, roughly double Denver's going rate. The Denver U.S. National Bank became the principal tenant, a move that prompted other local banks to keep pace by moving into other new buildings.

As Pei had predicted, the prestige associated with the open plaza more than recovered the revenue lost by moving the ground-floor stores. Mile High Center proved the premise that progressive architecture could be profitable.

Meanwhile, the courts had, after protracted delay, ruled that Courthouse Square, Zeckendorf's original acquisition, did not qualify as a public park and upheld his purchase in October 1949. Under a new contract with the city, Webb & Knapp was to begin construction by March 1, 1951, or pay an annual fine of $25,000. But the Korean War erupted in 1950, necessitating government restrictions on building materials. Faced with further delays, Zeckendorf, at the suggestion of Mayor Quigg Newton, reluctantly converted the square into a parking lot until ground could be broken. A *Denver Post* poll conducted in December 1950 found that only 20 percent of Denverites expected to see a building go up. Editorials insinuated that Zeckendorf, or "Parking Lot Bill," had never intended to build on the square, and called on Mayor Newton to reclaim the land by condemnation. Courthouse Square seemed cursed.

Zeckendorf refused to give up. Two and a half years later he returned to Denver and, speaking before a thousand business and civic leaders convened at a chamber of commerce luncheon, announced plans to erect on Courthouse Square an elegant 880-room convention hotel—Denver's first in forty years—opulently furnished with a block-long lobby topped by a luminous gold ceiling, two expansive banquet halls, a ballroom, sunken gardens, fountains, terraced dining rooms and shops. A plastic-enclosed pedestrian bridge would span a sunken skating rink and would lead from the hotel to a windowless aluminum-clad department store with a startling hyperbolic paraboloid canopy out front, all conveniently built over three levels of underground parking. It would be among the first complexes in the country to integrate stores, hotel rooms, offices and parking. Construction, he promised, would begin the following year. An impatient audience, having already suffered seven years of delay, gave him a standing ovation.

An unexpected bonus helped pay for what was then the biggest privately funded excavation in American history. When engineers struck the remains of an ancient creek bed forty feet down, Zeckendorf asked them to test their core samples. Sure enough, they found traces of gold. Workers dug up 600,000 tons of earth in all and hauled it to a 110-acre site on the outskirts of town, where sifting yielded $50,000 worth of gold. Zeckendorf saved a few nuggets and had them made into cuff links.

The windfall didn't prevent Zeckendorf from running out of financing, however. In 1958, with the hotel climbing to four stories without a backer, Zeckendorf sent Araldo Cossutta, a talented young Yugoslavian designer on Pei's staff, to Los Angeles for a meeting with hotel magnate Conrad Hilton. When Cossutta arrived at the newly opened Beverly Hilton, he found that the model had shattered in shipping. He frantically reassembled it in his room just in time for the big meeting. Zeckendorf subsequently acquired financing, and a slightly modified hotel—renamed the Denver Hilton—went up above the ancient creek bed.

Having worked in Le Corbusier's Paris atelier, Cossutta argued against making the hotel another Miesian box of glass and steel. He advocated instead the sculptural qualities of Le Corbusier's favorite material: concrete. That suited Zeckendorf, since the Korean War had created a lingering shortage of structural steel. So Cossutta trucked the sand and gravel excavated from the hotel site to Salt Lake City where a contractor molded the materials into four thousand reddish brown concrete window frames, which were reassembled on the site to form a rich waffle-textured slab. Until now Pei's work—the Gulf Oil building in Atlanta, the Webb & Knapp renovation and Mile High Center—had amounted to what Philip Johnson called "minor Mies." Cossutta helped to shift Pei away from the Miesian glass-and-steel aesthetic and into the more expressive plasticism of sculptural concrete that would characterize his work for years to come.

◄

Pei in a rare relaxed moment.

The Denver Hilton: "They said it couldn't

be done."

▼

When "Zeckendorf Plaza," as it was now called, opened in the spring of 1960, a full fifteen years after Webb & Knapp had acquired Courthouse Square, Zeckendorf ran a full-page newspaper ad with a picture of the new Hilton, with the Mile High Center down the street, accompanied by a one-line caption: "They said it couldn't be done."

Zeckendorf and Pei were credited with instigating Denver's ensuing building boom by breaking the local stranglehold on real estate. "With my tongue but partly in my cheek," Zeckendorf later wrote, "I can say that I found Denver brick and left it soaring steel, concrete, and glass—with here and there a touch of marble." Denver was a triumphant episode, but it was the last city in which Pei's collaboration with Zeckendorf would be profitable.

．　．　．　．

By the time the Denver projects were completed, Zeckendorf and Pei were already thickly embroiled in their most ambitious campaign: a master redevelopment of southwest Washington, D.C. When Major Pierre-Charles L'Enfant laid out his Baroque city plan across swamps and pastures in 1791, he expected this low wedge of riverfront land—bordered to the north by the Washington Mall and to the south by the confluence of the Potomac and Anacostia rivers—to become an elegant residential address. A scattering of wealthy citizens, including George Washington's granddaughter, did build homes there in the closing years of the eighteenth century, but the southwest quadrant suffered one fatal drawback: it was segregated from Washington proper by Goose Creek, which was later deepened into a canal, and, since 1873, by the Baltimore and Potomac Railroad.

Southwest, as the area is called, literally lay on the wrong side of the tracks. By World War II it had consequently degenerated into an industrial ash heap and the city's most notorious slum. Five thousand families, most of them black, lived in its tumbledown row houses and in wooden alley shacks with earthen floors. About half of the homes had no plumbing or heat. Worst of all, Southwest's squalor persisted in embarrassing proximity to our most cherished symbols of national glory.

Washington was no longer the sleepy southern town it had been when Franklin D. Roosevelt took office. The New Deal and World War II had spawned swarms of new federal agencies. As the bureaucracy proliferated, so too did lobbyists, think tanks, journalists and sundry associations. The once-sleepy capital suddenly resembled a bustling metropolis with big-city rents and wide boulevards jammed with traffic. To relieve congestion, politicians turned inevitably to the Potomac slum festering in the shadows of the Capitol dome.

In 1946, Congress created the quasi-governmental Redevelopment Land Agency, or RLA, to handle Washington's urban renewal. By the early 1950s, the RLA had expropriated nearly five hundred acres of Southwest through Title I (and in the process had prompted a Supreme Court ruling reconfirming the city's right of eminent domain), but the agency could not agree on a plan.

Washington Post president Phil Graham had heard Zeckendorf lecture at the Harvard Graduate School of Design, and he implored the developer to save Southwest from government inertia. Zeckendorf demurred. The best candidates for urban renewal, he had found, were cities ruled by autocratic mayors. Washington lacked any such central authority back then; it was, Zeckendorf concluded, a "headless monster" run by dozens of government agencies, each advancing its own obscure agenda. Besides, he considered the capital a dead museum town in which choice plots already belonged to the government. Zeckendorf demonstrated his lack of interest by dispatching Washington real-estate brokers to Webb & Knapp vice presidents down the hall.

Having received more than one such disappointed visitor, Zeckendorf's vice president of public relations, John Price Bell, noticed an article in a 1952 issue of *Architectural Forum* describing Southwest's blighted acreage. An accompanying photograph showed half-naked black kids standing in a garbage-strewn yard with the Capitol dome looming in the background. It was an image not easily dismissed, and Bell brooded over it for some time afterward.

Bell was a newspaper reporter by training. Despite his current employment, he disavowed any real-estate expertise. It was the public relations possibilities of redeveloping the capital's worst slum that enticed him to fly down to D.C. one morning for a firsthand look. By the time he stood where the photograph had been taken, he knew that he had uncovered a spectacular opportunity. It would take most developers a lifetime to amass this much contiguous acreage within a major city. Moreover, it lay within walking distance of the Capitol, and its entire southern portion bordered the river.

"Where have you been?" Zeckendorf demanded upon Bell's return.

"Bill," Bell responded, "whoever develops that area will visit the White House within thirty days and they will receive the best possible publicity." Zeckendorf's face lit up. He returned with Pei and toured the fetid slum by car and on foot. Brainstorming began on the spot.

In November 1953, RLA chairman John Remon visited 383 Madison to plumb Webb & Knapp's intentions. "We gave him a couple of dry martinis and a good lunch in the tower dining room over my office," Zeckendorf wrote. "Then, as proof of our interest, we unveiled a master plan for the entire area." Pei's blueprint reconnected Southwest to the city by broadening Tenth Street into a 300-foot-wide pedestrian esplanade lined with stately office buildings, sidewalk cafés and fountains. The expanded street would eliminate the district's historic isolation by spanning the railroad tracks and a proposed eight-lane highway with a pedestrian bridge and then continuing north to a monumental terminus at the Smithsonian's redbrick castle beside the mall.

Off this axis Pei envisioned spectacular vistas lined with three-story town houses wrapped around peaceful courtyards, tall apartment blocks, a symphony hall, an opera house, shops, schools, churches, a library, a planetarium, waterfront marinas and restaurants—a self-sufficient ward all but closed to car traffic. Pei hoped it would be the best of both worlds: the greenery and open space of suburbia combined with festive urban spaces and jobs within walking distance of home.

Southwest would be the largest Title I redevelopment project in the country, and Webb & Knapp proposed to build it according to the rigid geometry of neoclassical landscaping. Zeckendorf promised a select audience of congressmen and District of Columbia officials that the new Southwest would be to Washington "what the Champs-Elysées is to Paris and the Piazza San Marco to Venice." On July 8, 1954, Zeckendorf and Pei discussed the plan with President Eisenhower in the White House. The president's reaction, Zeckendorf told the press, "was far from unfavorable." With Eisenhower's blessing, the RLA signed a "memorandum of understanding" with Webb & Knapp in 1954 committing them to a year of study, later extended to eighteen months, during which the RLA agreed not to recruit competing developers.

At this point Zeckendorf's original misgivings about Washington proved prophetic. First, the prestigious Smithsonian Institution made it known that they considered the proposal an intrusion on their turf. They had their own plans for a new museum south of the Mall that would obstruct Pei's Tenth Street boulevard. Government mediators offered a compromise: Why not reroute the Tenth Street terminus around both sides of the new museum in a giant U? No, Pei said. He refused to sacrifice the monumental connection to the Mall. In that case, why not shift the whole plan over to Ninth Street? But that wouldn't work either: Tenth Street was the only place where the railroad tracks dipped low enough to allow an overhead bridge.

The plan languished in bureaucratic limbo while Webb & Knapp haggled with no fewer than twenty-seven government agencies. Who would be responsible for appraising the land value? Who would pay to maintain Tenth Street? The Washington bureaucracy addressed each question in its laborious manner. "There were moments during these Washington years," Zeckendorf later wrote, "when I felt we were part of some mad surrealist's real-life Monopoly set: every time we were about to acquire a key property or pass 'Go,' the 'Chance' card turned up reading 'Go back three paces.' "

One of the constant perils of urban redevelopment was the long delay between conception and completion, during which all sorts of homegrown resistance could arise. In this case, the protracted interlude cost Webb & Knapp crucial support as the project's original backers slipped away: President Eisenhower left office in 1961, John Remon died, and Phil Graham committed suicide. "We were accustomed to going in and getting things done quickly," said L. Peter Clow, a Webb & Knapp vice president. "Dealing with the government on their own territory was so time-consuming. The truth is, we just got tired."

Pei's master plan called for the Navy Department to occupy two buildings flanking Tenth Street, but in 1962 the General Services Administration's own architects surreptitiously floated a design for the Forrestal Building, which bridged the Mall, and hustled it through the Planning and Fine Arts commissions, thereby putting an end to Pei's plan for an open pedestrian axis leading from the whimsical Smithsonian castle to the Potomac. "A street that is subjected to the indignity of crawling under a massive government building is hardly an inviting gateway into a spanking new part of town," the critic Wolf Von Eckardt wrote in the *New Republic*. "It certainly is no esplanade."

At this point Webb & Knapp withdrew and other developers rushed in to scavenge their plan. In the muddled compromise that followed, Pei contributed only an apartment building and an office complex called L'Enfant Plaza, designed by Araldo Cossutta and built just a block west of where L'Enfant himself had envisioned a great square. In 1966, twelve years after hatching the scheme with Pei, Zeckendorf attended the groundbreaking ceremony.

"I'm the guy who got the girl pregnant," he told reporters. "Those fellows you see around here are merely the obstetricians."

．　．　．　．

Webb & Knapp's Washington adventure ended in a costly miscarriage. But neither this debacle nor Zeckendorf's ignominious descent into debt could diminish Pei's flourishing reputation for insinuating new forms—sheer towers of glass, steel and concrete integrated with open plazas and tunnels leading to stores and parking—among older city patterns. These great neutral presences altered the way people worked and shopped and entertained themselves downtown, but they were not loved. They stood coldly aloof from the surrounding city, from its particular flavor and street life. Nonetheless, city fathers, having seen the modern style ardently documented in *Architectural Digest* and *Life,* welcomed Webb & Knapp's strategy for urban rejuvenation, often reluctantly, as the new face of progress.

Montreal, like Denver, was an undeveloped gray-hued city of slightly more than one million with a melancholy sense of historic abandonment when Pei and Zeckendorf descended on it in the mid-1950s. No major building had gone up in fifty years, and with companies quietly relocating to Toronto, it was in danger of forfeiting its status as Canada's commercial capital. Many, in fact, were quietly dismissing Montreal as a loser.

Fifty years earlier the Canadian National Railroad had planned to build an elaborate station where tracks emerged from a three-mile tunnel under Mount Royal. But depression and war had halted the project, leaving a million-dollar hole sitting like an open grave in a crucial downtown site between Mount Royal and the Saint Lawrence River. In 1950 a tall, forceful Scotsman named Donald Gordon took over the railroad. His efforts to fill the embarrassing gulch with a bold, unified development of integrated parts were not encouraged by the conservative English-speaking establishment. So he turned instead to Zeckendorf, whom he had read about in *Life*. To his surprise, Zeckendorf immediately tried to sell *him* on the idea. After inspecting the site, Zeckendorf offered to have Pei design a master plan for the entire acreage at Webb & Knapp's expense, with no obligation to the railroad. They astutely named it Place Ville Marie, after the city's original missionary settlement, to assuage the French Canadian politicians and editors who complained when the railroad christened a new hotel beside its station the Queen Elizabeth.

Pei by now was so preoccupied with the burdens of constant reconnaissance and the management of dozens of projects and proposals that he struggled to find time for design. As he would throughout his career, he rose from his bed at odd hours to solve nagging design problems. "He needed eight hours of sleep," said Eileen, "but he often got only six. I would get up to go to the bathroom and find little pieces of paper all over the apartment reminding him to try this or that, or get in touch with someone." The bureaucracy associated with urban renewal required years of reconnaissance, politicking and public relations before anything tangible appeared on the site.

The pace of incoming work forced Pei to abdicate the actual design role beyond the early conceptual phase and to allow associates to shepherd the project along in his stead. He returned periodically to evaluate their progress and accompany the model into meetings with Zeckendorf's political allies and financial backers. He was so adept at explaining designs that nobody knew he was anything but intimately involved in their day-to-day gestation. As far as the public was concerned, these were Pei's designs.

In this case, Pei's design proxy was Henry Cobb. At age twenty-eight, Cobb was only six years out of Harvard when he began work on the largest complex of its kind in the world alongside Vincent Ponte, another former student of Pei's, who served as in-house city planner. While the DC-3 flew them to Montreal for lunch with a dozen local real-estate men, Cobb showed Zeckendorf a plan he had developed under Pei's supervision for two simple rect-

▲

A model of Place Ville Marie's forty-eight-story cruciform tower. The tallest building in the British Commonwealth, it changed Montreal forever.

◄

Henry Cobb shows Zeckendorf an early scheme for Place Ville Marie aboard Webb & Knapp's DC-3. "You don't make 'melly' out of blue-white diamonds," Zeckendorf said.

angular towers with a series of smaller subsidiary buildings. "It was a competent and a pleasant design," Zeckendorf recalled, "but as I stood up in the steeply banked airplane and looked out the windows to the winter-gripped city below, I was dissatisfied. Something was missing. Here lay this unexploited but potentially fabulous site which only we could develop, but what we proposed to develop lacked power. As I began to sense what was missing, I said, 'Henry, I want to tell you something . . . you don't make 'melly' out of blue-white diamonds.' The minute I explained that melly are merely the bits and chips left over when a great diamond has been cut, he saw what I meant. He, too, recognized that we needed something with enough critical mass to force changes on Montreal."

A few hours later, between dessert and coffee, Zeckendorf asked his lunch companions how big his building should be. The responses ranged from 300,000 to 750,000 square feet. "Gentlemen," he announced, "we're going to put up a building of four million square feet."

Zeckendorf later remembered that "the faces at that table turned green with horror."

"Place Ville Marie struck Montreal's deeply conservative business community like an earthquake measuring ten on the Richter scale," said one staff member close to the project. "It was as if Saul Steinberg had announced plans to build an office tower in midtown Manhattan four times the size of the Empire State Building. A Greek chorus of ill-wishers predicted its failure: 'They'll never expropriate the land. They'll never get tenants. They'll never get it built.' But they did."

Zeckendorf exhorted Cobb to generate a monumental landmark that would dominate the skyline like the Eiffel Tower or the Empire State Building. Cobb responded with a forty-two-story cruciform tower ballasted by layers of brightly lit underground concourses through which some 55,000 commuters would come and go comfortably catacombed against the icy winds blowing off the Saint Lawrence. It was to be the largest underground city in the world—three times the size of Rockefeller Center—lined with barbershops, bakeries, theaters, galleries and restaurants.

As Cobb originally designed it, Place Ville Marie would have been the tallest building in the entire British Commonwealth. Shortly after groundbreaking, however, the Canadian Imperial Bank of Commerce announced plans for a slightly taller tower nearby. Never one to be outdone, Zeckendorf waited until the rival project committed itself to construction before blithely restoring Place Ville Marie to preeminence by instructing Pei to add three extra stories. The Imperial Bank publicly accused Zeckendorf of altering his plan simply for the sake of publicity. Not so, huffed Zeckendorf. Nonetheless, it had become obvious, in Montreal and elsewhere, that Zeckendorf's strategy, and therefore Pei's, was aimed at being the most conspicuous. "Zeckendorf simply thought big, and that was rather infectious," said Cobb. "We wanted to think big as well."

The isolated behemoth was also planned as the focus point for an updated Montreal, with walkways snaking like ganglia beyond the property line to link up with a new subway system, suburban trains, surrounding streets, apartment buildings, shops, hotels, theaters and the nearby McGill University campus. It welded the retail district to the north with the financial district to the south.

The original floor plan carefully worked around the Saint James Club, an oak-paneled lair across the street where Montreal's Anglo-Saxon establishment had converged after work since 1863 to shoot billiards and peruse the financial pages. By coincidence, a street-widening had done away with the top French club across town. The French-Canadian mayor, Jean Drapeau, saw Place Ville Marie as an opportunity to retaliate by razing the symbolic headquarters of the English-speaking gentry. "We knew he was going to hit it," said city planner Vincent Ponte. A local cartoonist depicted the old gentlemen of the Saint James Club staving off bulldozers with umbrellas and blasts from seltzer bottles. Zeckendorf offered them a new clubhouse on Place Ville Marie's top floor with their own private elevator, but the members could not bring themselves to occupy the belly of the beast, no matter how panoramic its view. They relocated instead to an ordinary building across the street from their flattened roost.

The local financial institutions, many of them run by Saint James members, expressed a similar reluctance to forsake their spacious dark-paneled offices arrayed along Saint James Street for the high ground where Place Ville Marie stood. Montreal's devoutly conservative business community wasn't about to inconvenience itself on behalf of an American developer. Zeckendorf needed tenants in order to get financing, but he encountered a chilly reception wherever he went. In what amounted to an enormous gamble, he went ahead and borrowed the money to begin excavation. By late winter of 1957–1958 he had a $4 million hole and no major tenants.

One night, as his predicament grew dire, Zeckendorf complained by phone to James Muir, president of the Royal Bank of Canada, "Jim, you know we are not getting anywhere with this damn renting."

"Why the hell should you get anywhere?" Muir answered. "That goddamn Chinaman is stopping you."

"It's not Pei," Zeckendorf said. "It's you. You and your crowd are refusing to take any space down here." A short time later Muir's bank agreed to lease eight floors if Zeckendorf would buy their vacated headquarters. The commitment allowed Zeckendorf to borrow $75 million to finish the project.

When it opened in 1962, the *Montreal Star* effusively announced that "Place Ville Marie is now to Montreal what the Vatican City has long been to Rome." Some fifteen hundred invited guests and additional hundreds massed in the open plaza for the inauguration. Cobb was reportedly pleased sometime later when French-Canadian nationalists used the plaza to burn an effigy of Donald Gordon in protest of what they considered discriminatory hiring practices. Cobb thought this showed that the plaza was fulfilling its function as a gathering place.

Zeckendorf and Pei had found Montreal cloaked in redbrick provincialism, but they left it a rejuvenated city. Place Ville Marie shifted the financial district uptown and stimulated shopping. The tax windfall helped Mayor Drapeau raise enough capital for a clean, efficient subway system, which in turn helped the city win approval for the 1967 World's Fair. With its space frames, cantilevered pavilions, translucent tents and inverted pyramids, Expo, along with Place Ville Marie, made Montreal a showcase for progressive design. For fifteen years, city planners around North America offered incentives to developers if they agreed to connect mass transit, pedestrian walkways and shopping concourses.

For all its accomplishments, however, Place Ville Marie cannot be called beautiful. Nor has it settled gracefully into its surroundings. Its imposing shaft of glass and steel ruptures the fabric of nineteenth-century Montreal. Worse, a cluster of other cold boxes has sprung up around it. Montreal, like countless other cities, forfeited the local vernacular, its unique expression of its own location, for the dubious promise of modernism.

Place Ville Marie enhanced Pei's reputation as an architect who saw beyond the property line and concerned himself with the surrounding city, but Webb & Knapp paid a terrible price. Place Ville Marie cost $105 million, roughly double its original budget. The grim numbers confirmed what Zeckendorf's vice presidents had been warning him for years: Pei's designs cost too much for any fiscally responsible developer. "Place Ville Marie should have been built by the government or a Rockefeller," said

Peter Clow. "It wasn't the kind of project a real-estate firm should at-tempt."

．　．　．　．

Just as Place Ville Marie got under way, Zeckendorf and New York's master builder Robert Moses negotiated a rapprochement. In 1957 a scandal had erupted over the Title I projects conducted under Moses's auspices as head of the Mayor's Committee on Slum Clearance. Other cities relocated tenants and cleared the land before turning the site over to a sponsor responsible for building the approved development. In New York, though, Robert Moses had tried to hasten the laborious Title I process by turning the condemned plots over to sponsors before clearing the slum. The problem was that sponsors found it more profitable simply to collect rents from the impoverished tenants than to relocate them and proceed with the proposed redevelopment. In the meantime, they neglected to pay taxes. At a City Hall press conference a badly embarrassed Mayor Robert F. Wagner conceded that the sponsors had conned the city for five full years. Faced with long, politically damaging fore-closure hearings, Moses invited Zeckendorf to assume control of the wayward projects.

The architect Gordon Bunshaft of Skidmore, Owings & Merrill, designer of the landmark Lever House on Park Avenue and a city consultant for Title I projects, reportedly advised Pei to avoid what he considered a bureaucratic quagmire. "I went to Gordon Bunshaft," Pei said, "and I said, Gordon, what do you think? 'I.M.,' he said, 'don't touch it. That's not for architects. That's for lawyers.' At that time, architects like Bunshaft looked upon urban rede-velopment as work not worth doing."

Pei relayed Bunshaft's warning to his boss, but the irrepressible Zeck-endorf could not be dissuaded. He bought a majority control of three projects and paid their back taxes. Almost overnight, Webb & Knapp became a dominant New York redeveloper.

Pei encountered Bunshaft's quagmire for himself at Kips Bay Plaza, a project set among the brownstones of an old Italian neighborhood in Manhattan's East Thirties. All Title I buildings had to conform to convoluted specifications imposed by the Federal Housing Authority in order to qualify for mortgage insurance. These cryptic codes baffled architects who were unacquainted with their obscure logic. The FHA, for example, allotted money according to the number of rooms, but a balcony somehow qualified as a room while a bathroom did not. "It's a science, not an art," Pei told *Architectural Forum*, "but it's not a logical science. . . . It took me six months to even begin to understand it." What's more, Pei had to navigate these impenetrable specifications burdened by an unusually tight budget. While construction costs of up to thirty dollars per square foot were acceptable in speculative office buildings, low-income housing could afford only about half that.

Zeckendorf wisely retained the project's original architects to help guide Pei through the housing arcana. A wizened old veteran of New York redevelopment, Samuel Kessler, and his son Melvin had participated in more than half a dozen Title I redevelopments. They didn't offer much in the way of inspired design—they never claimed to—but they excelled in the art of bureaucracy. Over the years they had mastered the intricacies of red tape and carefully cultivated relationships with unions and Democratic party bosses. *Architectural Forum* called them "a combination of know-how and know-who." Their expertise freed Pei to pursue new ideas.

Pei asserted himself throughout his years with Zeckendorf as an architect capable of overcoming the impediments to quality imposed by budgets and bureaucracy. At Kips Bay, he was determined to show that imaginative design could raise the quality of middle-income housing and still prove profitable. First, he replaced the six buildings designated in the original master plan with twin rectangular slabs, and he arranged them so as to create a protected park out of the space left over. "The slabs do perform an important function," he said. "They enclose the park. If you go inside Kips Bay Plaza today you discover a world all by itself which is very pleasant." Pei wanted to adorn the park with a 30-foot-high Picasso sculpture, *Bust of Sylvette*. Zeckendorf gave him a choice: he could have the Picasso or fifty saplings, but not both. Pei chose the saplings.

At the Denver Hilton, Araldo Cossutta had experimented with window frames of raw, unfinished concrete. Pei speculated that he could make the same windows strong enough to support the building, thereby eliminating the need for expensive steel framing. They might also be attractive enough, in a rough, sculptural way, to stand without the bland cosmetic bricks that sheathed standard middle-income housing projects like Stuyvesant Town and Peter Cooper Village. In other words, Pei hoped to merge the skin and the structure into one unit, thereby hastening construction and freeing up funds for improved hardware and light fixtures. To maximize efficiency, he designed Kips Bay Plaza as twin twenty-one-story slabs enclosing a garden. "At that time," Pei said, "we had only one thing in mind: how to break out of the straitjacket of Peter Cooper Village and Stuyvesant Town."

Not everyone shared Pei's ambitions. Concrete is a notoriously unpredictable material prone to shrinkage, hairline cracks and damp Rorschach blotches. Webb & Knapp's own construction department inflated the estimated costs in an attempt to steer the project back to conventional bricks and mortar. "I realized there was a concerted effort under way to shaft the Pei concept," said John O'Mara, a vice president. "The construction department wanted no part of these Harvard-educated architects telling them how to do things. As far as they were concerned, you needed architects only to draw pictures and make sure the lines were straight. Pei's people handled themselves well. They kept their cool, and they did a damn good job of selling their ideas, and of romancing old man Kessler. Kessler realized that he was going to get paid and also profit from his association with this renowned young architect on his way up. It ended without blood."

Pei lavished extravagant care on the lowly genre of middle-income housing. His staff developed a special lightweight concrete and showed the contractors how to mix it. They inspected bags of aggregate to make sure the colors were consistent. They even filled little bottles with the mixture and examined them back in the office. Meanwhile, workers assembled the waffle-shaped facades by pouring concrete like Jell-O into molds right on the site. Because the window frames replaced beams and columns, the Kips Bay Plaza apartments were unusually spacious and illuminated by floor-to-ceiling windows. Pei even persuaded the FHA to award partial balcony credit for the deep-set windows by arguing that public money should not go toward anything as luxurious as balconies.

At $10.15 a square foot, Kips Bay Plaza cost more than conventional housing, but Pei was convinced that his cast-concrete innovations would grow profitable with refinement. Unfortunately, investors bet against Pei. Zeckendorf recruited the prestigious firm of Lazard Freres as an equity partner in a subsequent Title I project called Lincoln Towers, which was to go up behind Lincoln Center. Aware of Pei's overages at Kips Bay, Lazard senior partner André Meyer demanded to see for himself the design that Zeckendorf was touting as "one of the wonders of Manhattan."

"Pei produced this enormous model—it took up most of the back of a station wagon—and drove it down to 44 Wall Street," remembered Meyer's associate George Ames. "He carted it into a conference room and put it down on the table. When André came in, he was taken aback. He hadn't realized how large the project was. Rich, jazzy buildings covered half a dozen blocks. So André looked at I.M., and he said, 'Mr. Pei, I want you to remember to think of us as greedy Wall Street bankers.' I.M. wanders through life with a perpetual smile on his face, but on this occasion the smile disappeared totally. He persevered with his pitch, but it quickly became clear this was an expensive affair, and the project was eventually turned over to a cheaper architect."

Zeckendorf, of course, was crushed. "I am not proud of the final product," he wrote in his memoir. "I am ashamed of it. . . . The fact is, I was so enamored of Pei, of how he thought and the kind of work he could do, that no other architects could really interest me."

．　．　．　．

In the discredited nineteenth-century city, only important civic edifices like courthouses and city halls were given the right to stand in splendid isolation. Pei's generation extended that privilege to a wide range of structures. It became clear, in time, that few office buildings and apartment slabs mustered the symbolic weight to stand apart with anything but awkward monumentality. And their vast plazas too often became forlorn concrete plateaus, windswept and forbidding. As Lewis Mumford put it, Le Corbusier's City in a Park turned out to be a City in a Parking Lot.

By the late 1950s, the shiny promise that originally accompanied urban renewal had soured into simmering resentment. Edward T. Chase summarized the disenchantment with modernism's broken promises in a 1958 article published in *Commonweal:*

> Are we human beings of such staunch stuff that we can
> suffer unharmed such harsh antithetical relationships as are
> presented by modern architecture—the stark patterns of
> ninety-degree angles; the impenetrable, unchanging and
> silent facades of cruel smooth steel and glass; the monotony
> of geometric forms in simple repetition coldly applied to
> any site, anonymous, interchangeable, indifferent to the

indigenous; the tasteless, often ugly exploitation of new synthetic materials in jukebox fashion; and the trivial "functional" gimmicks tendered us apologetically as amelioration of these machine-engineered structures?

In 1961 a former newspaper reporter from Scranton, Ohio, named Jane Jacobs rallied a popular insurrection by lambasting urban planners in a manifesto entitled *The Death and Life of Great American Cities.* With reasoned irony she blamed all those responsible for gutting the vital undergrowth of old neighborhoods and extinguishing their flavorsome street life. "Low-income projects are worse than the slums they replace," she wrote, "middle-income housing is a marvel of dullness, luxury housing vulgar. . . . This is not the rebuilding of cities, this is the sacking of cities."

Jacobs upended the basic tenets of modern planning by glorifying the sidewalk as civilization's most vital institution, a stage set upon which a familiar neighborhood cast performs its daily rituals: swarms of children pass noisily to and from school, a housewife negotiates with the butcher, grandparents gossip on the stoop, pedestrians duck into a shop to elude the rain, and a boyfriend waits expectantly for his date at a prearranged rendezvous while the colorful pageant of everyday life passes by. What single planner could presume to replace the haphazard brilliance of the lively, jostling street?

Once heralded as the engineers of an improved society, modern architects and city planners were increasingly inveighed against as authoritarian figures imposing their manifestos on behalf of politicians and profiteers. Jacobs quoted the complaint of a tenant of a Manhattan housing project: "They threw our homes down and pushed us here and pushed our friends somewhere else. We don't have a place to get a cup of coffee or a paper even, or borrow fifty cents. . . . But the big men come and look at that grass and say, 'Isn't that wonderful! Now the poor have everything!' "

Nothing besmirched urban redevelopment more than the policy of forced relocation. Hundreds of thousands watched as bulldozers and wrecking balls destroyed their homes, schools and small businesses at a time when housing was already scarce. The redevelopment of southwest Washington alone uprooted no fewer than 24,000 people from a district which, despite its poverty, had provided all the incidental neighborhood benefits that a master plan could never replace: acquaintances chatting over a backyard fence, kids playing tag in a grassy lot, elderly folks waving to friends from the front porch. Federal law required developers to find them new homes close to their work. But displaced residents inevitably scrounged for new apartments at higher rents. Because more than half of all families forced from their homes were black, the policy developed a strong racial stigma. Urban renewal was privately referred to as "Negro removal."

As Americans came to hate the charmless slabs and forlorn plazas inflicted on them in the name of urban redevelopment, "developer" became a dirty word. As the most visible developer in the country, Zeckendorf was inevitably tarred by the backlash. A full-page cartoon published in a 1962 issue of *Horizon* magazine, for example, portrayed him as a monster, *"Zeckendorfus barbarus,"* devouring New York. "A burrowing animal, fully webbed and napped except for the sharp claws used in operating its famous game called 'urban renewal,' " read the caption. "Makes grunting noises that sound like 'Title I! Title I!'; abhors high ceilings, thick walls, and decorative architecture. Naturalists believe it instinctively builds drab buildings the way the beaver builds leaking dams."

Still, Zeckendorf is remembered as an enlightened developer committed to raising the standards of speculative building. "If you can raise the standards by even ten percent, it's no mean thing," Pei said, "and I think we did that."

Pei came from a civilization that built impossibly grand expressions of power—imperial palaces, vast burial tombs and the Great Wall. In America, Pei joined the forefront of a generation of architects and planners that unflinchingly imposed the theories of Gropius and Le Corbusier on real-life neighborhoods. Unfortunately, the idealized vision of an efficient, light-filled city rarely worked out in practice. Pei was perhaps the most prolific of those architects who surgically implanted towers and commanding plazas that ruptured historic patterns and opened the way to further development, which in turn erased much of the indigenous flavor of Boston, Montreal, Washington, Philadelphia, New York, Chicago and Cleveland. "It could be argued that Pei projects like Kips Bay Plaza and University Plaza at NYU offered their residences the best of both worlds: the human activity of nearby streets and the privacy of an isolated setting," said urbanist Philip Howard. "I don't buy that. If you removed them from the fabric of the city—from the retail wall of First Avenue and SoHo—they would simply be better versions of Co-op City or housing projects. These projects could not succeed without reference to the city whose character they deny. I think they're just boring, and I think most people would agree."

Pei expressed no remorse—except to say, "We would not do it the same way today"—and suffered little blame. "It just didn't occur to anyone to blame Pei," said Philip Johnson. "He's one of those totally blameless people. He is the kind of man that is unattackable. He's the sweetest guy in the world, and everyone loves him."

．．．．

By the early 1960s, Zeckendorf faced graver problems than public disapproval. Behind Webb & Knapp's guise of glamour and prosperity wobbled an increasingly unstable structure of mortgages and high-interest loans. His borrow-and-build strategy worked as long as land values continued their postwar surge. But on May 28, 1962—Blue Monday—stocks suffered their most precipitous drop since 1929, and real estate sank along with them. The plunge caught Zeckendorf badly overextended.

Webb & Knapp was already burdened by inordinate operating costs. Because his deals were so numerous and complex, Zeckendorf was obliged to pay legions of lawyers and accountants to mop up the details. Pei's design department alone cost a million dollars a year. Meanwhile, the advent of jet travel allowed executives to visit cities in a single day, reducing the occupancy rate in Webb & Knapp's nine hotels. Between 1959 and 1965 the firm lost a reported $70 million.

In order to satisfy encircling creditors, Zeckendorf reluctantly sold one property after another before it had matured into full profitability. Sadly, the sell-off claimed some projects that he had painstakingly assembled in collaboration with Pei, including Denver's Mile High Center, Philadelphia's Society Hill and Kips Bay Plaza.

Zeckendorf was temperamentally ill-suited for consolidation, and his prodigious imagination continued to outpace his purse. Eventually his reputation as a debtor eclipsed his reputation as a developer, and having exhausted all credit at conventional banks, he borrowed money at up to 24 percent interest from loan sharks to prevent his empire from collapsing like a house of cards. "I'd rather be alive at eighteen percent than dead at the prime rate," he said.

Throughout this perilous period Zeckendorf conducted himself with poise and good humor. When the head of Morgan Guarantee remarked that he looked like a million bucks, Zeckendorf responded, "I better—I owe you three million." And when an officer of Reynolds Aluminum told Zeckendorf that his firm netted about $9 million a year, Zeckendorf replied, "My God, I pay my shylocks more than that."

The financial community followed Zeckendorf's plight with morbid fascination. He defied expectations for a spell and dangled by a fraying thread, but he couldn't hang on forever. Zeckendorf's long high-wire act ended on a Friday afternoon in 1965. He was alerted by car phone while riding down the East River Drive in his limousine that Marine Midland Bank had called in an $8.5 million note. Webb & Knapp collapsed into bankruptcy with debts of $80 million. Zeckendorf's phones were disconnected. Appraisers tagged the company furnishings for bankruptcy sale. "Now all action ceased," Zeckendorf wrote. "I could no longer act for the company. I became, in effect, a bystander at the wake, and an official nonperson, a role both unfamiliar and unenjoyable."

Zeckendorf's troubles worsened after Webb & Knapp went under. In 1968 he declared personal bankruptcy, and his wife, Marion, died in a plane crash en route to Guadeloupe, where she was to meet him. Two years later he suffered the first in a series of strokes. The sixth killed him in 1976, six months after a Manhattan grand jury indicted him for failing to pay state income tax.

· · · ·

During the ten years before Zeckendorf's demise, Pei had grown increasingly mindful of the constraints of development work, and he had shrewdly distanced himself from Webb & Knapp well before its ignoble demise. "Working for Zeckendorf helped Pei and hurt him in different ways," explained *New York Times* critic Paul Goldberger. "It was their shared insight that there could be a point of intersection between serious modern architecture and real-estate development that others had not perceived. To make it work required a lot of compromise on both ends. Zeckendorf could not operate with as much pragmatism; Pei could not operate with all the freedom a serious architect could hope for."

Pei's association with Zeckendorf stigmatized him as a developer's architect. "I've heard of you," Frank Lloyd Wright reportedly told Pei. "You belong to Zeckendorf." It also disqualified him from consideration for coveted high-profile commissions like New York's Lincoln Center. "Pei saw that there were plenty of worlds to conquer," said Charles Urstadt, a Webb & Knapp vice president, "and he wanted to build up his own portfolio. It was natural for him to want to create his own image."

Pei decided it was time to step outside Zeckendorf's penumbra. "I expressed our restlessness to Mr. Zeckendorf around '55, '56, and he was very understanding, saying, 'You can take some outside commissions, but don't forget about us,' " Pei later recalled.

Pei's first independent job was a Washington, D.C., home for William Slayton, head of the government's urban renewal programs, consisting of three concrete barrel vaults with glass walls at either end. "We did it on the backs of envelopes," Pei said, "traveling from city to city."

His first big job in his own name came in 1959 when his alma mater, MIT, asked him to design a nine-story earth science laboratory. Pei persuaded them to build instead a twenty-story high-rise which, he promised, would act as an organizing landmark for the neoclassical campus. Banking on this single commission, Pei, at age forty-three, formally broke away from Webb & Knapp the following year. It was an amicable divorce of mutual convenience. Zeckendorf's tottering empire could no longer afford the luxury of a $1 million design staff; Pei, in turn, paid Zeckendorf a nominal rent for his studio space and offered his services on a contractual basis. Pei celebrated the formation of I. M. Pei & Associates, later changed to I. M. Pei & Partners, with a staff dinner at the Saint Regis.

Zeckendorf's downfall ironically helped Pei by granting him independence at a propitious moment. Webb & Knapp served as a booster rocket propelling Pei to a higher orbit before consuming itself in flames. "I felt trapped in the role of looking for jobs, being a procurer of commissions," Pei said. "While my people had the luxury of doing one job at a time, I had to keep track of the whole enterprise. My growth as a designer was stunted; I should have reached my maturity much earlier. In a way, Zeckendorf's financial

▶

Kips Bay Plaza with one apartment block
completed, October 1960. It ushered in a
new way of building.

◀

Araldo Cossutta and Pei inspect a model of
MIT's Earth Sciences building, December
1960. It was their first big independent job.

▶

An airport control tower in El Paso, Texas,
one of fifty built according to Pei's proto-
typical design.

problems were the beginning of my opportunity as an architect." By 1962, Pei had procured a handful of jobs that matched his elevated ambitions: a soaring chapel for a missionary college in Formosa in memory of the Reverend Dr. Henry W. Luce, father of Time, Inc., founder Henry R. Luce; a prototype for a five-sided control tower to be built at fifty U.S. airports; a master plan for downtown Boston; and a National Airlines terminal for New York's Idlewild (now JFK) Airport.

Once Pei's stock rose, he declined to participate in the projects his irrepressible former boss tried to generate after Webb & Knapp's fall. Instead, he referred Zeckendorf to promising younger architects. "I.M. knew none of them would be built," said Richard Meier, one such candidate. "He's very canny about what to do and what not to do. We all have a lot to learn from him in that way."

Pei's private life had also entered a new phase. For a decade he and Eileen had maintained a diminishing hope of returning to China. By the mid-1950s there was no longer any doubt that the China of their childhood had given way to the People's Republic. In fact, Pei's brother Y.K. had returned to Shanghai to build a glass factory after the Japanese surrender, only to leave a few years later in the face of threats. "The Maoists said, 'If you're not with us, you're against us,' " Y.K. recalled. "They called me an undesirable. Shortly after they came to power I told my family our lives might be in danger. So we left China."

On Veterans Day, 1955, I.M. and Eileen filed into New York's Polo Grounds where, speaking from a platform erected behind second base, U.S. Attorney General Herbert Brownell Jr. led 10,000 assembled immigrants in the oath of citizenship. Pei had mixed emotions about this experience:

> On the one hand, feelings of sorrow at having to abandon
> our culture, our roots, our ancestral home. On the other

hand, feelings of gratitude—more than happiness—that we had this wonderful country in which to live. Those mixed feelings disappeared about ten years later when President Lyndon Johnson invited me to a ceremony on Ellis Island. It was then that I felt very much like an American.

America has been a blessing to me. It has given me a dimension of challenge which I don't think I would have been able to experience anywhere else. For me, this is a country to which I owe nearly everything I have.

In 1952 Pei had built for his growing family a simple country home in the quaint Westchester town of Katonah, New York. Liberated in this rare instance from the external pressures that influence large-scale projects, Pei created an unpretentious wooden pavilion floating almost like a treehouse above a sloping acreage planted with Chinese pines. With its open plan, sliding doors and spare cantilevered space, the house could be described with equal accuracy as having been inspired by Mies or by the Japanese wood-frame tradition—a child of both East and West. The architect and critic Peter Blake called it "a marvel of restrained sumptuousness." It reveals a lightness and warmth not always evident in his more monumental creations.

Whatever its inspiration, the Katonah house was an exceedingly simple affair, not much more than a platform elevated on stilts with massive laminated pine beams stretched overhead and an encircling screened porch. "Like many things in his life, it was humble but elegant," said Pershing Wong, an associate who helped design it. Workers erected its post-and-lintel frame in a single day and covered it in a week. Pei and Wong attached the screens themselves. The four Pei children had beds on casters so that they could wheel themselves wherever they liked on warm summer nights. Light filtered into the house from theatrically illuminated trees.

Katonah became Pei's weekend retreat from the pressures of launching his own practice, for the burden of drumming up enough work to support a staff of seventy-five now fell on his own shoulders. He worried that his association with Zeckendorf, the spectacularly failed developer, would damage his reputation as an expensive architect. He was nonetheless determined to put redevelopment behind him and advance to more prestigious commissions. "The area of speculative real-estate building does not alone interest me anymore," he told *Time*. "It's too hard to make good architecture out of real-estate buildings."

Pei's search for a new direction was informed by the need to instill modern forms with sculptural drama. In 1951, the Peis toured Europe on a Harvard fellowship. "Instead of visiting cathedrals and palaces," Pei said, "I spent most of my time drinking my way through the Rhône Valley." One landmark he did observe was Chartres Cathedral, and it instilled in him an appreciation for the sonorous light and power at play in the historic buildings Gropius had expunged from the Harvard curriculum. It was a galvanizing encounter. "That's when my architectural education began," Pei said. "My eyes were opened for the first time. . . . If it had happened later I would have been too formed. If it had happened earlier I wouldn't have gotten as much out of it. The timing was perfect."

Pei's breakthrough into a new direction came when a panel of deans from seven architecture schools headed by Pietro Belluschi of MIT picked him in 1961 to design the National Center for Atmospheric Research from a list that included such stalwart candidates as Edward Larrabee Barnes, Skidmore, Owings & Merrill and Eero Saarinen. A memo issued by the committee concluded that "the project would be for [Pei] a quite new challenge and would provide personal and professional advantages and satisfactions that could lead him to be tremendously involved."

The National Center for Atmospheric Research was fathered by Dr. Walter Orr Roberts, a Harvard-trained astrophysicist who rose through the research ranks to become one of the science community's foremost statesmen. As his wrinkled wardrobe and sandals suggested, Roberts was an independent thinker and a visionary. He virtually invented the field of atmospheric science and brought it credibility and substantial funding. "We live on the earth," he liked to say, "but we live *in* the atmosphere."

Twenty years earlier, Harvard had sent Roberts to establish a high-altitude observatory in Colorado. With his bride of a few weeks in the passenger seat and a precious device used for photographing the sun packed in the back, Roberts drove west through the midsummer heat in a dilapidated Graham-Paige, a vintage automobile that required constant repair along the way. The newlyweds spent their first year in a little house adjoining the observatory dome on an isolated mountain peak perched above the remote mining town of Climax. Over the years, Roberts built Colorado's high-altitude observatory into one of the most respected scientific institutions in the country.

Roberts selected for the National Center for Atmospheric Research a site of awesome beauty perched fittingly between land and sky: a 6,200-foot-high mesa in the tree-studded Rocky Mountain foothills overlooking Boulder and the Great Plains stretching eastward. The selection was dictated in part by convenience: Boulder was a rare high-altitude university town. But the real impetus was the site's natural beauty, which Roberts had admired for years through his living room window. The mesa was blanketed by more than five hundred acres of waving meadow grass and wildflowers patrolled by deer and coyotes. Architect and client tramped through the fragrant sage grass and prickly pears discussing the project—Roberts in his customary wrinkled pants and sandals, Pei in a meticulous suit and fine leather shoes. "I went and slept on the mesa," Pei said. "I don't know how many times I walked the mesa, and I drank a lot of wine on that mesa. It was almost a religious experience, the early part of it, to try to really get a feel of nature."

Dr. Roberts was the first in a succession of remarkable clients with whom

Pei forged working relationships so intimate they might almost be called collaborations. "Before I.M. gets into the subject of business, he befriends the client," said Richards Mixon, a designer who worked on the research center. "It's characteristic of upper-class Chinese. They get to know each other. They test each other's humor. This intimacy allows him to explore business issues more deeply."

In the course of their mesa walks, Walt Roberts outlined his vision of a think tank, medieval and monastic in its isolation, where scientists released from the workaday burdens of the university could ponder the mysteries of cloud physics and atmospheric chemistry. While the center would have to contain its share of laboratory clutter and masticating computers, it would, as Roberts envisioned it, be first and foremost a beautiful temple of contemplation.

During the Webb & Knapp years Pei had reluctantly withdrawn from day-to-day design work. He had appraised large acreages like Place Ville Marie and Kips Bay, formulated a design concept and left the rest to Henry Cobb or Araldo Cossutta. With the research center, he returned to the intimate details of design. "I had always looked over the shoulders of the architects working with me," he said, "and I would participate in the concept and occasionally draw a line to test out an idea or to help someone consolidate his own direction in a design. But it wasn't until [the National Center for Atmospheric Research] that I was thrown fully into the process once again."

Ironically, the drama of the site paralyzed Pei. His precocious portfolio contained only city buildings composed according to the urban scale of doors, windows and floors. These proportions turned balky against the hyperscale of the surrounding Flatiron range. Pei stayed up nights concocting some fifteen abortive schemes. Low sprawling buildings, tall towers—the mountainous backdrop dwarfed them all. Pei has always seemed to know just how to proceed; we see him here in a rare state of uncertainty. "I was floundering," he acknowledged. "I was groping for straws."

▲

The National Center for Atmospheric Re-

search in Boulder, Colorado, an early exam-

ple of Pei's meditative geometry.

About that time Pei and Eileen toured the Southwest by car. In the southern corner of Colorado they visited Mesa Verde where, in the thirteenth century, the Anasazi Indians had constructed a honeycomb of mud-and-stone dwellings nestled harmoniously within immense sandstone caves. Pei observed how the Anasazi, not unlike Frank Lloyd Wright, blended their shapes and colors with the surrounding landscape. The ruins were *of* the land as well as *on* the land. "I saw that the Indians, instead of fighting their background, made it a part of their building," he later said. "Their success stemmed from using indigenous materials, then tucking their structures into the mountain. It looks as if it was carved out of the mountain." It reminded him of the high Andes Inca settlement of Ollantaytambo, which he had seen the previous year. Pei's road trip inspired him to move beyond the stiff inhibitions of his Bauhaus schooling and explore the meditative geometry that became his trademark.

Pei's research center proved faulty in several respects, however. The roof leaked, the fountain had to be shut down and cracks in the concrete required elaborate repairs. But for all its technical shortcomings, its cluster of rusty pink concrete ramparts are weighted with a mysterious, glowering power. They stand assuredly among the purple-brown cliffs like a romantic fortress on a hill, a New Age acropolis. Philip Johnson called it "the first postmodern edifice." The National Center for Atmospheric Research was a transforming event that provided the first glimpses of a mature Pei. From then on, he gave himself license to indulge his taste for drama.

"I began to know how little I knew," Pei later recalled, "and, finding that out, I acquired an appetite for designing more—much more."

6
THE KENNEDY
BLESSING

In the anguished days immediately following President John F. Kennedy's assassination, the widowed First Lady planned a funeral of dark European pageantry. Upon her personal directions, the mahogany coffin was carried through the hushed streets to Saint Matthew's Cathedral on the same glistening black caisson that had borne FDR's coffin eighteen years earlier. Behind the horse-drawn caisson walked a riderless black gelding with a pair of military boots reversed in the stirrups to signify the fallen leader. The widow herself followed, her veiled head lowered.

When her public obligations were completed, Jacqueline Kennedy withdrew into private mourning. Aside from her children, John and Caroline, her main preoccupation became the planning of a more enduring reminder of her husband's place in world affairs, which she pursued with the same careful attention to ceremonial detail. Hundreds of memorials were under way within weeks of the assassination, but the Kennedy Library on the banks of the Charles River would be by far the most prominent.

One month after the funeral Mrs. Kennedy summoned her husband's closest aides to the Georgetown home she had borrowed from Averell Harriman. One by one they assembled in her adopted living room—the slain president's brothers, Robert and Ted, Arthur Schlesinger, Jr., John Kenneth Galbraith, Ted Sorensen and McGeorge Bundy. What ensued, remembered Galbraith, was

◀ **Pei with Jackie Kennedy.**

"an intense discussion of the library and its higher educational purpose. . . . We all had the idea from the very beginning that it should be more than just a repository for the letters and documents of the presidential papers."

A monumental statue like the one in the Lincoln Memorial seemed pretentious and inappropriate for a president who was informal by nature. Had he lived, JFK would have enlivened his library with people and scholarly discourse. As if to compensate for his absence, his survivors added a school of government—"a meeting place," Harvard president Nathan Pusey called it, "between the academic world and the world of public affairs"—to inspire younger statesmen to enter public service and a museum to tell JFK's life story. They envisioned a bustling, utilitarian memorial that would perpetuate the excitement of the man for whom it was named.

In mid-January Mrs. Kennedy appeared live on television to thank the 800,000 Americans who had sent condolence notes. Speaking in her trademark whisper, she promised that each letter would be preserved in the library, where it would be "treasured, not only for my children, but so that future generations will know how much our country and people in other nations thought of him. . . . I hope that, in years to come, many of you and your children will be able to visit the Kennedy Library. It will be, we hope, not only a memorial to President Kennedy but a living center of study of the times in which he lived and a center for young people and for scholars from all over the world."

Jacqueline Kennedy had every reason to expect the library to be completed by 1970, if not sooner. Announcing a fund-raising goal of $6 million, Robert Kennedy said his brother had "been deprived of the personal enjoyment of such a library, but its speedy completion would be his dearest wish." What followed resembled nothing so much as another political campaign waged with the Kennedy clan's vigorous group purpose. Mrs. Kennedy trolled for contributions among wealthy acquaintances while her brother-in-law

Stephen Smith worked Manhattan. The president's mother, Rose, attended a fund-raising rally in North Carolina with evangelist Billy Graham and Governor Terry Sanford. Ted Kennedy flew to Paris to thank the French government for its $100,000 donation, then on to Germany to talk with fund-raisers in Munich, students in Hamburg and labor leaders in Frankfurt. He even visited the Vatican to discuss the project with the pope. Meanwhile, IBM chairman Thomas Watson Jr. sought donations from U.S. corporations, and chief fund-raiser Eugene Black, a former World Bank president, canvassed foreign embassies.

"I have never had a job as easy as this one," Black remarked as thirty million individual donations, ranging from a few pennies to a quarter of a million dollars, swamped the Boston post office. The Red Sox donated the proceeds from their opening game of the 1964 season, a 4–1 win, and the AFL-CIO collected fifty cents from each member. An exhibit of JFK memorabilia embarked on an international fund-raising tour. Thousands lined up at every stop to view the empty rocking chair and the famous photograph of John Junior peeking out from under the president's desk. "Dear Mrs. Kennedy," wrote one young donor, "I am donating a nickel which I earned Sunday. I behaved like a gentleman while visiting my aunt." The most demonstrative donation of all came from a young Japanese man who had hiked eight hundred miles to board a U.S.-bound ship. He then trekked across America, wearing out five pairs of shoes en route, to present Jackie Kennedy with a string of pearls for the library fund.

Where would the Kennedys find an architect worthy of such an outpouring? Jackie turned for guidance to William Walton, a muscular, sandy-haired family friend who had parachuted into France on D day as a war correspondent for Time-Life and covered the combat with his friends Robert Capa and Ernest Hemingway. He later became an accomplished painter and a trusted Kennedy campaign organizer in Wisconsin, West Virginia and New York.

Kennedy had used Walton's Georgetown home as an office the day before the inauguration.

Walton declined White House jobs, but he agreed to chair the Fine Arts Commission, a group that monitored the quality of federal architecture. As the administration's point man on the cultural front, he helped preserve Lafayette Square, a quadrangle of old buildings across from the White House, and informally helped Jackie select paintings for the White House renovation. She clearly recognized in him a kindred taste. It was Walton whom she dispatched to the White House library the night of the assassination to research Lincoln's rites, and it was Walton who draped the East Room in black curtains to receive his friend's remains.

Now, in the melancholy afternoons of mourning, Secret Service agents escorted her across Georgetown to Walton's P Street home where the two sat ruminating over the library plans. Walton dissuaded her from staging a formal design competition. Better to choose your own architect, he argued, than to relinquish the power of selection to outside judges. Instead, they summoned eighteen world-renowned designers to Boston's Ritz-Carlton in April 1964 for two days of informal consultation. Architecture's own best and brightest paraded into town from all enlightened corners: Sir Basil Spence from London, Kenzo Tange from Tokyo, and Sven Markelius from Stockholm. The Americans included Mies van der Rohe, Louis Kahn, Hugh Stubbins, Pietro Belluschi, John Carl Warnecke, and, by dint of his prolific portfolio, the comparatively unknown I. M. Pei, a man whom Walton had met when Dulles Airport built a control tower based on the prototype Pei had designed.

"In welcoming this group of architects," Ted Kennedy told them upon arrival, "I must say you are dealing with a family that has very limited knowledge and understanding of the wonders of the architectural world. Without exception, all of us have lived in rented houses." Afterward they visited the site beside the Charles River that JFK himself had selected for his presidential library the previous May. The White House had tried to keep his trip quiet that day, but a throng of several hundred was waiting on the lawn outside the Harvard Business School when his marine helicopter touched down from Hyannis Port. The president walked the measure of the lawn, a raw spring breeze tousling that distinctive shock of boyish hair. Across the Charles River the cupolas and white spires of Harvard peeked above a canopy of sycamore leaves. The expansive view included Winthrop House where JFK had lived as an undergraduate. The crowd chanted, "Speech, speech, speech!" The president acknowledged them with a smile and ducked into a waiting limousine.

Presidential libraries were still a relatively new concept when Kennedy made that visit. Every retiring commander in chief since George Washington had deposited his documents with the Library of Congress without ceremony or had toted them home, where many were lost, auctioned or burned, until Franklin D. Roosevelt established a special archive for his papers in a Dutch Colonial house he had designed on his family's Hyde Park estate. Like Truman and Eisenhower, Kennedy would follow FDR's precedent—but that still seemed a distant consideration. JFK would presumably win reelection and serve until 1968, then retire to his presidential library where, at age fifty-one, he would have plenty of time left to write his memoirs, teach Harvard seminars and pursue his prolific correspondence.

Kennedy saw the site just once more, in October, after attending the Harvard-Columbia football game. A few days later, back at the White House, he signed papers officially reserving the riverside site for his library. It was a providential transaction. Only one month later his open limousine wheeled into Dallas's Dealey Plaza.

After visiting the president's riverside site, the architects sat down to watch film clips of JFK, and Schlesinger, Galbraith and Sorensen briefed them on the library's contents. "John Kennedy was a man who never wore a hat," said Harvard Professor Samuel Beer, a Kennedy confidant. "So this library should be a building of simple and direct lines . . . a library without a hat."

The group was "deeply moved," Sir Basil Spence recalled, when someone produced a handwritten note the late president had sent to an architect who was designing a federal building. It contained a single quote from Pericles: "We do not imitate, for we are an example to others."

"That," Spence concluded, "should be the motto for this building."

Out of the Kennedys' earshot, the architects complained to Walton of being put on the spot. They could advise the family on design, but they were reluctant to recommend specific names. "It was, in the architectural profession, an unprecedented proceeding—to ask architects which of their brethren should be so honored," Walton said. The foreigners insisted on limiting the search to Americans. It was therefore agreed that each would anonymously nominate three U.S. architects for the family's consideration. Walton collected their sealed envelopes as they filed aboard the Kennedy plane, *Caroline,* en route to a clam chowder lunch and a walk on the beach at the family's Hyannis Port compound. Walton tallied the ballots in a nearby hangar and then burned them to ensure secrecy. The names that appeared most often were Mies van der Rohe, John Carl Warnecke, Gordon Bunshaft, Paul Rudolph, Louis Kahn, Philip Johnson and I. M. Pei.

Jackie, accompanied by William Walton and her sister-in-law Jean Kennedy Smith, studied elaborate workbooks filled with photographs of the candidates' work. They inspected buildings in Chicago, New Haven and Philadelphia and interviewed each nominee in his office. Mies van der Rohe was the most prominent, but at age seventy-eight he was encumbered by ill health. He puffed cigars throughout the interview with an air of detached interest. An architectural jury might well have selected the Philadelphian Louis Kahn, whose Richards Medical Research Building at the University of

Pennsylvania had made Pei's Colorado research center possible. Kahn stood at the forefront of second-generation modernists reinterpreting the strict Bauhaus legacy. The architectural historian Vince Scully had championed him in 1961 as "unquestionably first in professional importance among living American architects." But Kahn's shy, quixotic manner, his metaphysical musings and his awkward appearance and demeanor—he was a short, disheveled man with a high, reedy voice and a complexion badly disfigured by childhood burns—all but disqualified him from consideration.

If Kahn was all wrong for the Kennedys' genteel popularity contest, the charming, self-assured Pei was just right. "So often in architecture the messenger himself is the message," observed the architectural historian Spiro Kostoff. "Poor Louis Kahn was one of the visionary architects of his time. He had something to say, but he couldn't say it. He stood there in front of audiences with his pockmarked face mumbling mysterious things. He was not an easy guy to love. Pei, on the other hand, comes into a room and the light comes with him. He's full of pep and confidence. He dazzles. Who would *you* choose?"

This was exactly the sort of monumental commission that had eluded Pei under Zeckendorf's aegis. Moreover, it would erase the lingering stigma of having worked for a developer. Pei consequently prepared for his interview as if for a royal visitation. His office couldn't compete with Gordon Bunshaft's endless rows of drafting tables or with Philip Johnson's glamorous glass-walled suite in the Seagram Building on Park Avenue, a building on which he had collaborated with Mies. Pei's office operated out of the humble working studio leased from Webb & Knapp where draftsmen crammed six to an alcove amused themselves by rolling balls of tape down the hall into the corner office Pei shared with his secretary.

But Pei adroitly turned his modest, informal quarters into an asset. On the appointed day his staff set about the freshly repainted studio stashing assorted paraphernalia and dusting half-forgotten models. There was great deliberation over what to exhibit in the conference room. "We were all so concerned with the arrival of Jackie Kennedy," remembered Harold Fredenburgh. "None of us fathomed the meeting's professional significance. But I.M. must have. He always, *always* looks ahead to where he wants to position himself."

Mrs. Kennedy's car inched its way up Madison Avenue through a solid mass of gawkers who had somehow been alerted to her appointment. Police escorted her to the elevator through an impenetrable throng massed on the sidewalk and inside the lobby. "We had a tiny little reception area with a big bouquet of flowers in a clear glass bowl for her arrival," remembered Don Page, the graphic designer. "She came in and said, 'My, that's a beautiful bouquet. Do you always have those?' Pei said, 'Oh, no, we only got those for you.' Most people, of course, wouldn't have been so honest."

Pei acknowledged with winning modesty that he was no celebrated form-giver like Kahn or Mies. "The big commissions of the monumental sort," he said, "they usually don't come my way." Nonetheless, at age forty-seven he had established himself as a national presence with work in more than a dozen American cities, and his expanding portfolio suggested a young architect on the verge of greatness. "Mr. Pei," she said, "where did you find the energy to do all of this?"

"The day Mrs. Kennedy came into my office," Pei said, "I told her, 'I have no big concert halls to show you. No Lincoln Centers. My work is unglamorous—slum clearance projects like Kips Bay in New York, the Hyde Park area of Chicago.' She didn't say much, but kept asking, 'Why? Why? Why?' about what I'd done." In those days people still believed that modern design was the remedy for urban ills, and Pei's portfolio conferred on him the aura of a young man of social conscience.

While the other candidates conjured up elaborate descriptions of their imagined library—the situation seemed to demand some display of advanced thinking—Pei stated with disarming honesty that it was too soon for him to say what he would do. But he left no doubt that he was a young man on the brink.

His carefully understated performance was a tour de force. Mrs. Kennedy left convinced that Pei was the one. He was the same age as her husband—they were born just one month apart—and, like JFK, he had prepared at Harvard for a career in which he advanced rapidly among much older men. There was about him the same aura of a young gentleman endowed with a certain worldliness, breaking down barriers in the postwar world. Best of all, Pei was not a respected elder whom she was obliged to defer to. On the contrary, he was an effusive sprite, a man of humility and Oriental playfulness with whom she could converse—a potential friend.

"Jackie and I interviewed a lot of architects for the Kennedy Library," Jean Kennedy Smith said. "When we saw I. M. Pei there was no question he was it. His work is like he is—the poetry comes through."

Pei was vacationing in Italy with Eileen and their four children in midsummer 1964 when a telegram arrived from his administrative partner, Eason Leonard: "Please telephone Mr. William Walton . . . in Washington immediately." Pei spent most of a day in a small-town café outside Pisa trying to get through on the telephone while his family tarried around the town square. Finally he received Walton's long-distance congratulations. Pei later described it as the most thrilling moment in his career. "I had been conditioned by my mother to believe this was inevitable," said Pei's eldest son, T'ing. "There was tremendous expectation of my father's success. I felt that sooner or later he would break into the sunshine."

Robert Kennedy publicly announced Pei's selection at a press conference at New York's Pierre Hotel. "I suppose the choice was a little unorthodox,"

◄

President Kennedy's survivors rejected the riverside lawn, LOWER RIGHT, in favor of the car barns of the Massachusetts Bay Transportation Authority, CENTER.

Jackie Kennedy and Pei at the 1964 press conference called to announce his selection. "I suppose the choice was a little unorthodox," she said.

▼

Jackie told reporters. "After all, some of the others were much better known. All those we considered are fine architects. But Pei! He loves things to be beautiful. People say, why didn't you find someone more established? We felt that Pei's best work, as John Kennedy's was in 1960, is yet to come."

Pei smiled under the klieg lights of national attention for the first time that day, a new celebrity anointed by the queen of Camelot herself. He had come to that place where all architects strive to be, and he had arrived at an unusually young age. The ensuing project proved to be a national showcase for his uncanny mastery of propriety and politics. "That's when he became Mr. Diplomat," remembered Philip Johnson. "All his jobs are feats of diplomacy. He performs incredible political footwork that none of the rest of us have any idea about."

. . . .

No sooner had Pei won the commission than he expressed doubts over the site. The two-and-a-half-acre lawn sufficed for the modest 100,000-square-foot library the president had envisioned, but an archive, a museum and a school of government would need three times the space. Why settle for a cramped acreage disturbed by road traffic on both banks of the Charles when they could demand any site they wanted in the assassination's emotionally charged aftermath? Who would dare to deny the Kennedys in their tragic hour?

Pei promptly flew to Boston to confer with Governor Endicott Peabody and officials of the Massachusetts Bay Transportation Authority about shifting the site across the Charles River to a sprawling asphalt trolley yard known as the car barn. Cluttered with subway tracks and repair sheds, the car barn occupied twelve acres strategically situated between Harvard's residential colleges, the river and Harvard Square. JFK himself had considered the site ideal, but he had dismissed it as politically inexpedient. It was the last adjacent real estate onto which Harvard could expand, and the university had coveted it for years. "I told Robert Kennedy that I'd been trying to acquire that land forever," Harvard president Nathan Pusey remembered. "He said, 'I hope you won't be offended if I say that John Kennedy's name might hold more sway than John Harvard's.'"

Robert Kennedy was right. Cambridge's Irish Democrats were not about to relinquish the car barn to Harvard, but they were only too eager to accommodate a martyred son. The city council passed a resolution pledging to "do everything in its power" to situate the library in Cambridge, and a *Boston Globe* editorial called the proposal "nothing less than inspirational" and "a challenge the people . . . will certainly rise to without complaint. Their eternal gratitude to John Fitzgerald Kennedy demands no less."

The *Globe* also endorsed a bill authorizing the state to buy the twelve-acre site. When a special legislative commission accorded the bill a hearing in October, a single witness rose from a front row State House bench to testify. It was the president's mother, Rose, whose own father, John "Honey Fitz" Fitzgerald, had been one of Boston's most flamboyant mayors and a hugely influential figure within the city's Irish Democratic machinery. "My son never thought in terms of a memorial to himself," she said in a quavering voice. "The Kennedy family decided that a library along the Charles River would perpetuate [his] principles better than anything else. It is the only Kennedy memorial for which we have asked support." It took just eighteen minutes for the commission to vote in favor of the $7 million car barn purchase. Nothing again would go so smoothly.

Pei called the move "fundamental to the Kennedy Library's progress," and the Massachusetts Bay Transportation Authority obligingly agreed to vacate the site as soon as it found an alternate plot—by 1970 at the very latest. The logical candidate was Codman yard, a facility the Authority already owned in the outlying neighborhood of Dorchester, but the move encountered virulent opposition from resentful locals. Nine hundred foot-stomping residents turned up at a public hearing, and their local legislators blocked the move on grounds that the resulting clatter would disturb a nearby hospital. So the Transportation Authority shifted its sights to a marshland in Milton, but this time environmentalists objected. Plans also fell through at Mattapan Square and South Braintree. Finally, after an agonizing six-year search, the Authority announced that it had secured a narrow strip on the former Penn Central switchyards in South Boston.

Even this belated resolution came into question when Boston Mayor Kevin White argued that a city agency should not claim taxable land. After much vigorous lobbying, Ted Kennedy mustered sufficient support to close the deal over White's objections. (A few years later Kennedy blocked George McGovern from picking White as his vice presidential running mate in a move widely interpreted as revenge for impeding the library's progress.) "The end is very clearly in sight," Senator Kennedy told the *New York Times*. "Now at last we are reaching the bricks and mortar stage."

· · · ·

As long as JFK's blood remained vivid in the American memory, mountains could have been moved on his behalf. But the project had by now squandered much of its precious impetus. By the time the battered trolleys finally vacated the car barn the psychic shock of the assassination had receded into history and been supplanted by the more immediate horrors of Vietnam, the arms race, Watergate, revelations of JFK's personal life and brother Ted's Chappaquiddick misadventure.

Camelot had lost much of its mythic allure, and an antiauthoritarian spirit was hard upon the land. Nobody confronted the cultural shift more abruptly than Defense Secretary Robert McNamara, a Kennedy appointee who was forced to take refuge on top of his car after being chased by some eight hundred Harvard protesters in 1966. From this undignified perch he feebly attempted to conduct a dialogue with his captors until cops drove a wedge through the crowd and escorted him away, harassed and humiliated. Three years later students seized an administration building in Harvard Yard, evicted eight deans and renamed it Che Guevara Hall. Their long list of demands included the abolition of Harvard's "expansionist" approach to its urban surroundings.

You didn't have to be a student to resent the "improvements" inflicted by development. The great sea change of the sixties engendered new forms of political expression and empowered ordinary folks to decide for themselves what their neighborhoods would be. Organized voices of protest unthinkable a few years earlier were now commonplace. Nowhere was the new preservation practiced with greater militancy than among the vintage neighborhoods surrounding Harvard Square, where traffic congestion and real-estate speculation threatened Colonial side streets lined with bookshops, coffeehouses, antique stores and historic ivy-covered homes. Cambridge developed a heightened awareness of the drawbacks of development, and it was one of the few cities to flat out reject an urban renewal project.

So the library emerged from years of political dickering only to encounter a chilly reception from Cantabrigians whose dread of further development overshadowed their traditional loyalty to the Kennedys. If an estimated three million people visited JFK's Arlington gravesite each year, would similar numbers inundate Harvard Square? Would garish souvenir stands and fried-chicken franchises displace the bookshops and cafés from their fragile back streets? Would huge parking garages and Howard Johnson motor lodges wall off the grassy banks of the Charles?

In keeping with the prevailing mood of grassroots activism, the city council appointed a nineteen-man task force to address these concerns on behalf of the community. The task force convened in 1971 on the naive assumption that the Kennedys would welcome its thoughts on how best to integrate the library into the neighborhood's historic atmosphere. But the cordial working relationship it envisioned was not to be. "Instead," wrote *Boston Globe* architecture critic Robert Campbell, the Kennedys "began with the idea of building a monument, and with an attitude toward the community that was for a long time uncommunicative at best."

After Robert Kennedy's 1968 assassination, control of the library corporation, the project's guiding body, passed to his brother-in-law Stephen Smith, a smooth and efficient New Yorker who had masterminded the finances and administration of JFK's 1960 presidential campaign and, in subsequent years, managed the Kennedy investments and the frequent family crises with an unflinching instinct for hard-nosed tactics. "People call *me* ruthless?" Robert Kennedy used to say. "They ought to see my brother-in-law Steve."

Smith ran the library corporation from the president's former Bowdoin Street apartment across from the State House, the same apartment the young JFK had taken when he returned from the war and maintained as his legal address until his death. Under Smith's stewardship the apartment became, increasingly, a kind of Kennedy bunker besieged by overwrought opponents. As the consummate operative for the country's most powerful political family, Smith was not inclined to grant the task force or the coalescing neighborhood groups the planning role they presumed to take upon themselves. In his mind, the Kennedys did not have to brook dissension in their own backyard.

Community peevishness made Pei's assignment more ticklish. He had won the job without having said much about what his library might look like. Now he had to produce a suitably monumental design, something that would reflect the infatuation with JFK's life without offending Cambridge's precious pride of place. Pei has admitted to experiencing some anguish over the dilemma. He had more city planning experience than any other candidate, but until now his buildings had stood as isolated, self-absorbed sculptures, aloof and unaligned with the urban grain.

"This was a deeper, more complex problem," observed task force member Morse Payne, an architect who practiced in partnership with Walter Gropius at The Architects Collaborative. "How do you plant a new physical form into a setting that dates back to the 1630s? You have to get down off your horse and walk in the street and participate. Pei's grand pieces had never required him to do that. Pei was the right architect politically, but the demands of the site ran counter to everything he was about. He didn't know how to blend in."

JFK's widow had conceived of the library in concert with his inner circle as an unpretentious living memorial enlivened by the bustle of students, curious children and other visitors. But Pei thought of the library as a monument. "Pei said to me once that he felt that the building was the memorial," remembered library director Dan Fenn. "I said, 'No, the *institution* is the memorial.'"

After a private presentation at Mrs. Kennedy's Fifth Avenue apartment, Pei unveiled his long-awaited design on what would have been JFK's fifty-sixth birthday "with all the finality," wrote critic Jane Holtz Kaye, "of a pharaoh presenting a fait accompli to generations as yet unborn." A widely published UPI photograph showed Senator Ted Kennedy, Eunice Shriver and fifteen-year-old Caroline Kennedy admiring an enormous plastic and wood model of a concrete building encircling an 85-foot pyramid flattened at the apex. Critic Wolf Von Eckardt bemoaned the "banal symbolism of the pyramidal power of John Kennedy's achievement tragically truncated by fate."

Pei's imperial design revealed how far the library had strayed from FDR's unassuming Hyde Park prototype built like a private home with fieldstone walls, small windows and simple white-painted woodwork. Pei seemed to have reverted to the monuments of bygone centuries. "It's the last thing John

Kennedy would have wanted in relation to the historic Harvard he loved," said his friend, John Carl Warnecke. "It wasn't modest. It screamed, 'Look at me! Look at me!' "

"It startled me," concurred Morse Payne. "It was bigger than we ever imagined and not at all simpatico with the Harvard buildings. Most architects who have poked away at Harvard Square have tried to complement it, to work on its behalf. This scheme didn't seem to want to do that; it wasn't at all harmonic. It was like living in a sleepy small town and hearing that a major shopping center is about to be built. It was that kind of shock."

J. Carter Brown, then director of Washington's National Gallery, was suffering from jet lag in a London hotel shortly after the unveiling. He arose midway through a sleepless night to compose a letter to Pei. "Even the great have their Bay of Pigs," he wrote. "As a friend, I do earnestly pray this building won't, in the judgment of history, be considered yours."

"I was afraid it was the right building in the wrong place," he later explained. "I was worried for both Harvard and I.M."

When the task force had asked to review Pei's plans, Smith had replied that none existed yet. The task force accepted his explanation until the supposedly nonexistent plans appeared in the *Boston Globe*. That was a turning point. "They lied to us," said Father Richard Shmaruk, an associate pastor at Saint Paul's Rectory, located just off Harvard Square. "That's when we got angry. We knew we were going to have to fight them on the same level."

Community concerns had originally focused on traffic and parking, but the infelicitous image of a pyramid rising above historic Harvard galvanized a wider opposition. "He did the project a tremendous disservice," said Dan Fenn, who was not shown the design before its public unveiling. "That pyramid became just one more club to beat us up with."

As early as 1967 the British columnist Henry Fairlie had written a pair of articles, reprinted in the *Washington Post* and *Philadelphia Inquirer*, in which he attributed the entire project to the Kennedys' thirst for glory and castigated Harvard for accepting "a formal endowment that no major university should accept." Pei's pyramid now reinforced the impression of an institution designed to immortalize. "All of us had the greatest respect for the memory of John Kennedy," said Father Shmaruk, "but they commissioned Pei to build more than a library. It became a mausoleum, a monument not just to JFK but to Bobby and Teddy and the whole family. Ted was going to be president, too, so that pyramid would have to contain three ghosts. So it *had* to be big."

With groundbreaking one year away, concern spread throughout Cambridge that the library might become a New England version of Disneyland. The lawyers, architects and professors residing in spacious houses set back from fashionable Brattle Street conjured up nightmarish scenarios of unchecked development and midwestern tourists in Bermuda shorts clogging their redbrick streets with Winnebagos—"like Goths overwhelming the intelligentsia," wrote architecture critic Ada Louise Huxtable—and strewing fast-food containers along the banks of the Charles. The most militant critic of all was Pebble Gifford, whose husband, Dun, had once served as a top aide to his friend Ted Kennedy. Frustrated with the sluggish bureaucratic channels, Mrs. Gifford wrote her husband's former boss letters complaining about the "gum-chewing, paper-throwing, sneaker-wearing crowd."

Stephen Smith dismissed these gripes as the sanctimonious mewlings of effete cocktail-party liberals with a snobbish distaste for Middle America. Support remained strong, he argued, throughout the city's blue-collar periphery: the working-class Irish and Italians, Kennedy's firmly Catholic constituency.

Legitimate or not, Smith's contention was soon undermined by a second front of opposition arising among the outlying black communities of Riverside and Cambridgeport, which had battled Harvard expansion for years.

Saundra Graham, a black city council member who was notorious for having seized the microphone at a Harvard commencement to scold the university for ignoring its underprivileged neighbors—"Now, you listen to us, Harvard!"—loudly warned that the library would inevitably inflate property values and lead to higher rents and evictions. Things sure had changed. A few years earlier the Kennedys had practically owned Massachusetts. Now here was Saundra Graham denouncing the president's library as another "two-bit development."

Graham's participation prevented Smith from dismissing his opponents as a privileged bow-tie crowd. With a black woman aboard, the neighborhood groups won the support of a cheering section sympathetic to an underdog fighting New England's two most powerful institutions—Harvard and the Kennedys. By the late spring of 1973 even the *Boston Globe,* which had originally supported the library, was chastising the Kennedys for being "evasive" and insensitive to "community reaction."

In response to these combined pressures, Pei retracted his beleaguered design and replaced it some months later with a politely reduced version, which he defended during a rare city hall press conference as "much more modest" and "appropriately woven into the fabric of the city." He replaced his oversized concrete facade, its back to Harvard Square, with two redbrick triangular buildings facing each other across a corridor of open park connecting the banks of the Charles with the square. Moreover, the new version stayed respectfully within the cornice height established by the adjacent Harvard houses. The new version dispensed altogether with the misbegotten pyramid—though Cambridge residents were amused to see it reappear more than a decade later at the Louvre in Paris.

These concessions failed to appease Pei's critics, however. A smaller library, they argued, would attract the same number of visitors. In fact, Pei's alterations reinforced the impression of a facility for tourists rather than

▲

Pei with Mies van der Rohe.

▼

Pei's first scheme featured a truncated glass pyramid rising from a circular courtyard. Cambridge erupted.

▲ Eileen and I.M. at a Boston art opening.

▼ Pei's politely scaled-down versions failed to appease critics.

scholars by relegating two-thirds of the 21 million documents to a temporary archive established in a Waltham warehouse while still finding room for a ceremonial reception area dominated by an imposing bust of JFK. Indeed, Pei's revised scheme was not a library at all so much as a tabernacle of warm remembrances in which carefully curated memorabilia—the famous rocking chair, the desk from Choate, the coconut on which he carved a call for help after PT-109 sank off Guadalcanal—would perpetuate JFK's cult of personality. "One is tempted to conjecture in all this that the memorial is really being designed by a committee of aging advance men," Father Shmaruk wrote in a front-page article in the *Harvard Crimson*, "who think that the measure of President Kennedy's greatness in history will depend on the size of the crowd they get out, just like in the old days."

It fell now to Pei to perform his inimitable missionary work among the disgruntled natives. He dutifully rode the shuttle up from New York as often as once a week to dispense palliatives at innumerable meetings held in churches and private homes. Looking slightly out of place in his elegant Madison Avenue suits, he attended to their grievances with the formal bedside manner of a dignified Old World physician. "Watching what he did in those endless meetings and listening to what he said taught me some unforgettable lessons, not the least of which was that there's a lot more to being a great architect than just making drawings," remembered William Walton. "His patience, his tact, his insights into the city and university problems and his skill in dealing with people were impressive. And finally I understood one of the reasons for his greatness—maybe one of his secrets—that he becomes a citizen of every city where he builds."

However conciliatory Pei seemed, he presented his designs to those within the library's Bowdoin Street office as inviolable and nonnegotiable. "Pei is so charming and so articulate and so pleasant," said Dan Fenn, "but there was absolutely no way he was going to budge on that design. He was going to put there what *he* wanted. No way was he going to negotiate with Pebble Gifford."

If Pei adroitly played good cop, Smith became bad cop. Opponents say that Smith tried to bully them and, on one occasion, threatened "to build the library over your dead body." When Pei presented his revised scheme at city hall, a reporter asked task force chairman Oliver Brooks if he'd seen it before its unveiling. Yes, he answered, he'd viewed it in a back room at Pei's office. "The next morning at eight o'clock I got an angry call from Steve Smith," Brooks said. " 'Ollie, what the hell are you trying to do?' he said. 'It sounds like you're trying to make trouble.' Clearly, as a political operative, the phrase 'back room' rang a bell with him. It hadn't occurred to me that it might have any derogatory insinuations, but Steve took it as a declaration of war. It seemed to me a ridiculously paranoid response."

Smith's intemperate remarks reflected his frustration at relocating to Cambridge only to have the door inched shut as construction costs soared and the worst inflation since the Korean War eroded building funds. Meanwhile, Lyndon Johnson's monumental library at the University of Texas designed by Gordon Bunshaft was attracting almost as many visitors as all the other presidential libraries combined. Smith was so desperate to advance his project that he reportedly considered firing Pei, but William Walton dissuaded him.

The community, meanwhile, was equally frustrated by the Kennedys' refusal to address their concerns. "They didn't do their homework, and they didn't make any concessions," complained Pebble Gifford. "Wherever we turned there weren't any answers to our questions. They were stonewalling us."

By 1974 things had clearly reached an impasse. Both sides summoned their own statistics to support their claims, but the Cambridge-Kennedy contretemps had arrived at that irreconcilable stage where numbers ceased to matter. They might just as well have been speaking different languages.

Mercifully, the stalemate was to be arbitrated once and for all by an environmental impact statement, a procedure that community groups had correctly demanded, since the library would pass to the federal government upon completion. Both sides agreed to abide by the results.

But matters got worse when the General Services Administration contracted the environmental impact study out to C. E. Maguire, Inc., a consulting firm that had been accused of altering an earlier statement on behalf of the Massachusetts Port Authority. Nor was the firm's dubious reputation enhanced by a *Boston Globe* report that one of Maguire's politically connected staff members, a former state representative, had phoned Father Shmaruk and threatened to donate a large sum to the diocese with a request that it "do something about" him—a threat that was subsequently denied.

Needless to say, these allegations strained Maguire's credibility. One task force member told the *Harvard Crimson* that he expected the report to consist of little more than "wads of wet toilet paper."

Sure enough, the 600-page study released on January 21, 1975, concluded that, despite nearly a million annual visitors arriving by car, the library would have a "negligible impact" on its historic neighborhood. It was an absurd assertion, and suspicious opponents immediately suggested that the report was rigged in the Kennedys' favor. "The document seems to be very clearly painted as a kind of advocacy of the library and not an objective analysis," said Ben Thompson, who served as chairman of the department of architecture at Harvard from 1964 to 1968. A *Boston Globe* editorial called it "so contradictory in its facts and its findings and so clearly slanted toward a preordained conclusion that it threatens to discredit the whole process of environmental impact statements."

The study was further undermined when, one month later, the *Harvard Crimson* reported that Stephen Smith had reviewed preliminary drafts. It was also revealed that the General Services Administration had almost entirely omitted a damaging 250-page planning report submitted by a Maguire consultant named Ecodesign. More suspicious still, Ecodesign's office had been ransacked twice while its staff members were preparing their findings. On behalf of a neighborhood group, Harvard Business School professor Paul Lawrence invoked the Freedom of Information Act in federal district court, demanding access to all background data.

These developments caused much hand-wringing at the library's Bowdoin Street office. The continuing imbroglio threatened to become a damaging endgame. Smith forestalled further embarrassment by announcing, just hours before the judge's ruling, that the museum portion would not be built in Cambridge after all. Ted Kennedy cited a "small and vociferous group that was prepared to entangle" the project in lawsuits for years. Instead, they would consider two options: move the entire institution to a new site or keep the archive in Cambridge while building the museum portion elsewhere. Pei had by now labored on the project for a dozen years and produced some fifteen or twenty different designs, only two of which were released to the public. "I'm not going to touch my pencil," Pei said, until all the factions agreed on what they wanted.

Robert Wood, an old Kennedy friend and former head of the Massachusetts Bay Transportation Authority, had played a key role in helping the Kennedys acquire the car barn site for the library. A decade later Wood was president of the University of Massachusetts, and his career intersected with the wayward library once again. "Years after I left the MBTA," he remembered, "Steve Smith called me and he said, 'Pebble Gifford has screwed us in Cambridge and now the library is up for other offers.'"

Wood pounced on the opportunity to pluck the library away from Harvard. Like most state universities, UMass was bracing itself in the late-1950s for a wave of college-bound baby boomers. If colleges were to accommodate them within the state system, they would have to expand. So UMass transformed itself, with generous infusions of state funds, from a tiny cow college ("Mass Aggie") of 6,500 students nestled in the rolling farmlands of Amherst into a sprawling center of liberal arts study with three times its earlier enrollment. The expansion included a scrappy commuter campus for low-income students built on an isolated windswept marsh called Columbia Point located on the "wrong" side of Boston Harbor. For decades this swampy peninsula had been Boston's gulag, home to such undesirable facilities as a garbage dump, a prisoner of war camp and New England's largest low-income housing project. Students enrolled at UMass's Columbia Point campus enjoyed no wood-paneled clubs or book-lined studies, no vintage bookstores or plush common rooms. In the heartland of privileged private schools, this was a no-frills blue-collar institution of parking lots and cold concrete buildings.

UMass needed an infusion of prestige to overcome its inferiority complex, and nothing wielded more prestige in Massachusetts than the Kennedy escutcheon. So Wood mounted a swift pursuit. Smith called him on a Friday; by Monday he'd dispatched letters to Kennedy insiders describing UMass as the kind of forward-looking public-spirited institution JFK would have liked. Unlike Cambridge, he promised, UMass and the adjacent Dorchester neighborhood, where Rose Kennedy had grown up, would welcome the library as an unalloyed blessing. In the following days he used his wide range of political and academic contacts to lobby with strategic precision.

Wood courted Pei along with the rest. He flew the architect to Amherst to inspect the UMass campus and to Boston to see Columbia Point. Pei, a discerning reader of institutional prestige, was appalled.

He also had professional motives for resisting the move. Because Harvard and MIT considered themselves enlightened patrons, they had over the years commissioned progressive works by Walter Gropius, Le Corbusier, Eero Saarinen and Alvar Aalto. The Kennedy Library was to have been Pei's chance to slip his own trophy into the showcase. "Pei was so committed to

Cambridge," remembered Dan Fenn, "that he didn't even want to think about Columbia Point. The key people kept asking him, 'What about it? What would the library look like on Columbia Point?' He would say, 'Awful! A terrible site! Can't do *anything* there.' "

Wood devised a clever way of soliciting Pei's cooperation. He contacted the architect Hugh Stubbins, an older Gropius protégé, aboard his sailboat in Nantucket and invited him to demonstrate, purely as an academic exercise, that a distinguished building could be designed for Columbia Point—with or without Pei. "I knew that if I could get Pei into the same room with a competitor, I could get action," Wood said. "And I was right."

Wood summoned the library trustees to a private room at New York's 21 Club, where he showed slides of Columbia Point and introduced Stubbins, who unveiled a model of a long, low building extending over the water on enormous piers. "I.M.'s face was typically impassive, and his manners were impeccable," Wood said, "but within twenty-four hours one of his people showed up in our office and began to work with us. Then Stubbins faded away." Pei would later accuse Stubbins of "being opportunistic."

In the course of planning, Wood entertained Pei's team at his home in Lincoln, Massachusetts. Wood's wife, Peggy, remembers talking to a Pei staffer sprawled on the couch with a drink. "Who are you?" she asked at one point. "Define yourself."

"I'm a slave," he responded, "in a geometry factory."

Up until then Harvard had not expended much effort to keep the library in Cambridge. Harvard president Derek Bok and his predecessor, Nathan Pusey, were content to remain above the fray, confident that at least the archive portion would inevitably land beside JFK's prestigious alma mater. "Harvard existed before there was a United States," Pusey said, "and it's going to be there for a long time to come. I told them that locale could not help but enliven and perpetuate his memory." As long as the library stayed in

Cambridge, the university would shed no tears if the vilified museum portion, with its sentimental bric-a-brac, moved elsewhere. One possible home for these artifacts was the abandoned Charlestown Navy Yard where the USS *Constitution* had become the centerpiece of a historic park.

Harvard's arrogant assumption rankled the Kennedys, particularly Jackie, who privately suggested that perhaps Jack and Bobby had been too enthralled with the university's aura. She also resented Harvard's snobbish disregard for memorabilia, as if what sat on her husband's desk was entirely too unimportant for them. Why hadn't Harvard gone to bat for the library? Why hadn't it donated some of its own acreage to help resolve the parking dispute? Where was Harvard when the Kennedys were deflecting flak from Pebble Gifford and Saundra Graham?

It was with mounting disenchantment, then, that she and Ted Kennedy arrived in Boston to inspect their options. Either by happenstance or by design, they were escorted to the Charlestown Navy Yard at the height of rush hour and they proceeded to Columbia Point at the most flattering time of day. The sun was setting over the water, and the Boston skyline rose up in the dusk. Out beyond the lapping waves lay the shipping lane known as President's Road. "This is the most beautiful place I've ever seen," Jackie said.

Derek Bok enacted a flurry of desperate countermeasures, offering the Kennedys a series of alternate Harvard sites, including the same business school lawn they'd forsaken ten years earlier.

A few days after the twelfth anniversary of the assassination the library trustees convened for the decisive meeting at Pei's Madison Avenue office. (Pei's receptionist reportedly scolded Jackie for arriving twenty minutes late.) A conference table was scattered with models and site maps. After a general discussion of the pros and cons, during which Jackie stated her preference for Columbia Point, the family withdrew to caucus among themselves. After more discussion, they voted to abandon a dozen years of planning and award the entire institution to UMass. "I remember I.M.'s face when Steve brought the family back in and announced that it was going to be Columbia Point," Fenn said. "He was one heartbroken man."

When Robert Wood informed students assembled in a Columbia Point building called College One that their fledgling scrap of landfill had prevailed over the most prestigious university in the country, they understandably performed the celebration of underdogs. A stunned Derek Bok responded with a one-sentence statement wishing the project well. "It was a major shock for them," said Robert Wood. "For several years I wasn't warmly received at Harvard, even though I had taught there once."

Now that the acquisition of the Columbia Point site was a fait accompli, Pei had to acknowledge its benefits: the waterfront setting evoked the personal, contemplative side of JFK's persona and his love of the sea dating back to his boyhood on Cape Cod. UMass wasn't Harvard, but it was still a university. And its remoteness allowed Pei to indulge in his brand of monumental image-making unencumbered by community grievances.

Stephen Smith's aide, Jack Fallon, had reservations about the specific site on Columbia Point, which had been chosen for its proximity to a school cafeteria and a parking lot. He argued, and Pei agreed, that the library would be dwarfed by the forbidding hulk of UMass on one side while overlooking an odoriferous tidal flat on the other. They preferred a nearby point extending into Boston Harbor, and to dramatize their case Pei had a platform erected to show what the view would be from his preferred location. Having already suffered through more than ten years of hair-pulling hindrances associated with two aborted sites, the trustees wearily clambered up onto the platform. There they saw a poetic vista extending through the low hills of the deserted harbor islands to the open sea beyond. They quickly acceded. The groundbreaking occurred thirteen years and six months after the assassination—the duration of Kennedy's political career.

◄

The 110-foot atrium is undecorated, save for an American flag hung from its upper reaches.

▶

The Kennedy Library's final incarnation opened October 20th, 1979, sixteen years after the assassination.

▶

Pei inspecting Columbia Point. In the end, Pei had to acknowledge that its setting evoked JFK's love of the sea.

Pei's third and final design combined a squat cylinder with a space-frame box and a ten-story concrete tower that commanded the point like a light-house. This was a shrine designed to awe and immortalize. After witnessing JFK's achievements in a half-hour film and admiring emotionally charged memorabilia—including Jackie's dresses and a U.S. marshal's helmet dented in a civil rights riot—exhibited in a darkened basement, visitors emerge into a soaring atrium minimally adorned with an American flag hung from its up-per reaches. It is the last space visitors experience before they leave. Outside sits JFK's little sloop, *Victura,* her bow pointed to the open sea. "This," wrote Ada Louise Huxtable of the *New York Times,* "is consummate theater, art and politics. . . . what this building demonstrates conclusively is that architecture is a powerful instrument of symbolism and an extremely effective shaper of the environment and emotional responses."

Scholars and archivists meanwhile were consigned to the triangular tower. "I didn't see the Columbia Point scheme until two weeks before it was un-veiled to the family," said Dan Fenn. "I said, 'This is a pretty weird space. What am I going to do with these triangles and odd corners? How about just squaring off one of those corners?' I.M. was not going to have any of that. That idea disappeared extremely quickly—like in one second."

Critics noted a slight staginess, as if the interminable years of delay had sapped the conviction from Pei's pencil, leaving a formal gesture of monu-mentality—a hollow, manufactured Camelot castle. "That Pei can do much better is evident," wrote the critic Charles Jencks, "but that he has a weak-ness for corporate reticence is also clear. Good taste and expression fight it out in the large corporate practices—and usually boredom wins."

The lukewarm plaudits were subsumed by relief when, after sixteen years of infighting and controversy, the library finally opened on October 20, 1979, the kind of nippy fall day that suggests touch football. Seven thousand in-vited guests, including Kennedy cousins and aging New Frontiersmen, listened to the Boston Pops beneath a blue-and-white canopy and then heard speeches from President Jimmy Carter and Senator Ted Kennedy. (Their proximity that day was a matter of some awkwardness, since Kennedy was about to declare his intention to unseat the president.) There was a public reading of the quotation from JFK's inaugural address, which was inscribed on the atrium wall: "All this will not be finished in the first one hundred days. Nor will it be finished in the first one thousand days, nor in the life of this Administration, nor even perhaps in our lifetime on this planet. But let us begin." The words suggested nothing so much as the library's own stormy gestation.

"Perhaps not since the pharaohs," Stephen Smith quipped to the press that day, "has an architect had such a long, long ongoing relationship with a client."

7

I. M. PEI &
PARTNERS

Shortly after I. M. Pei began work on the Kennedy Library, his partner Henry Cobb designed a Title I housing complex in Boston called Harbor Towers in the rough cast-concrete style of Kips Bay Plaza. It was the Pei firm's last urban housing campaign, and its least successful. "If there's one project I have a deep sense of regret about, it's Harbor Towers," Cobb said. "I was unable to overcome the disability of a poor client. The disjunction between our aspirations and theirs was so extreme that it shows in the results. It was abominably executed. It just so happened that it was built on the same waterfront site as my thesis project at Harvard. This caused me a great deal of pain."

The developer probably would not have hired such an exacting architect had it not been for Ed Logue, the powerful chairman of the Boston Redevelopment Authority. As one of the most imposing figures in urban renewal, Logue compelled developers operating on his turf to seek his cooperation by using architects he liked. Even before Jackie Kennedy thrust Pei into the limelight, Logue had hired him to draft a $90 million downtown master plan known as Government Center, one of the few urban renewal projects actually built as planned.

Logue admired the Pei firm's work, but he shared Cobb's disappointment in Harbor Towers. One day he asked Pei what went wrong. "Pei said some-

◄ **I. M. Pei: "For him, it was effortless."**

thing unbelievable," Logue remembered. "He said, 'At that point I was no longer interested in housing.' "

Pei was not the only architect to turn away from housing in the mid-1960s. After reaching its apogee under the Kennedy administration, funding for urban housing dried up, and the subject shifted to the periphery of architectural discourse. Architects focused instead on prestige jobs that brought opportunities for self-expression. As the heroic posturing of early modernism faded, its imagery—rectangular volumes sheathed in undecorated neutral surfaces of steel, glass and concrete—persisted among the richly endowed museums, city halls and conspicuous corporate headquarters that are the Notre-Dames of our money culture. No architect did more than I. M. Pei to make modernism the official style of institutional America. "He's always on *this* side of authority," said Calvin Tsao, a former senior associate. "He's always glorifying the people with power. He's never a renegade."

The fact that Jackie Kennedy chose him ensured Pei's candidacy for the prize jobs, and their enduring friendship conferred valuable social connections on him. "We have that chemistry," Pei said. "We understand each other." Regardless of the library's problems, he became one of the most sought-after young architects of the late 1960s and the recipient of an abundance of top-tier commissions. "Every day you could see I.M.'s fame rising a little more," said associate Fred Fang, "but he never let it go to his head. He was the same old I.M." Within a few years, Pei's partner Araldo Cossutta was assembling a thirty-two-acre Christian Science vatican surrounding the mother church in Boston. Cobb built a thirty-two-story office tower on Baltimore's inner harbor. Pei himself designed an addition to Eliel Saarinen's Des Moines Art Center, an office for Polaroid, an art museum for Cornell University, a chemistry building for MIT, and, ironically, a Dallas city hall commissioned in the hope of improving the city's damaged reputation in the wake of the Kennedy assassination. "It seemed like every week something exciting

▲

The Dallas City Hall, one of many prize jobs
awarded to Pei in the wake of the Kennedy
Library commission.

happened," remembered designer Ralph Heisel. "It was like the world was opening up to us. Everyone was working together in a spirit of camaraderie. This was architecture at its best."

The glut of incoming work doubled Pei's payroll. He now employed one hundred architects, planners and draftsmen aided by a back-office staff of fifty. In 1966 he moved by necessity into an office building at 600 Madison, a few steps from the fashionable intersection of Madison and Fifty-seventh Street. Here Pei's firm assumed the trappings of a large corporate practice. Elevators opened onto a spacious reception lounge with the obligatory white walls and tubular-steel chairs. Carpeted corridors contained rows of color transparencies of the firm's work mounted on light boxes. Pei himself occupied a spare corner room dominated by a wall-sized geometric mural painted by his friend Al Held. Miniature versions of the Calder and Picasso sculptures he had installed beside his buildings at MIT and NYU sat on a counter. A trim, compact bookshelf contained Bauhaus monographs, volumes on the architectural history of Rome and catalogs of his own work. He eschewed the conventional desk in favor of a black lacquer table piled with clippings and correspondence. Associates came in ones and twos to confer with him on the widening array of projects.

Pei chose this juncture to change the firm's name from I. M. Pei & Associates to I. M. Pei & Partners to reflect, however cryptically, the growing contributions of Cobb, Cossutta and their administrative partner, Eason Leonard. Cossutta felt that architecture was an individual act, however, and he was reluctant to stay on as an anonymous "partner." But Pei was reportedly displeased when a construction-site placard identified Cossutta as the partner in charge of the Christian Science project. So it surprised no one when Cossutta left in 1973 to start his own practice. His place was filled by Jim Freed, a tall, bearded German immigrant who had joined Pei in 1956 after helping Mies complete the Seagram Building. Though the public perceived the Pei firm as a one-man act, it operated in reality as a troika: Pei, Cobb and Freed worked semiautonomously on their own jobs with their own teams. Their backgrounds could not have differed more—the mandarin, the Boston Brahmin and the Jewish refugee from Nazi Germany. Their unlikely union was based on a mutual concern for crisp, uncluttered geometries, an aversion to the extraordinary and a reputation for laboring obsessively toward a refined, logical result. All three conducted themselves as decorous gentlemen; they were cautious, considerate, patient, thorough and diplomatic. "They share an attitude toward life and work," said the architect James Polshek. "It's like a quiet, discreet men's club. Everybody understands the unspoken rules of the place. Pei doesn't have to worry that anyone is going to go off the deep end and do this year's trend."

If Pei's partners exemplified the happy cohabitation of opposites—the managerial equivalent of yin and yang—so too did his practice: he wanted to compete for both the large-scale commercial jobs that sustained big firms and the small institutional gems that garnered attention and made reputations. He combined a tough pragmatic mind with a delicacy of touch. "Pei always wanted to have the best of both worlds," Cobb said. "It's perfectly obvious he wanted to be a star, but he also wanted to work on a prodigious scale." The firm Pei fashioned in the late 1960s was the perfect apparatus for realizing these ambitions. He amassed great expertise within a large staff without sacrificing personal loyalty and esprit de corps. No firm was better at turning talk into concrete. Of course, prosperity inevitably imposed a new sense of hierarchy on a firm that was outgrowing the informal atelier atmosphere.

The partners allowed the assignment of responsibility to remain ambiguous, a tactic that ensured everyone's best effort. "They always had two people charged with identical assignments so that the partner would be the final arbiter," said one former employee. "It resulted in an enormous amount of angling." The inevitable office maneuvering ensued: Who would occupy the politically advantageous desk? Who would work on the most prestigious jobs? "It had all the aspects of a big family that's been together a long time," said former senior associate Marek Zamdmer. "And all the tensions—who's the favorite child?—were set against a background of discretion and good manners."

Pei kept everyone together by sheer force of personality and a rare gift for inspiring loyalty. He showed that he believed in the young talent around him. They repaid his faith by rising to the occasion. "I.M. was the father of a great institution," said designer Karen Van Lengen. "One aspect of his genius was that he understood how to create a positive climate to work in. Instead of making you work, he made you *want* to work."

Young designers came to Pei for the security of a firm with plenty of commissions and the chance to apply their pencils to high-profile jobs. Pei offered the additional inducement of working in teams that saw projects through from conception to final debugging, thus exposing them to a wide range of skills while their counterparts at other large firms languished on esoteric technical chores, like amassing specifications for bathroom fixtures. For those assigned to Pei's own team, there was the added exhilaration, which for many proved addictive, of working on the most coveted jobs in close collaboration with the master himself.

Pei was an inspiring presence. He moved about the studio looking over shoulders, offering ideas and squeezing arms in encouragement. He took every decision seriously, no matter how small. He listened closely. "Some architects running their own shop don't want to hear different ideas," said designer Ralph Heisel. "Pei was inclusive. You never got the sense that he was the boss and you were the employee. He always brought out the best in people and used their talents."

An almost palpable sense of mission—a romance of purpose—quickened the pulse of the ambitious young graduates of Ivy League design schools who filled the cubicles at 600 Madison. Pei had a way of recognizing their particular talent and providing a way for them to use it. "You are the *only* one who can do this," was a favorite exhortation. He had a gift for making subordinates feel like crucially important collaborators even as he quietly, almost imperceptibly, made the decisions himself. "He does give you the feeling of contributing," said Pei's son Sandi, who joined the firm in 1976. "It's a discovery process. He never gives you the solution. He gives you the clues."

Employees savored the glamorous world Pei created for them. He knew how to pamper their egos with perquisites. On Saturdays, for example, he often rounded them up for long lunches at Gino of Capri, a favorite Lexington Avenue restaurant. "Afterward we'd go home," remembered Harold Fredenburgh, a former associate partner, "and complain to our wives how hard we were working." They flew first-class and stayed in the best hotels while meeting with museum directors, CEOs and heads of state on jobs with seemingly unlimited budgets. "It's exciting and habit-forming," said Marek Zamdmer, "to work in an office where the news is from London and Paris instead of, say, Long Island City."

Pei also won his staff's affection—a rarity in a profession known for exploitive prima donnas—with infusions of personal warmth. He chatted with them in the elevator, administered grandfatherly scoldings for working on weekends, even though that was a tacit obligation, and went out of his way to admire babies brought in for a visit. He never affected hauteur; he never treated them as lesser creatures. "He gives the impression of humility and delicacy," said Jennifer Nadler, a former employee. "He's gracious and mild-mannered in the way he moves about the office. He harbors a certain twinkle in his eye."

Although rarely demonstrative, Pei was capable of the touching personal gesture. "In the early sixties, shortly after we left Webb & Knapp, my first wife learned that she had breast cancer," remembered Eason Leonard. "I realized this was going to take a great deal of attention away from this firm. I told I.M. the problem, and he said, 'Do what you have to do. That's what partners are for.' One can never, never forget that."

Pei tempered his warmth with occasional flashes of cold, dismissive authority. "Quite a few people in the office are deathly afraid of I.M. shooting out a little dart at them," said one former senior associate. "He can destroy someone with a word, and I've seen him do it, even to his own sons. Of course, he can also charm them with a word. It's a great skill, and it enables him to get the best out of his people. It was like receiving a little holy water to get I.M. to smile."

Most of all, Pei endowed his office with a certitude of taste that went beyond design to include a Confucian code of manners. "Pei is a person of complete honesty," Marcel Breuer observed in 1967. "His personality and his architecture have a total identity. There is no fakery or facade." A mandarin's sureness of touch extended to all things. "Even if you didn't make much money," said designer J. Woodson Rainey, "you wanted to live on that plane of clarity."

"In those early days we were more of a family," said Jim Freed. "It was a golden age of innocence. We used to go down to Chinatown for dumplings on Saturdays and Sundays. I.M. told me many things about Chinese food that still remain in my mind. One always learned from I.M. about things, things about life. He tells stories like nobody else I know. He has a way of looking at things. Some artists live just inside their work, but he understands that architecture is not all of life. You have to see him laugh to understand. The only way I can put it is this: he's very comfortable in his own skin."

Pei handled all problems with unflappable composure. The increasing demands on his time did not alter his habitual disregard for daily schedules, as if his eye were trained on a distant star. "Well," he said one day after missing the bus to attend an event at his son's school, "I'm Chinese." He seemed an oasis of calm in the eye of a hurricane of calamity.

His secretary was forever hustling him off to some impending appointment or to the airport for a flight departing half an hour hence. "Oh, that's all the time I need," he would say. One day Pei lingered precariously late before leaving with his associate Kellogg Wong to meet the architect Pietro Belluschi on a flight to Syracuse. "We got in a cab and headed off," Wong remembered. "I was in a panic. LaGuardia Airport was under construction, so the cabdriver wanted to let us off some distance from the terminal, but Mr. Pei instructed him to go through a barricade. We ran by the check-in counter to the wrong gate, had to run to another gate. When we finally stepped on the plane the other passengers applauded. Belluschi said, 'I told you Pei would make it.' I was exhausted, but Mr. Pei was hardly panting. For him it was effortless."

◄   **Pei on a mid-1960s vacation in Europe**

with the Breuers.

8

WINDOWS OVER
COPLEY SQUARE

One day I. M. Pei arrived at a luncheon in Boston to find his MIT classmate, Frank Sargent, by then governor of Massachusetts, holding forth. "As Pei came in," Sargent recalled, "I said, 'I would like to apologize for my former classmate for being late, but he's been puttying windows over at the John Hancock Building.'"

It was a slightly cruel joke. Pei's plums included a nearly fatal commission to build an audacious glass tower, New England's tallest, for the John Hancock Mutual Life Insurance Company on Boston's historic Copley Square. Like the Kennedy Library, the Hancock Building was nearly defeated by its own ambitions. It became one of architecture's most excruciating fiascoes and a grave challenge to Pei's otherwise charmed career. "The story of the Hancock Tower is endless," *Boston Globe* critic Robert Campbell observed, "and wherever you probe it, there's no limit to the disasters and tragedies and miscalculations and beauties and wonderful examples of professional conduct by engineers and architects. It's a door opening onto a room with another door and another door and another door."

The Hancock was the latest in a long line of insurance towers. Unlike the other great nineteenth-century industries, like steel, coal and railroads, life insurance purveyed no tangible product. It dealt in trust; it relied on a fragile public confidence. This faith had suf-

◄ **The Hancock Tower in the early stages of dismemberment.**

fered when, in the financial turmoil of the 1870s, one insurance firm after another folded with policyholders' money—an offense that was well documented by the press. The surviving companies were quick to use architecture to impart an aura of solidity and civic responsibility. Thus early insurance towers like New York's Equitable Life Building (1868–1870) and Chicago's Home Insurance Building (1883–1885) were designed as reassuring reference points of community stability. "The idea," the president of the Prudential wrote in 1892, "is to construct a building which shall typify and symbolize the character of the business of the Prudential, exemplify its all-pervading spirit of beneficence and its ingrained love of the golden rule."

Hancock also favored hefty, four-square edifices. When the firm outgrew its downtown Boston headquarters in 1922, for example, a caravan of forty trucks escorted by police transported five tons of bonds and other documents generated by 1,800 employees to a new ten-story home office on Copley Square, the hub of Boston's Back Bay gentility. Set amid carefully scaled town houses with mansard roofs and polished brass doorplates, the Hancock Building was a solid, imposing affair and an architectural prizewinner.

Hancock had outgrown its office by the 1940s and commissioned another headquarters next door with double the office space. Their new counting-house was an Art Deco stone tower modeled on the civic landmarks of the 1930s, with a distinctive pyramidal roof topped by an observation deck and a glass tower from which colored lights were displayed to designate weather conditions. It was a throwback compared to the severe boxes Walter Gropius was by then espousing a few miles away at Harvard. "I have not been able to stand in awe before the stone and steel which constitute the housing of the John Hancock Company," president Paul Clark said at the dedication. "It is dwarfed by the magnificence of its basic concept—the life insurance idea. The most efficient working space must pale before the emotion the miracle of life insurance excites—confidence in the present, hope for the future, education, home solidarity, sunshine and play, and, most of all, self-reliance and determination to make our lives in our own way."

Hancock's stocky tower stood as the tallest building in Boston until 1964 when Prudential built a fifty-two-story slab a quarter mile away designed by Los Angeles architect Charles Luckman. The newcomer towered so awkwardly above the redbrick village of Back Bay that *Globe* critic Robert Campbell named his annual list of ugly architecture the "Pru Awards" in its honor. Ugly or not, it earned bragging rights as the tallest in town. Hancock officials were, of course, aghast that their Newark-based rival would build a regional office of such overwhelming proportions on their home turf. Worse, the Pru boys were said to be relishing the slight. From their new aerie they derided the Hancock as "the midget."

Hancock chairman Robert Slater endured the humiliation for one year before hiring Pei in 1965 to put the Pru in its place. Though young and still relatively untested, Pei was by now an established name in Boston, in part because Ed Logue had hired him to produce the master plan for Government Center. "Hancock knew that architectural quality was of concern to me," Logue later said, "and that John Collins, the mayor, backed me up on that. They knew I would approve Pei's selection. And they knew they needed special approvals to get a sixty-story building built."

Nobody had to instruct Pei to surpass the Pru's height; it was a tacit responsibility. All six of his preliminary sketches stood about sixty stories, the last of which, completed in the summer of 1966, was a concrete shaft with one flattened glass side facing the state capitol. (The design was derived from a cardboard roll Harold Fredenburgh had sliced lengthwise and carried into Pei's office.) Hancock liked the design and planned to demolish its 1922 headquarters to make room for two low buildings at the base of the tower enclosing a triangular plaza facing the landmark Trinity Church.

"I was invited to the Hancock boardroom to see a model of the area and of the building which was proposed to be built," Logue remembered. "Pei and the president of the company were sitting on the sidelines of the boardroom, and the president said to Pei, 'Do you think he'll like it?' And Pei said, 'Don't worry. Ed likes anything I do.' "

Logue gave his informal approval, despite the height, saying, "It seemed clear to me that if the Prudential, a foreign company from our perspective, got fifty-two ugly stories, then the Hancock should get more. Local preference."

Pei's design was poised for its public unveiling when Logue unexpectedly announced that he was resigning from the Boston Redevelopment Authority to run—unsuccessfully, as it turned out—for mayor. His departure changed everything. As long as Logue presided over Boston real estate, he had enforced strict limits on development. With Logue gone, Hancock was free to build higher, so they retracted Pei's concrete shaft and hired Maxwell Philipson, a hard-nosed New York real-estate consultant, to help formulate a new plan.

Buoyed by the upturn in postwar birth rates, Robert Slater, the firm's youngest chief executive, had expanded the old-line company throughout the 1960s into new fields, like mutual funds and variable annuities, and reorganized its operations around the computer. Philipson persuaded top management to pursue a bigger, more iconic tower capable of symbolizing Slater's aggressive new Hancock. Besides, with Logue gone and the firm sprouting subsidiaries at a rapid clip, management might as well grab for all the space it could. Hancock came back to Pei after one full year with a more ambitious mandate: they wanted 2 million square feet instead of 1.5 million, and they wanted it on half of the original site.

A spate of new jobs had arrived in Pei's office during the year's hiatus. In addition to the Kennedy Library and the Dallas City Hall, he was busy with a renewal project in Brooklyn's Bedford-Stuyvesant, launched at the behest of Senator Robert Kennedy, and a commercial complex in Toronto for the

Canadian Imperial Bank of Commerce. In fact, Pei had so many jobs under way that he was hard-pressed to choose which to personally direct and which to delegate. It was decided that Pei would take on the Toronto project while his long-term design partner, Henry Cobb, started from scratch at Hancock.

Top billing came slowly for Cobb, a painfully shy Boston Brahmin who, along with Cossutta and Freed, quietly generated much of the firm's design work while Pei, the high-profile front man, performed his diplomatic rounds. In tortoiseshell glasses and tweed, Cobb could have passed as John Chancellor's soft-spoken brother.

It is probably no coincidence that Pei chose Cobb as his professional alter ego. Together they formed the kind of yin and yang symbiosis that exists between opposites: Pei is spontaneous and outgoing while Cobb is reserved; Pei had avoided academic discourse while Cobb became chairman of the department of architecture at Harvard's Graduate School of Design; Pei trusted his eye while Cobb trusted logic; Pei was an immigrant while Cobb was a New England aristocrat with ancestral roots in the Yankee headwaters of Portland, Maine. "As a Chinese in America, I.M. felt that he had to have an Anglo-Saxon base," observed the architect Paul Rudolph, who had known both men at Harvard. "Harry was that base."

Cobb's retiring manner and halting, deliberate speech hindered him from courting his own clients, so it was convenient for him to rely on the self-possessed Pei. Typically, Pei handed new jobs to Cobb or Freed for development and reappeared as little as an hour prior to big client meetings. He easily grasped their concepts in time to present them himself. It was under this somewhat subservient partnership that Cobb designed many of the early works credited to Pei, including Place Ville Marie and the May D & F department store in Denver's Courthouse Square.

The partners anguished over whether to proceed with the commission under Hancock's expanded specifications. "As a native of Boston it was of some concern to me," Cobb said. "Many acquaintances there felt that I should have refused the commission."

As a conservative town flavored by colonial continuities and genteel understatement, Boston was slow to accept the skyscraper as an exuberant expression of prosperity. On the contrary, provincial city fathers viewed the early prototypes proliferating in Chicago and New York with cool Yankee skepticism. They guarded their own Victorian skyline against such intrusions by enacting America's first height limits, and they had maintained those restrictions throughout most of the building boom that preceded the Depression. As late as 1919 the tallest building in New England stood in Hartford.

Back Bay, in particular, resisted alterations to its nineteenth-century plan patterned after Second Empire Paris—a deliberate departure from the English styles favored on Beacon Hill—with graceful church spires and domes rising above a level mass of five-story town houses bisected by broad tree-lined boulevards. As old money and nouveau riche alike gravitated to Back Bay, it emerged as the center of Boston's intellectual and cultural life. A cluster of institutions and churches formed haphazardly on the less expensive land around Copley Square.

The Acropolis of the New World, as Bostonians boastfully called Copley Square, contained America's first public art museum, the New Old South Church and, one block away, a natural history society. The jewel of the square was undoubtedly H. H. Richardson's Trinity Church of 1877. By reviving a blend of Spanish and French Romanesque, Richardson, the preeminent American architect of his time, guided his colleagues out of the doldrums of Victorian Gothic into a Renaissance phase that endured well into this century. In 1885 a panel of distinguished architects voted Trinity Church the country's most significant building.

Trinity's richly carved tower and mass were balanced in 1896 by McKim, Mead & White's serenely classical public library, the largest of its kind in the world. These two great public edifices faced each other across one of America's most celebrated public spaces as if challenging passersby to take sides. So firm was the collective resolve to preserve what amounted to an outdoor museum of period architecture that when the ornately Gothic Westminster Chambers Hotel of 1903, built on the future Hancock site, exceeded the ninety-foot height limit by six feet, Boston prosecuted the case all the way to the U.S. Supreme Court, where, in a landmark zoning case, the justices affirmed the city's right to impose height restrictions. The hotel's owners were consequently obliged to strip off four feet of cornice and two feet of roof.

Pei and Cobb's misgivings were overshadowed by their appetite for large-scale undertakings and by their certainty that if they didn't build the Hancock Tower, somebody else would. "Harry and I came to the conclusion that Copley Square, in spite of these two great buildings by Richardson and McKim, Mead and White, lacked the enclosure of, say, the Place Vendôme," Pei said. "Maybe what it needed was a twentieth-century addition to create a new space rather than preserve the eighteenth-century-drawing-room scale, which could no longer be. So we decided to go ahead and do it."

Cobb approached the drafting table for the biggest job of his career at a time when the worn-out glass box, replicated monotonously throughout the 1950s and 1960s, was mutating into a late modern species—Philip Johnson called it "shaped modern"—incorporating picturesque chamfers and cuts, undulating glass walls, geometric setbacks and notched corners. These corporate crystal palaces, with their seamless "slick-tech" sheaths, were partly a reaction against the boredom of the box and partly a self-conscious demonstration of the new ability to construct continuous reflective surfaces. Because floor-to-ceiling glass panels made a cheap skin for a metal frame, the mirrored glass building with its cool, neutral presence became commonplace.

For Cobb, slick-tech offered an added benefit: its mirrored curtain wall would, theoretically, reflect the rich Romanesque carvings and Florentine arches of Hancock's landmark neighbors while the tower itself would melt into thin air like a shimmering mirage. It was the same vanishing, immaterial quality Pei would invoke years later at the Louvre. Cobb sublimated his building to best effect by banishing any hint of grillwork or mullion. In the ultimate application of "less is more," the eye perceived only the floor-to-ceiling windows, duplicated 10,344 times over thirteen seamless acres, rising like an undifferentiated sheet from the gray granite plaza in unrelenting muteness. "In a certain sense," Cobb said, "the Hancock is an impoverished architecture. Only by a certain deliberate reductionism was it possible to make a building of that scale in that particular place. It has no spatial presence, only a presence as an object, and then only as a plane. Everything about the building is *reduce, reduce, reduce.*" To further disguise its overwhelming bulk, Cobb configured his tower as a rhomboid with its thin end rising 800 feet above Copley Square like the bow of an enormous elegant ship.

Hancock disclosed the design on November 27, 1967, as a symbol of Boston's revival from economic doldrums. Senator Ted Kennedy, Mayor John Collins and Mayor-elect Kevin White—Boston's biggest guns—showed up to praise the company for demonstrating confidence in the city's future at a time when other businesses were relocating to the suburbs. The next day Hancock chairman Robert Slater hosted a luncheon for a thousand government officials during which Pei delivered an illustrated talk and Governor John A. Volpe presented Slater with a "Faith in Massachusetts Award." By hiring Pei, Hancock officials felt that they would not only surpass the hated Pru, they would enhance the skyline as well. In their minds, they were performing a public service by vanquishing the ugly interloper from Newark and restoring Boston to its natural order.

No chorus of gratitude resounded, however. Architects in particular—and Boston is said to harbor more architects per capita than any other city—

howled in collective protest. "A more massively inappropriate structure for the site could not be imagined," one local architect wrote to the *Boston Globe,* "and that this should have come from the office of our respected colleague could scarcely be believed." The Boston Society of Architects issued a statement condemning the design. "We had hoped in this time of urban unrest and crisis," it said, "for something other than an egotistical statement."

Ed Logue was unaware of the redesign until the *Globe* printed a rendering on its front page. "I called Pei," he recalled, "and I said, 'What the hell happened? That's not the building I approved.' To me, the essential point to understand is that the Hancock and its consultant, Philipson, didn't give a damn about the outline of the building. Harry was left free—extraordinarily free, considering the location and the scope of the building—to do exactly what he pleased. Perhaps all of this will help you understand why I so deeply and fervently believe that you can never trust an architect or developer, no matter how reputable, to protect the public interest."

Even with Logue gone from office, Hancock faced some restrictions. One week after Hancock unveiled its plan, the city denied it a building permit due to "possible zoning violations." Because Hancock owned adjacent property, and was therefore capable of swapping zoning credits from one plot to another, there was never much doubt that it would eventually get its permit, but the controversy dragged on contentiously through public hearings and appeals for nine months. City officials promptly issued the permit when Hancock, the city's largest private employer, threatened to move its headquarters to Chicago.

Problems arose, however, almost as soon as construction began in August of 1968. Back Bay rests unsteadily atop layers of sand and gravel dumped into the pungent tidal flats of the Charles River basin. Shortly after excavation began, a poorly braced retaining wall collapsed inward, shifting the sodden landfill for acres around. Sidewalks buckled, and utility lines snapped.

Already incensed by the noise of pile drivers, the adjacent Sheraton Plaza Hotel filed a lawsuit claiming $750,000 in damages. But Hancock's real-estate subsidiary bought the hotel from Sheraton for $6 million and, not surprisingly, dropped the lawsuit against itself.

Meanwhile, Hancock's monument to mammon not only dwarfed Trinity Church, Richardson's Romanesque jewel, it nearly destroyed it. Trinity rests upon 4,500 wooden piles driven into the unstable landfill. As the subsoil shifted, at least a dozen cracks appeared in the transept walls and on six John La Farge murals of the prophets that grace the spandrels of the massive main tower. The transept itself leaned precariously close to an angle at which it would no longer support the roof. Meanwhile, a water bucket dropped from the skeletal tower burst through a stained-glass window and a doorframe plummeted into the chancel's roof. Debris continued to rain down until a protective scaffolding was built around the church. After fifteen years of litigation, Trinity recovered $13 million in damages from Hancock, but the court rejected Trinity's suit against Pei.

Meanwhile, the glass tower taking shape above Copley Square struck many as an Orwellian monster. The supposedly unobtrusive glass sheathing affixed to the steel frame suggested the uncaring, neutral detachment of a corporate limousine at a time when institutional authority was viewed with suspicion. "It was, for a while, the building that people loved to hate, having been built exactly at the time when everything big was bad," remembered Cobb. "Abbie Hoffman stood in Copley Square shaking his fist at the building and said, '*That* is the enemy.' "

Nobody paid much attention when a few of the 5-by-11-foot glass sheets—the largest ever installed in a tower—popped out in the summer of 1972. Hancock dismissed the breakage as "normal construction damage" and replaced the $750-per-unit Thermopane windows with plywood. Every time the wind gusted up, however, more plywood appeared. The breakage was caused by construction debris blowing off the upper floors and nicking windows on the way down, Hancock assured the press. The problem would abate when glazing concluded in December.

One month after workers gingerly placed the last pane in its aluminum frame, the first winter storm of 1973 rumbled in from the northwest and lashed the tower with gale-force winds. Morning light revealed more than sixty broken windows and hundreds more damaged by falling shards. It was now clear that something was terribly wrong.

Hancock had already sensed a gathering crisis and quietly summoned Professor Robert Hansen of MIT, a structural engineer who had worked on the company's Chicago office tower. While workmen carted broken glass away in wheelbarrows, Hansen's MIT associates placed seventy hand-sized wind sensors in strategic locations around the tower's exterior and strung them together with some eleven miles of electrical cable leading to a central instrument room on the thirty-fifth floor where they amassed oceans of data on the building's conduct in the stiff New England winds. They also set up a scale model of Back Bay in MIT's Wright Brothers Wind Tunnel and subjected it to 150-mile-an-hour winds.

Meanwhile, the notorious building became the object of public curiosity. Plywood by now covered most of the tower's lower third (thirty homes could have been built with the lumber, according to one estimate), and it resembled an enormous boarded-up storefront. Police rushed to cordon off Copley Square whenever the wind gusted to forty-five miles per hour. Adding insult to injury, the Boston fire marshal ordered them to cover the plywood with a layer of black fire retardant paint, which only deepened the tower's aura of disuse and disaster.

The unrelenting media, meanwhile, spun the Hancock failure into a modern morality play, a comeuppance for overreaching corporate ambition. Walter Cronkite interviewed Hansen live on CBS. *Time* covered the story with a slightly wry tone, as did *Newsweek*, the *New York Times* and the *Wall Street Journal*. Editorial writers everywhere composed lessons on the Tower of Babel and people who live in glass houses. The building generated enough print coverage to fill twenty-three oversized black binders shelved in Hancock's public relations office, where spokesmen busily denied rumors that the entire building would be torn down.

Boston cabdrivers brightened their days by coining nicknames, like the Plywood Palace, the U.S. Plywood Building and Termite Heaven. Bostonians traded quips about woodpeckers and the world's tallest outhouse. "Came into town and saw the Hancock Building," Bette Midler told a Boston audience. "Like, wow. *Too* much."

"Can a structure that regularly loses face enhance the image of an insurance company?" wondered *Boston* magazine. "We would suggest we look immediately to the advantage of aluminum siding. . . . Or how about going Colonial and covering the building with cedar shingles?" Cobb endured meetings during which panicky Hancock officials openly discussed firing him. His daughter presented him with a "Ply in the Sky" T-shirt she'd bought in Harvard Square.

If it was agonizing for Hancock to watch its high-profile headquarters degenerate into a laughingstock, it was worse for Pei to see it erode his reputation for technical expertise. "The firm underwent a great trauma," remembered one senior associate. "Memos went out to employees asking them not to talk to the press. Harry, of course, labored under extreme pressure. He spent six hours a day with Michael Flynn [Pei's in-house engineer]. You could travel to any city in the country and tell a cabdriver you worked for I. M. Pei and they'd laugh about the Hancock."

The Hancock continued to shed its slick skin as if the unweary ghosts of Old Boston were intent on repelling the intruder. Well-intentioned suggestions arrived by the mailbagful: drill tiny holes in the windows, install curved glass, wrap the windows in chicken wire. . . .

The plywood blocked light from entering the lower half of the tower, and the building was consequently almost pitch-black inside. Wind whistled through chinks in the wood and rattled the boards against their narrow aluminum frames. From a makeshift office on the thirty-third floor, Harry Cobb directed a squadron of subcontractors and engineers in pursuit of a solution. Associates praised Cobb, whose father died during the ordeal, for conducting himself with astonishing equanimity and professionalism. One engineer called his performance "inspirational."

"It was quite humiliating," Pei said, ". . . humiliating when people sort of look at you, and architects particularly are very, very sympathetic, you know. It's compassion, but that's not what you need at that time."

By October 1973, engineers had at last uncovered the cause of the problem. The breakage, they concluded, was not caused by high winds or foundation settlement, as was initially assumed, but by defects in the manufactured windows. Engineering schools offered courses on the properties of steel and concrete, but glass was not considered a material so much as a manufactured product, an uncertain technology residing on the margins of structural inquiry. Besides, there was no scientific way to test new windows, except by trial and error. Double-glazed windows had been available since the early 1930s, but Pei's office, in its urgency to erect an 800-foot mirror, had ventured to the perilous edge of glass technology by requesting double-layered windows with a reflective coating. Light entered the outer pane, bounced off the silver lining on its inner surface, and passed through the outer pane again on its way back out. Detective work revealed that the lead spacer separating the two sheets of glass refused to flex when the outer pane expanded in the warmth generated by the light's round trip, and when the entire unit vibrated imperceptibly, as all windows do thousands of times daily. As a result, the brittle lead spacer developed microscopic cracks that were transmitted through the soldering to the glass itself. This tiny flaw resided in every pane.

This monstrous technical goof was never disclosed to the public. Shortly after Pei's colleagues presented their findings, Hancock announced plans to replace all 10,344 windows while concealing the specific problem behind cryptic press releases. The decision was made by Slater's successor, Gerhard Bleicken, a tough, conservative manager installed after Hancock's board of directors grew disenchanted with Slater's expansionist program. Consistent with his campaign of prudent consolidation, Bleicken considered subdividing each window into thirds on the theory that a more conventional appearance would help restore confidence in the building at a time when two major tenants had canceled their leases. "Had that happened," Cobb said, "the Hancock Tower would have been one of the worst buildings in modern times. When you deal with minimalism, everything counts. There's very little there—just certain shapes and proportions. If you modify those elements you destroy the architecture."

In the end, Bleicken overruled his advisers and honored Cobb's request for costlier windows capable of restoring the tower's shimmering appearance. Cobb called Bleicken's trust in him after his personal ordeal "the achievement in my life of which I'm most proud." Down the freight elevators came the defective 400-pound windows—many of which were sold as souvenirs— and up went tough, specially tempered single-pane replacements similar to those used in fire doors.

For months uniformed guards scanned the curtain wall from surrounding sidewalks with binoculars in search of the color change that signals imminent cracking. A few panes did shatter, but no more than was normal. The demons had been exorcised; quiet reigned once more on Copley Square.

Management had hoped to open the tower soon after the replacement windows were installed, but tests undisclosed to the public revealed that the tower was swaying so wildly in windstorms that occupants of the upper floors might actually feel seasick. The movement was so pronounced that engineers warned Pei's office not to install chandeliers in the top-floor boardroom and they jokingly recommended seat belts for secretaries.

William Le Messurier, the dean of Boston structuralists, stabilized the willowy tower by installing a "tuned mass damper," a device he had invented to calm the Citicorp Building in Manhattan. His remedy meant retrofitting the Hancock's fifty-eighth floor with two lead blocks, weighing about 300 tons each, attached to the steel frame by springs and shock absorbers. As the tower leaned in one direction, inertia dragged the blocks the opposite way across greased metal plates. The blocks thus acted as a corrective ballast, pulling the building back into plumb. Le Messurier tested the gargantuan device one night by tugging the building to and fro like a solo sailor maneuvering an enormous ship.

Le Messurier quieted the gyrations, but questions persisted about the tower's safety. "The situation was getting out of hand," Le Messurier said, "and finally Harry Cobb decided that he would get a high-level opinion from somebody of impeccable credentials outside the usual circle of consultants in this country."

At Cobb's urging, Hancock engaged Bruno Thürlimann, a Zurich-based expert on tall building behavior. Over the winter of 1974–1975, Thürlimann performed what is believed to be the most thorough structural examination ever conducted. Like everyone else, he assumed that if the building fell, it would land on its wide side, like a domino, and he judged the building sufficiently braced against this possibility. Just before flying to the United States to pronounce it safe, he made an astonishing discovery: in extreme winds— what engineers call "the hundred-year storm"—the tower could overturn on its *narrow* end, a danger nobody had considered. His analysis persuaded Hancock to stiffen the steel skeleton by adding 1,650 tons of diagonal steel struts from top to bottom at a reported cost of $5 million. "It was," said Pei's in-house curtain-wall specialist, Michael Flynn, "like putting your socks on after your shoes."

One morning shortly after this happy resolution Hancock ushered the press up to the sixtieth-floor observatory and offered them coffee, Danish pastries and reams of carefully crafted press releases emphasizing the "pleasing office environment" with its "brightly colored acoustical screens and various species of live plants." Almost all of the visitors that day, consciously or not, rapped the windows with their knuckles.

Bleicken sought to reimburse himself for a budget that had swelled from $75 million to something north of $125 million by issuing a spate of multimillion-dollar lawsuits against nearly everyone involved. Pei was charged with submitting designs that were "not good and workmanlike" and that failed to represent "an adequate determination of the forces and conditions to which the curtain wall would be subjected."

This was only the opening round of the most elaborate web of litigation in architectural history. The Toledo glass manufacturer Libbey-Owens-Ford countersued Hancock for damaging its reputation and Pei for "serious errors and defects" in his wind load specifications. Pei, in turn, sued the contractor and Libbey-Owens-Ford for withholding evidence of defects in its Thermopane windows, which, Hansen learned, had failed elsewhere. Pei further disavowed any legal responsibility for design and specifications, since Hancock had cleared them with outside consultants.

The litigious wrangling continued until 1981, when, after lengthy negotiations, all parties agreed to a settlement that required them "to refrain in perpetuity from any public discussion of the building's problems." As a result, it appeared that the mystery would never be formally solved.

Architects and engineers, denied the opportunity to learn from Hancock's

▼

Boston grudgingly accepted Cobb's Han-

cock Tower, despite its overwhelming scale.

H. H. Richardson's Trinity

Church is at center.

spectacular failure, engaged in half-informed speculation until, in 1988, *Boston Globe* critic Robert Campbell managed to break the code of silence by publishing interviews in the *Journal of the American Institute of Architects* with curtain-wall specialist Victor Mahler and structural engineer William Le Messurier, both of whom had helped to stabilize the tower without signing the gag pact.

The delicacy of the site had moved Pei's office to venture to the brink of the safely established state of the art. "We had a situation where really everybody reached to the edge," Mahler said. "It was like the Gothic cathedrals in the old days, and you know Beauvais—it fell down once, it fell down twice, okay, now let's try a third time. Finally they got it."

With these calamities quietly resolved, the Hancock Tower opened in October of 1976 at roughly double its original budget and five years behind schedule. "We came to realize," Gerhard Bleicken said at the dedication ceremony, "that people who build glass houses are bound to lead fragile existences."

In time, the plywood faded from memory and Bostonians came to appreciate the Hancock Building. It is an abomination to walk by, but to drivers entering town in the late afternoon it stands like an ethereal glowing screen, almost spiritual in its cool prismatic detachment. "What the church steeple is to the New England village," Robert Campbell wrote, "the Hancock is to the Boston metropolitan area. It signals presence, magnetizes space." It has come to be accepted as Boston's equivalent of the Eiffel Tower or the Empire State Building: an identifying icon.

"I lived in Boston for four years in an apartment building that was designed by Harry Cobb also, and it was located almost exactly one mile due east of the Hancock Tower," said Peter Blake, an architect and former editor-in-chief of *Architectural Forum*. "I lived on the thirtieth floor, and my living room had a panoramic view of the Boston skyline with this tall sliver of reflective glass precisely at its center. I saw this incredible building every day and every night in every conceivable kind of light. At sunrise and sunset, in clear skies and in violent storms. I never tired of it. Not for one moment."

It was fitting that Cobb should receive a measure of credit for the building's eventual success, since he had fielded the flak when things went wrong. In a series of closed-door meetings after the windows began falling, Pei had reportedly told his partners that, for better or worse, his name alone graced the letterhead and it was therefore in the firm's best interest for his reputation to remain unsullied. "Pei accepted the accolades when they came in," said one source who was privy to these discussions, "but when the blame came in, he stepped aside."

"Somehow, I.M. came out smelling like roses," said the architect Richard Meier, "while Harry suffered greatly." One unplanned consequence, however, was that Cobb's name emerged from anonymity.

Virtually every staff member who is asked says the two partners were never again comfortable in each other's presence, but Cobb himself denies any ill-feelings. "The whole episode was so notorious and so high-profile that it naturally generated a lot of gossip," he said. "I.M. probably did give the impression that he was actively disassociating himself. I know that the Hancock people felt that way and resented it. It has never been a source of friction between us."

▶

Pei signs the topping-off beam, 1971.

9

THE MOST
SENSITIVE SITE IN
THE UNITED STATES

"You know," Pei told a friend during the Hancock troubles, "that building is not going to do my reputation any good." He was making an astonishing understatement. Architectural reputations are highly perishable, and the prestigious clients who had flocked to Pei following his Kennedy appointment abandoned him in the aftermath of Hancock. Word spread throughout the incestuous business fraternity that Pei was a risk. He has estimated that the Hancock fiasco caused him "immeasurable damage" in lost commissions. Nobody would hire an architect accused of malpractice, and the settlement that ended the litigation never clearly absolved him of blame. So Pei was blacklisted. He could not even rely on the kind of commercial jobs he had performed with Zeckendorf. "By then people had forgotten that we actually did investment buildings—and a lot of them," Pei said. "No developer would come to us anymore. We wanted them to remember that's how we started."

The whole pattern of Pei's life until Hancock had been a succession of sure-footed advances from one benefactor to the next: Dean Emerson to Walter Gropius; Gropius to Zeckendorf; Zeckendorf to the Kennedys; the Kennedys to high-profile clients like the city of Dallas and the Christian Science Church. Daniel Burnham liked to say that 75 percent of an architect's fate lay in his ability to get jobs. Nobody was better at procuring plum jobs than Pei, and nobody navigated political roadblocks more gracefully. "I.M., one feels, is at least as much interested in the diplomacies of architecture, and in the strategies employed, as in the final result," wrote the architect and author Peter Blake. "He is a kind of Chinese Metternich, let loose on the urban American scene."

Boston broke Pei's chain of success with cruel abruptness. It was an ironic stumbling point, for this was the city of the scholarly elite, the American mandarins, to which the eighteen-year-old Pei had gravitated from Philadelphia in the 1930s; where he had drafted his earliest architectural impulses; where he and Eileen had established their first home; and where their sons had gone to college. What should have been a triumphant homecoming degenerated into an Icarus-like fall from grace.

Pei inherited from Zeckendorf a tendency to go beyond the ordinary. One of his greatest talents was his ability to befriend the right clients and, with a persuasion verging on sorcery, exceed their original ambitions on the theory that good designs would recoup their cost. After Hancock, a chastened Pei found his current clients newly reluctant to proceed. IBM, for example, had hired him in 1969 to design an office tower at the corner of Madison Avenue and Fifty-seventh Street, a few steps from Pei's own office. Pei's partner Jim Freed sketched a dark glass rhomboid tower facing the intersection. Freed later called it "my last Miesian gasp," and it did impose an unrelenting geometry. The corridors encircling the elevator banks became rhomboids too, and rhomboid offices reportedly contained rhomboid desks. IBM would normally have asked for a redesign, but in light of the firestorm surrounding Hancock, it quietly sought to replace Pei with Edward Larrabee Barnes, a reliable practitioner known for stylish modern buildings delivered on budget. "To my amazement, IBM wanted to come in and talk," remembered Barnes. "There was no question they were calling because of John Hancock. So I put them off. I called I.M. and said, 'What's going on? I'm not going to take their calls until you tell me to.' About ten days later he said go ahead."

There were other disappointments as well. In early 1974, John D. Rockefeller III selected Pei from four dozen candidates to build a new Park Avenue home for the Asia Society, a cultural institution he had founded in 1956 and to which he was donating his $10 million collection of Oriental art. Few projects suited Pei more perfectly than an Asian art gallery on Park Avenue for the Rockefellers. He literally whistled as he drafted an expansive glass facade designed to draw pedestrians into an airy garden atrium.

Pei invariably plays the boardroom to perfection, so his associate Thomas Schmitt was surprised when Pei emerged from a crucial presentation in Rockefeller's office with a furrowed brow. "I.M. was very upset," Schmitt remembered. "He said, 'I'm getting no reaction at all. He's very cool. He's diffident.' We did another scheme. Again there was a strange noncommittal response. We presented scheme after scheme, none of which seemed acceptable." Although he did not express it to Pei, Rockefeller found Pei's expansive lobby extravagant for a nonprofit organization dependent on donations. Trustee Margot Wilkie urged Rockefeller to voice his reservations before it was too late. "We know that you have been too generous," she wrote him, "and unselfishly reticent about the choice of architects and that, alas, unless you make a firm statement about not liking the Pei building . . . the present plans will roll on into becoming reality."

In the end, Pei let Rockefeller off the hook by tendering a gracious letter of resignation. "Given the program," he wrote, "I sincerely believe we have explored every alternative appropriate to the site." Asia House, like IBM, went to Ed Barnes.

.   .   .   .

Pei was never inclined to mind his fiscal boundaries as prudently as he might have. He preferred to run I. M. Pei & Partners as a design studio, an atelier, tolerant of creative waste. He was notorious for refining right down to the wire on the theory that overages would be forgotten but architecture was for the ages. "If you make decisions based on the bottom line you might just miss the best solution," he said. "You spend whatever time it takes; you don't ask how much it costs. Architecture is only fun if there's some satisfaction on the other end."

Pei could afford sweet inefficiency so long as admiring patrons brought a wealth of unsolicited commissions to his door. When the inquiries tailed off, however, Pei was left without a steady diet of corporate work to sustain him through hard times. Smaller firms could survive the recession by accepting campus jobs or by designing the odd office building, but I. M. Pei & Partners was a hungry machine of one hundred fifty employees. It needed a prodigious workload. "Pei was interested in the jewels at the top," said office veteran Preston Moore, "but we never had a base of work to keep us going. It had become well known that you didn't hire Pei if you wanted to keep the job on budget."

Pei's fall from grace, combined with the withering downturn in the building economy of the mid-1970s, nudged him perilously close to the tar pits of insolvency. Pei's financial larder grew so bare during the 1970s drought that he struggled to make payroll and fell precariously behind in payments to various consultants on lighting, mechanics and other technical matters. Architects routinely delay outgoing checks until clients pay them, so an accumulation of arrears normally indicates no particular distress. But this time word spread through the office that Pei was unable to make good on his debts. Salaries were frozen and overtime work went uncompensated. "The firm was damn near bankrupt," recalled one senior associate. "It was terrifying."

Pei was not one to wring his hands in the face of adversity, though. His ingratiating, soft-spoken ways and his unimposing physical appearance disguised a strong will. "Pei can be as hard-edged as his buildings," said Robert Geddes, former dean of Princeton's architecture school.

Pei persevered in an Eastern way: he prevailed without overt force or intimidation. "Be possessed of the strength of the male," advised Lao-tzu, "but display the weakness of the female." The objective was to be like water—soft and passive, but strong enough to erode mountains. Pei himself flowed effortlessly through life, even in the face of physical danger. In the late 1950s, for example, he arrived in Hawaii with his administrative partner, Eason Leonard, to find that the first three floors of their Waikiki hotel had been evacuated in anticipation of a tidal wave induced by an earthquake in Chile. "I have to see this," Pei declared.

"So we did," Leonard said. "At three A.M. we stood in a totally deserted lobby stripped of furniture. We had received word that the tidal wave had hit the east coast of the Big Island a few hours earlier. Several people were killed. However, we were curious and determined to hold our ground until we saw what a tidal wave looked like. Our only protection was to hang on to concrete columns, and they were too wide to get our arms around. The wave arrived right on schedule in the form of a huge swell which sucked water out a thousand yards, exposing the surfing reefs. Then there was a sound like a locomotive, and the water rushed back. To our disappointment, it was not spectacular. It salt-watered the lawn, but it didn't reach us in the lobby. However, several days later the same wave hit the coast of Alaska with substantial damage, and a week later it hit Japan with major damage and loss of life. We were lucky—we just didn't know what we were dealing with."

Leonard remembered another dangerous situation Pei met with sangfroid. In 1970 he flew to Cambodia with Eileen, their daughter, Liane, and their friends the Salgos to tour the Hindu ruins of Angkor Wat, the intricately carved temple buried in the banyan jungle two hundred twenty-five miles north of Phnom Penh. They awoke one morning to find their hotel practically abandoned. A Communist incursion had seized the road leading to Phnom Penh, and a panicky evacuation was under way. Nicolas Salgo telexed the French ambassador, who advised them to flee westward. Abandoning their luggage, they squeezed into a hired car and drove a hundred miles down a hot, dusty road to the Thai border. The Salgos were clearly Western, but this was a grave juncture for the Peis: if their passports were confiscated, they could be mistaken for fleeing Cambodians. Pei nonetheless chose this moment to stop at a roadside fruit stand to sample durian, an Asian melon filled with a creamy pulp as rank as Limburger cheese.

The Peis arrived safely at the Bangkok airport and, after bathing in the bathrooms, flew on to Tokyo, where tailors replaced their wardrobes. "In two days they were elegantly dressed and on their way to Paris," said Eason Leonard. "They arrived slightly shaken but handsomely outfitted in their new clothes. I remember I.M. had the most natty coat; he looked dapper as hell."

Pei was equally composed in the face of professional peril, and he maintained his equanimity throughout his firm's difficulties. Fresh flowers had been an office tradition since Jackie Kennedy's famous visit, and bouquets still arrived on schedule. A uniformed maid continued serving coffee to visiting clients, and tuxedoed waiters poured champagne and carved roast beef on silver servers at the company Christmas party. "We tried to keep an even keel," said Eason Leonard. "We tried to keep spirits up."

Pei has always been adept at negotiating his way out of setbacks. His first rule was not to waste time on brooding and regret. "Be not ashamed of mistakes and thus make them crimes," Confucius advised. Instead, Pei employed a chess player's ability to think several moves ahead, to see beyond the small dips in fortune and focus on the next opportunity. In this case he knew better than to expect any major commissions in the United States. Encumbered with a staff of one hundred fifty that he was loath to dismiss, he began looking overseas.

Fortunately for him, the island of Singapore was then transforming itself from a colonial outpost into a prosperous Pacific Rim hub complete with subways, shopping malls and golf courses. Pei had entrée among the Singaporean bankers who knew his father. By the mid-1970s Pei was at work on a fifty-two-story headquarters for the Overseas Chinese Banking Corporation and an extravaganza called Raffles City that integrated a hotel, offices, a convention center and a shopping area. In addition, a wealthy Singaporean shipping magnate hired Pei to build a speculative office building overlooking New York's South Street Seaport. "One project after another started to come in from that part of the world," said Kellogg Wong, who supervised much of Pei's Far East work. "There's no question it allowed us to survive the troughs."

Pei also scouted for work in the Middle East, where OPEC profits were funding colossal desert complexes. "Pei and I were invited to Kuwait to judge a competition for a bank," remembered the architect Paul Rudolph. "For two or three days we did this, dining at the ministry of culture and so forth. I admired Pei for knowing all the government officials and talking to them all. At breakfast one morning I complimented him on this ability. 'You know what I was doing,' he said. 'I was thinking of where the next job is going to come from. I have all these people working for me, and I have to worry about that.' "

His reconnaissance paid off in Kuwait, where he built the Al Salaam shopping arcade, and in Iran, where the Shah's headlong pursuit of a European standard of living had led to a vast spread of offices and apartments called Kapsad covering thirty-six acres northwest of Tehran funded by an Iranian dentist turned cookie magnate. "The Iranians loved I.M.," recalled one senior associate. "They loved his sense of ceremony. He was a perfect reflection of Iran: he's incredibly devious, and he can negotiate his way through a storm. We were about to leave after negotiating a multimillion-dollar contract when at the last minute the client said, 'The only remaining issue is reimbursable expenses. We'll let some of you fly first-class, but not all.' We're talking about no more than a few hundred thousand dollars spread over many years, but they loved that Mickey Mouse stuff because it established hierarchy. Divide and conquer. Fight. Negotiate. I.M. looked at them and said, 'Nobody flies first-class.' It completely undercut them."

In Iran, as elsewhere, Pei attuned himself to the local sources of power. A fortune-teller approached his table one night as he dined with three associates in Tehran. The fortune-teller rolled brass dice across the table and divined a secret about each one—a heartbreaking teenage romance, a job offer, an extramarital affair. Despite their laughing denials, the pronouncements were surprisingly accurate. "This is a famous person," the fortune-teller said of Pei. "Very distinguished. Very talented. His real interest here is to meet the king and queen."

"Of course, I.M. vehemently denied it," one companion remembered. "He said, 'I'm here to help the country.' But everybody knew it was true. I.M. was dying to meet the Shah."

As excavation on the huge project got under way, associate partner Preston Moore, who by coincidence had once gone to school with the Shah, sensed gathering political unrest. After conferring with the U.S. ambassador, he advised his associates in New York to demand payment in full and get out. A short time later the Islamic Revolution swept the Shah from power.

· · · ·

Though overseas jobs helped keep I. M. Pei & Partners afloat, what Pei needed to rescue his imperiled career was an enlightened client committed to a spectacular public building. That savior appeared as if by a deus ex machina in the person of Paul Mellon, a cultivated patrician and a patron who was utterly impervious to the sticker shock that accompanied Pei's work. Mellon's Gulfstream jet conveyed him from his town houses in Washington and Manhattan to a four-thousand-acre horse farm in Virginia and to retreats in Antigua and Cape Cod. When the dunes on his oceanfront property struck him as deficient, he trucked in two thousand tons of sand. "*We* couldn't afford Pei," investment banker and Metropolitan Museum of Art president C. Douglas Dillon once told a Harvard official. "*You* couldn't afford him. But *Mellon* can afford him."

Mellon planned to build an addition to the National Gallery, which his father, the Pittsburgh banker and industrialist Andrew Mellon, had built on the Washington Mall. The elder Mellon had negotiated the terms of his gift while sipping tea with President Roosevelt in the White House library shortly before Christmas of 1936. Their agreement was that Mellon would pay for the gallery and stock it from his own atticful of masterpieces, many of which he had shrewdly acquired when the Soviet Union needed hard currency after the revolution. The gallery would operate as a bureau of the Smithsonian maintained by federal funds but governed by an independent board of trustees.

Mellon and Roosevelt agreed on this rare mix of public ownership and private control during a discussion described as cordial but strained. Mellon was exactly the sort of financial baron New Dealers abhorred—FDR himself called them "malefactors of great wealth." As treasury secretary to three Republican presidents he had presided over spending cuts and tax reforms that were beneficial to corporations and stockholders. Mellon consequently found himself the victim of what he termed "a campaign of character-wrecking and abuse." In January of 1935 the Internal Revenue Service, which Mellon himself had once governed, accused him of tax evasion (the charges never stuck).

Mellon's flamboyant defense attorney, Frank J. Hogan, disclosed his client's gift to the nation in his opening remarks before a crowded Pittsburgh courtroom. "God doesn't place in the hearts and minds of men such diverse and opposite traits as these," Hogan told the room while Mellon sat nodding in approval. "It is impossible to conceive of a man planning such benefactions and at the same time plotting and scheming to defraud his government."

When the time came for Mellon to decide what sort of gallery to build, he shunned the modern style that was overtaking the country. He felt that a literal classicism was the only acceptable vocabulary for an institution residing in the bosom of official Washington. "Mr. Mellon felt that people, especially in America, have a need for buildings more magnificent, more spatial, and less utilitarian than the apartments and small houses they usually inhabit," wrote John Walker, a childhood friend of Paul Mellon's who became gallery director.

Mellon consequently hired America's leading practitioner of Beaux-Arts classicism, John Russell Pope, whose portfolio included the Jefferson Memorial and the richly decorated National Archives building, to design an Ionic temple with a domed rotunda, porticos and fountains, sweeping stairs and barrel-vaulted corridors. It was the last great essay in classicism, a temple to antiquity baptized on the eve of modernism.

The long months of planning sapped Andrew Mellon's strength. After a few fainting spells and a fall resulting in a cut chin, he agreed to escape the summer heat at Bonnie Dune, his daughter's Southampton home. He was pleased to see that excavation was under way as he rode down Pennsylvania Avenue en route to a private railroad car waiting for him at Union Station. That casual glimpse was his final inspection. He died of bronchial pneumonia at Bonnie Dune on August 26, 1937, two months after the groundbreaking ceremony. Pope died the next night in Newport, having postponed a cancer operation in order to complete the drawings for what he hoped would be his masterpiece.

The $65 million collection Mellon left the gallery was the largest individual gift ever bestowed on any government, and it included works by the most exalted names in Western art, from Turner to Titian, El Greco to Botticelli. If the collection was big, the gallery was far bigger. When it opened on a frigid Saint Patrick's Day 1941, all of Mellon's painstakingly accumulated masterpieces filled only five of the one hundred thirty-five rooms sprawled along two lengthy blocks. A joke went around suggesting that the guards were hired to guide visitors from one artwork to the next.

The gallery didn't stay empty long, though. In an astonishing gesture of modesty, or farsightedness, Mellon had omitted his name from the entablature. The patriotic implications proved a powerful enticement; those who might not have donated to the *Mellon* gallery gave generously to a *national* gallery. Within thirty years the collection had grown from a nucleus of 133 pieces to more than 30,000, all privately donated.

Fortunately, Andrew Mellon had anticipated the need for expansion. His deed of gift stipulated that Congress reserve an adjacent patch of swampy land at the foot of Capitol Hill, where early congressmen had paused to shoot ducks en route to the White House.

By the 1960s these nine grassy acres, occupied by nine tennis courts, were the last undeveloped spot on the north side of the Mall. Gallery director John Walker began to worry that Congress might renege on its pledge and assign it some other use, so he steered Mellon's son, Paul, outside for a look. "If we don't use that land," he warned, "someone's going to take it from us." Walker recounted how his mentor, the esteemed art historian Bernard Berenson, exhorted him upon his appointment to build an American center of learning comparable to the ancient library at Alexandria.

"Yes, that's a good idea," replied Paul, who succeeded his father as gallery president. "How much will it cost?" Twenty million dollars was Walker's estimate. Mellon pledged half, so Walker consulted Mellon's sister, Ailsa Mellon Bruce.

"Paul thinks it's a good idea," she said. "You think it's a good idea. I'll give you ten million too."

Having planted the seed of what came to be known as the East Building, Walker left the planning to his protégé, J. Carter Brown, a deputy director slated to succeed him in 1969. Brown was a lanky, curly-headed scion of one of Rhode Island's founding families (Brown University was named after an eighteenth-century ancestor) and a precocious young scholar with a hyper-buoyant manner. He expressed his many enthusiasms in the lock-jawed cadences of Groton, where he had graduated first in his class at age sixteen, and Harvard, where he was summa cum laude and Phi Beta Kappa. Like Walker, Brown had spent childhood summers on Fishers Island, an old-money enclave off the eastern tip of Long Island. Also like Walker, he had studied art history at I Tatti, Bernard Berenson's villa in Florence.

Brown embodied New England–bred aristocracy, but he also belonged to an emerging generation of curators eager to democratize the dark, musty repositories of past riches frequented by privileged patrons on rainy Sunday afternoons. Nationwide museum attendance had quadrupled during the National Gallery's first twenty-five years as a growing college-educated audience blessed with leisure time stormed the gates of culture. Art viewing had become a great American pastime, and Brown hoped to accommodate this new constituency without sacrificing scholarly standards.

No curator reshaped a museum for popular appeal more sensationally than Brown's New York counterpart, the adventuresome Thomas P. F. Hoving, a young medievalist and former New York City parks commissioner who was installed as director of the Metropolitan Museum of Art in 1967. A self-confessed publicity hound (he joked that his middle initials stood for Publicity Forever), the youthful Hoving enticed the largest possible audience by livening up the old hallways of contemplative silence. Under his tempestuous tenure the moribund museum became a bustling theater of activity, a place of diversion as well as enlightenment. He paid colossal sums to acquire masterpieces, drafted a master plan for expansion into Central Park, introduced pop and minimalism and hyped unconventional shows like *Harlem on My Mind* with glittering opening-night parties.

Hoving attracted unprecedented crowds: his first year surpassed previous attendance by more than a million. Sixty-two thousand spun the turnstiles on a single record-breaking Sunday. Hoving begat a new breed of museum, box-office conscious and merchandise-savvy, in which the actual viewing of art was only part of the experience. After wandering through exhibits equipped with recorded tours and explanatory placards, visitors swarmed around display cases stocked with Egyptian pottery, postcards and the familiar Winslow Homer prints, or lined up at cafeterias and movie theaters.

"The museum has very largely supplanted the church as the emblematic focus of the American city," critic Robert Hughes observed. "In doing so, it has adopted, partly by osmosis and partly by design, the strategies of other mass media: emphasis on spectacle, cult of celebrity, the whole masterpiece-and-treasure syndrome. Only by these means can it retain the loyalty of its unprecedentedly large public, or so it thinks."

For all his gentlemanly polish, J. Carter Brown was a determined competitor and, armed with a degree in business administration from Harvard—a credential his predecessors had never found necessary—he was eager to shed the National Gallery's reputation as a sedate dowager of old masters and challenge New York's supremacy in the visual arts. He had a lot of catching up to do. Washington has always been a provincial city of transient bureaucrats with no permanent community of wealthy donors to enrich local institutions. Brown hoped to compensate by taking full advantage of the capital's diplomatic ties as well as his own social connections. He was willing to play lobbyist and diplomat to bring the gallery up to date and lure spectacular shows from abroad. "Washington," he wrote, "is still something of a sleeping princess in terms of scholarly exploitation."

Brown also had to overcome the gallery's deep-seated conservatism. Its marble hallways lined with ancient pictures embodied the unhurried, unchanging nineteenth-century museum. The longtime director, John Walker,

was an unabashed elitist. He believed that "the success or failure of a museum is not to be measured by attendance but by the beauty of its collections
and the harmony of their display." Rather than antagonize politicians like
Representative George Dondero, who had denounced modern art on the floor
of the House as a Communist plot, he confined himself safely to the past. For
years the gallery had refused works by artists who had been dead less than
twenty years; it acquired Picassos and Matisses up to about 1940, but very
few of more recent vintage.

The proposed East Building conveniently suited Brown's ambitions, for
there was no better way to win patrons and boost attendance than to build a
high-profile showcase of institutional grandeur. If the National Gallery was to
be an anthology, Brown told trustees, its collection should not stop at some
arbitrary point. The East Building should extend the collection to include definitive modern works. And the building itself should be a self-confident declaration that the gallery was at last entering the twentieth century. "The
original gallery is wonderful," he said, "but America finally has enough confidence to build in its own style."

Brown needed an architect who could navigate the arduous politics required to insert a distinguished modern edifice in a city that resisted all but
the most lackluster modern buildings. Where would Brown find an architect
who could bring Washington up to the present? In 1967 he solicited a dozen
portfolios, which he compiled into a small exhibit for the trustees who, in
turn, whittled the list down to four: Louis Kahn, Philip Johnson, Kevin Roche
and I. M. Pei.

Kahn was already designing a gracious gallery to house Paul Mellon's vast
collection of British art in New Haven, directly across Chapel Street from
Kahn's brick addition to the old Yale Art Gallery. The Yale Center for British
Art was arguably closer to Mellon's heart than the National Gallery, for he
was, by his own description, "a galloping Anglophile." He had begun col-

lecting English hunting prints and illustrated books while at Cambridge University, not as an investment but as a reflection of the British countryside he loved. While the rest of the world vied for French Impressionists and Picassos, Mellon quietly acquired the most systematic assemblage of eighteenth- and nineteenth-century British art outside London's Tate Gallery.

Kahn enshrined Mellon's collection in a gallery as urbane and understated as the patron himself. It is a masterpiece of serenity and sunlight, at once intimate and grand, organized around two fifty-six-foot-high courtyards and sheathed on the exterior in slim panels of unpolished stainless steel. "On a gray day it will look like a moth," Kahn said. "On a sunny day like a butterfly." *Time* critic Robert Hughes called it "a four-story box, dedicated to light: a building without gimmicks or stylistic narcissism, low-key but explicit, whose pale concrete, blond wood and natural linen wall coverings provided a strictly subordinate background to the paintings. This unpretentious exactness of taste was much in keeping with Mellon's general style of philanthropy: the ambition being, in a phrase often heard by the curators and museum directors who have dealt with him, to do it right, and not skimp, but within budget."

Although the Yale Center for British Art was one of the most revered museums of recent times, Kahn was never a serious candidate for the more visible National Gallery job. As a professor at Yale and later at the University of Pennsylvania, he developed an idiosyncratic architectural philosophy based on his infatuation with ancient forms: "I asked the brick what it liked, and the brick said, 'I like an arch.' "

Architecture's deep-thinking oracle, however, was grievously incapable of selling himself. He never learned to mask his personal awkwardness and baffling wordplay, and uninitiated patrons found him flaky. Nor did his portfolio inspire confidence, for Kahn concentrated on places of reflective congregation, like synagogues, churches, laboratories and classrooms instead of the obvious emblems of architectural success, like skyscrapers and corporate office buildings. Having absorbed the scale and shape of antiquity while attending the American Academy in Rome, he favored big, hefty forms built of humble materials like concrete, brick and wood. They were not serene or pretty in any conventional way.

"When we invited architects to submit their work, Kahn was a disappointment," Brown said. "He didn't pursue it with much vigor. I suppose he expected that people would have seen his work in the Middle East and La Jolla, but that didn't give me much to work with in terms of the trustees." Nor was Brown impressed when he climbed the dark stairwell to Kahn's Philadelphia studio, located above a cigar store, where casually dressed acolytes worked among old furniture and cheap partitions. "He had some sidekicks," Brown recalled, "but he didn't seem to have any organization. He was the perfect poet for a small, Yale-sized museum, but not for the overwhelming programmatic requirements we were considering."

As with the Kennedy Library, Pei excelled in all the ways Kahn failed. He was an acknowledged master of propriety backed by an impressive Madison Avenue studio bustling with a refined corps of ambitious young architects. While Kahn was a rumpled Jewish intellectual and academic, Pei associated himself with clients like the Kennedys, the city governments of Dallas and Boston and the Christian Science church. His discreet geometries embodied high-toned civic architecture: they were bold but never disconcerting, striking but well mannered. And they came with Pei's famous knack for diplomacy and protocol. It didn't hurt that Pei's wide circle of friends included the columnist Joseph Alsop and *Washington Post* publisher Katharine Graham. "Kahn and Pei were alike," said architect Robert Stern, "but Kahn was an outsider. . . . Pei was an aristocrat."

Mellon, Brown and trustee Stoddard Stevens embarked in Mellon's private jet to see Pei's work for themselves. His candidacy grew stronger at every stop. "Each of his buildings demonstrated his ability to solve one of our problems," Brown said. At the unfinished Everson Museum in Syracuse, they saw four cantilevered blocks of reinforced concrete surrounding a courtyard. The rhythmic play of solids and voids inspired Brown to write Pei a letter comparing his composition to the movements of a quartet. "It's not a large building," he later said, "but it has majesty. Visitors understand they're in a special place."

If Everson proved Pei could design a work of art encasing art, his deferential addition to Eliel Saarinen's Des Moines Art Center showed that he could add to a museum without upstaging it. Indeed, Pei's addition is virtually invisible from the entrance.

The coup de grâce came at the National Center for Atmospheric Research where they inspected laboratories and picnicked with Dr. Walter Roberts on the surrounding mesa. "We were blown away," Brown recalled, "by the urge to go into those carrels and start studying. The forms had an unerring sense of proportion and scale—monumental but user-friendly. Paul Mellon has a laconic manner he inherited from his father. He turned to me and said, 'Carter, I'm impressed.' I knew then that Pei would be it."

Brown invited Pei to Washington to meet Mellon. The patron greeted them at the door of his Whitehaven Street home and, bypassing more formal rooms, led them to a round corner table beside French doors overlooking a garden, exactly the spot Pei himself might have chosen. Pei was "an easy sell," Brown said. "Architect and patron struck up a quick rapport. Both are sons of emotionally detached bankers. Both are a bit reticent. The chemistry was super; they just hit it off. I.M. must have known this was a seminal moment in his career."

Mellon chose Pei, and the trustees followed with their pro forma blessing in July 1968, thereby duplicating Andrew Mellon's decision, made three decades earlier, to build in a conservative style associated with institutional America.

▲

Paul Mellon, J. Carter Brown and Pei

inspect the finished atrium.

Pei now inherited one of the most irregular patches of real estate produced by Pierre L'Enfant's 1791 city plan: a trapezoid where the axial reach of Pennsylvania Avenue converges at an awkward 19.5-degree angle with the green longitudinal thrust of the Mall. Building an ungainly wedge burdened with three facades and no backside would normally have posed no problem for the facile Pei, but this was the last in a procession of showy Mall-side monuments after which visitors looked up to the Capitol dome. Its privileged site among seats of power demanded a monumental flourish. "My own father warned me," Brown said, "make sure it doesn't look as if the National Gallery had a pup."

The site required monumentality, but it also demanded modesty. After all, it would be unseemly for the new kid on the Mall to call too much attention to itself. "I was unnerved by it all," Pei later confessed, "but especially because the Mall is full of tradition and sacred to so many Americans."

"This," he told associates, "is probably the most sensitive site in the United States."

If these weren't obstacles enough, Pei also had to find a graceful way to stitch his new building to its older sibling. "From the beginning, I.M. argued that the old gallery was closed and complete, that we shouldn't add to it," Brown said. "I.M. is very intuitive, and he understood that Paul grew up in his father's shadow. Paul wanted to differentiate his own building from his father's. But somehow they still had to be integral."

Pei is neither a distinguished draftsman nor a theoretician. He has instead a rare ability to assemble labyrinths in his mind and rotate the parts until they fit. He can lead elaborate tours of buildings that do not exist, even on paper. "If you're not able to draw in your mind, you're not able to tackle these problems," he once explained. "They are too complex. You've got to train your mind to see space. When you have two lines you have a plane; when you have three lines you have space. You've got to see it."

Pei's visceral gift allows him to digest a client's needs—what architects call "the program"—and translate them, often right on the spot, into a three-dimensional revelation, which he releases across the boardroom like a balloon for all to admire. "He can sit down and listen to a group of people talking about a building project and can then summarize in one or two minutes the basic conceptual idea that would solve the client's problems," said architect Ulrich Franzen. "I think that's how I.M. wins a lot of his major commissions. He walks into a board of directors meeting, listens to what they have to say, and then says, 'This is what you need.' "

The challenge for Pei is to "find the essence." He sometimes tunes out in the middle of conversations. A glazed expression comes over him. A woman who served on jury duty with Pei once saw him tracing lines in the air, oblivious of his surroundings. It is a fitful, even anguished process: "I get into a great inner turmoil when I have to find the right design for a building. It absorbs me completely, and I can't think of anything else. This may be a matter of hours or it may take as long as a month of sleeping badly, being irritable, sketching ideas and rejecting them. I am useless to everyone else. It is traumatic for my wife."

After a few weeks of distracted inner debate, Pei usually produces a quick, crude sketch containing the gist of an idea. He drew the concept for the Everson Museum, for example, on a napkin while lunching with Eason Leonard.

Pei's solution to the complicated demands of the East Building site came with a few Euclidean strokes of a red ballpoint pen unsheathed for some in-flight doodling on a return flight to New York shortly after his appointment. "I sketched a trapezoid on the back of an envelope," he said. "I drew a diagonal line across the trapezoid and produced two triangles: one for the museum, the other for the study center. This was the beginning."

Pei entrusted his sketch to two of his brightest young lights: Yann Weymouth, then married to *Washington Post* publisher Katharine Graham's daughter, Lally; and William Pedersen, a talented Minnesotan whom Pei had

▼ **The axial reach of Pennsylvania Avenue**

converges with the mall, producing

one of the city's most irregular patches

of real estate.

met while serving on the jury that awarded Pedersen the Rome Prize, a sabbatical in Italy conferred on one young architect each year. Pei summoned Pedersen for a job interview upon his return from Italy, and they became so engrossed in talk that Pei waved off his secretary, Leicia Black, when she warned him of an impending appointment with the National Institute of Arts and Letters. "Oh, that isn't important," he said, and resumed the discussion. Pei thus conscripted Pedersen into the royal guard of favored employees who help convey his diagrams into concrete.

As was often the case, there was something indisputably right about Pei's triangulations, as if they were the only possible plan for the place. "I.M. didn't even need to see the site model," Pedersen recalled. "He knew exactly what he wanted to do. He presented us with a diagram that was challenged only briefly. Its logic seemed incontestable. . . . From then on, the scheme assumed a life of its own. It was just a question of working it out dimensionally."

The ingenuity of Pei's plan lay in its ability to echo the neoclassicism of Pope's Roman temple without stooping to literal imitation. The wide side of the larger triangle became a broad post-and-lintel entrance sympathetically facing its older counterpart across a four-acre courtyard warmed by a door-to-door carpet of cobblestones. Facades of father and son thus faced each other from a respectful remove, separated by one generation and a revolution in style. They were joined by means of a subterranean concourse—a couple holding hands under the table.

Pei perpetuated the Mall's longitudinal thrust by tapering the nestled triangles to a wedge aimed at the Capitol. "The new building, whatever the style of architecture, has to recognize the axis of the old building," he explained. "You see, the axis of this entrance and the axis of the Pope building actually line up. From that point on, it takes on its own life."

While the East Building upheld the prevailing classical order, it was unmistakably its own self, a smooth prismatic iceberg anchored at three corners by diamond-shaped towers protruding like upturned table legs. Although Pei might never acknowledge it, his gallery building re-created the dramatic spatial progression of churches. One entered beneath a low narthexlike entryway and advanced from a compressed introductory space into a giddy, eye-popping atrium, the high-flung equivalent of a Gothic nave animated by staircases, bridges and what Brown called Romeo and Juliet balconies. This lofty court was Pei's answer to Pope's central rotunda, but it also suggested the uplift of Victorian train stations, John Portman's soaring hotel atriums and Frank Lloyd Wright's Guggenheim Museum, a favorite weekend haunt of the Pei family.

Unlike Pope's oak-paneled rooms, arranged for solemn encounters with old masters, Pei's East Building is a pulse-quickening bit of multilevel crowd manipulation in which oversized abstract artworks stand among the viewers. "The building has to be designed in such a way that young people will find it interesting to go there," Pei said. "Otherwise the whole purpose is lost; they will spend five minutes there and then go to the Air and Space Museum to look at the moon rocket. This is our problem: you have to think in terms of the public."

Pei's scheme was a chancy departure. He could find few triangular buildings in architectural history books, and for good reason. While conventional orthogonal space advances toward clear vanishing points, like an altar or a staircase, triangles offer *three* perspectives. Pei worried that multiple vanishing points might produce a disorienting, kaleidoscopic space in which each wall would read as a continuation of another. "Pei was nervous about it," Brown recalled. "He'd never done a triangular building before. The wide end tends to be a horizontal space and the narrow end tends to be a vertical space. The visitors, therefore, are driven into a corner. I.M. said he couldn't sleep at night until he saw the model. I.M. has as near a perfect visual pitch as anyone I've met, so I didn't worry too much."

Besides, Brown found the unsettling perspectives appropriate for twentieth-century art. "The theory of relativity emerged at exactly the same time as the birth of Cubism," Brown wrote. "Our world, then, is one of multiplicity and simultaneity, and our approach to it assumes not one point of reference but many."

Triangular space was hard to visualize, so Pei recruited a gifted illustrator named Steve Oles who, as an undergraduate, studied at Texas Tech under professors who still taught the discredited art of Beaux-Arts drawing. On this and many other projects, Oles served as Pei's insightful pencil. Once or twice a day he translated the team's progress into lifelike renderings that stimulated further rounds of refinement. The team huddled around his drawings until someone proposed an alteration and the others followed, Oles said, "like a school of fish."

Carter Brown felt that even hard-core museum visitors grow foot weary within forty-five minutes. He therefore gave Pei the paradoxical job of accommodating a mob scene while preserving the intimacy of the European house-museums he loved. "Large art needs large spaces," he said, "but I think art looks best in the home or chapel it was designed for." To illustrate his point, Brown took Pei on a three-week museum marathon, from Greece to Denmark. "I.M. has enormous energy," Brown recalled. "He wanted to see everything. But not at the expense of lunch hour."

The most inspiring museum was Milan's Poldi Pezzoli, the home of a nineteenth-century collector who had furnished his small, exquisite quarters with Renaissance paintings, porcelain, clocks and bronzes. "Carter said, 'Wouldn't it be wonderful if our museum could be like that?'" Pei remembered. "Of course it had to be twenty times the size of that museum, yet somehow we continued to come back to it to see if it was possible to create a very large museum with small spaces within it." Pei's answer was to tuck three self-contained Pezzolis into the corners of the triangular atrium and link them with

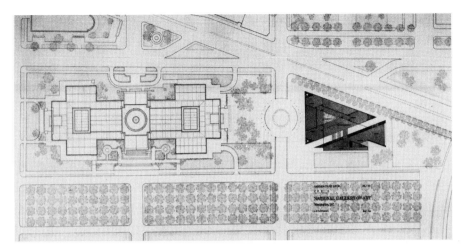

▲

Pei perpetuated the mall's longitudinal
thrust by tapering the nestled triangles
to a wedge.

"I drew a diagonal line across the

trapezoid and produced two triangles,"

Pei said. "This was the beginning."

▼

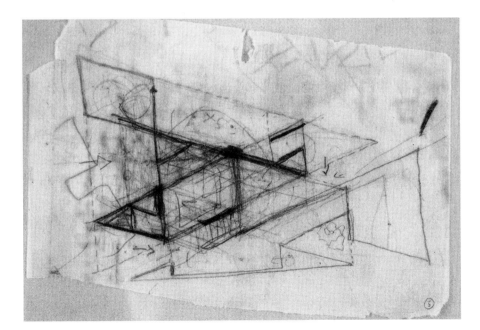

bridges and balconies. These human-scaled galleries, or "pods," were small enough to offer visitors digestible shows, after which they could return to the light-filled atrium refreshed and ready for something new.

Pei submitted all this to the trustees in 1969. Afterward Pei retreated to a stone bench in the West Building rotunda while his protégés paced the marble floor. They had cause to be nervous: there was nothing obvious or easy about the scheme the trustees were debating behind closed doors, and Pei had no way of knowing what sort of reaction lay beneath Paul Mellon's famously impassive demeanor. Fortunately Pei had a persuasive advocate in Carter Brown. After an agonizing wait, Brown emerged wearing a broad smile: the trustees had approved the design in toto. Pei's entourage decamped to columnist Joseph Alsop's home to celebrate. There Pei sipped champagne and, in his excitement, sketched his plan on a yellow legal pad. Alsop later sent the page to Pei with an inscription: "In memory of a happy afternoon." Pei returned the drawing with a rejoinder: "This sketch clearly shows the effects of bottles of Dom Pérignon—and what vintages!"

Having cleared the first hurdle, Pei's proposal advanced to the Commission of Fine Arts, Washington's arbiter of architectural taste, which approved it in February of 1970 by a four-to-two margin. The dissenting votes were cast by Aline Saarinen, widow of Eero Saarinen and a *New York Times* art critic, and the commission's chairman, William Walton, Pei's ally throughout the long Kennedy Library ordeal. "The building is a beauty—strong, subtle, imaginative, a marvelous combination of all the qualities I have long admired in your work," Walton wrote Pei by way of explanation. "What worries me is its height. . . . Both Archives and the National Gallery dome are higher, it is true, but the silhouette of your new building is entirely different. It is a strong unbroken line at the cornice, whereas the others are both broken, varying in shape and mass, giving an overall impression of lower height.

"I feel that the new building," he continued, "will be a harsh, over-assertive terminus to the long line of buildings leading toward the Capitol whose environs are a very touchy matter, both aesthetically and politically."

"Your criticism about the excessive height of the design does not surprise me," Pei answered, "for the problem has been a matter of great concern to us from the very beginning. The final resolution, however, is the result of a great deal of deliberation."

Many Washingtonians failed to see the virtues of an unconventional design that departed so radically from the bland neoclassical diet to which they were accustomed. Congressmen and their staffs mourned the loss of a much-loved plot of open space with tennis courts at the foot of Capitol Hill. Even the gallery's planning consultant, David Scott, used to park his car and stare at the site, trying to imagine the structure's finished form. "It was very hard to visualize the sheer elegance of the building," he acknowledged.

Pei might have faced another public relations disaster had it not been for a vigorous endorsement from Ada Louise Huxtable, architecture's most influential critic. "The rigid rule of mediocrity through uneasy compromise with an uncertain past that has characterized the best and worst of Washington construction in our day will be broken by the new East Building," she promised shortly after the plan's 1971 unveiling. "Let's go even further: it can be a great building for all time."

10
A BUILDING FOR
THE AGES

After three years of planning, Paul Mellon turned the first spadeful of dirt at a midday groundbreaking for the East Building on May 6, 1971. Pei and Eileen sat on folding chairs one row behind William Mann, a local builder hired to manage construction. "I turned to Pei and I said, 'I.M., why aren't you up on the stage?' " Mann recalled. "He said, 'This is Mr. Mellon's day. My day will come later.' . . . Pei introduced me to his wife, and he said, 'This is the man who will make my dreams come true.' He knew how to make a slave, you see, real quick."

It was a daunting challenge to build Pei's irregular geometries. The plans contained not a single right angle above ground. The triangle had become an obsessive motif—one critic called its proliferation "Pei-nful"—dictating even the smallest details: columns, ceiling panels, bathroom tiles and stairs. Even the doorframes and elevators were installed on a bias. It was hard enough to reconcile all those diagonal lines on paper; to build them required pinpoint precision. "It caused a chaotic condition among the carpenters," Mann recalled. "They're used to working with tools that are made for rectangles, not triangles. So our surveyors had to lay out everything for everybody—all the electricians, the mechanical people, everything—because none of them had the expertise to lay out a triangle.

The East Building atrium, a central court animated by staircases, bridges and Romeo and Juliet balconies.

"I felt that I had to do something to generate accuracy," he added. "How do you motivate a union guy? He gets paid the same amount whether he does a lousy job or a good one. . . . That's why I took them all over to see the model and pointed out their part in it, and pointed out to them how proud they would be that they had a part in the structure. It was in a room off a gallery. I remember the painting on the wall outside was of the matador who's lying there dead [Edouard Manet's *The Dead Toreador*]. I told them, 'That's a picture of the project manager by the time the job's done.' "

Excavation began before Pei's team finished its design. As a result, the plans changed and evolved throughout construction. The pressure to stay one step ahead of the builders provided what project manager Leonard Jacobson called "a little extra battlefield excitement."

Mann called Pei's plans "funny papers" because "they were so incomplete that it was very difficult to get the idea of what he was trying to do without having talked to him. . . . We felt that we were always pushing I.M. for more information. We weren't getting it fast enough! From his standpoint, his designs were very complicated, very innovative, and they took time."

Mann visited Pei's office as often as twice a week to solicit details. "These meetings we would have were well orchestrated," Mann said. "Pei would often make models of what he proposed. He would talk to the structural engineer ahead of time to learn if there were any pitfalls along the way so he could modify it. By the time he brought it up at a meeting, he'd already done his homework. He would say, 'Can you build it?' I'd turn to the structural engineer and say, 'Can you design it?' He'd say yes. I'd say, 'If you can design it, I can build it.' "

In the 1930s, John Russell Pope had delegated the job of selecting the West Building's rose-colored marble facing to a young architect named Malcolm Rice who had demonstrated a sure eye for subtle hues of stone while supervising the construction of the Jefferson Memorial and other Washington landmarks. Rice inspected each slab extracted from the hills of eastern Tennessee and assigned its location so that the gallery walls grew imperceptibly lighter as they progressed upward from the base to the shell-pink dome. The calculated gradation avoided a patchwork effect and created a subliminal air of solidity.

Thirty-five years later Rice came out of retirement to perform the same task for Pei. Now in his early seventies and sporting a thatch of silver hair, he reopened dormant quarries to find that many of the twenty-one gradations he had originally chosen among were no longer to be found. He spent five years painstakingly grading the remaining hues and assigning each piece a location. Workers quarried the specified slabs with equipment left over from the 1930s and trucked them to a mill where saws sliced them like bread. Rice signed each finished piece before sending it north.

The slabs Rice had quarried for the West Building at the tail end of the Depression were a solid foot thick. Not even Paul Mellon could afford such heft in the inflationary 1970s. Instead, Pei hung three-inch marble cladding on brick bearing walls. To fortify the illusion of solidity, each precisely cut panel slid snugly into its predetermined place like a jigsaw piece with a mere one-eighth inch to spare on each side. These slim sheathings were more likely to swell and shrink than the heavy pieces next door, so Pei cushioned the interstitial spaces with specially developed neoprene strips—a crucial innovation, since Pei's vast stretches of smooth, unmodulated marble contained no pilasters or moldings to hide expansion joints. Pei upheld the fiction by wrapping carefully cut pieces around the sharp exterior corners where conventionally mitered joints would have betrayed the thinness of the sheath.

Even thin marble was too costly to use throughout, so Pei resorted to exposed concrete for the floors and long trusses spanning the atrium. Concrete was considered a crude material prone to unsightly cracks and disfigurements, but Pei's in-house technicians had learned to execute blemishless sculptural forms from this messiest of materials over a series of poured-in-place experiments dating back to Kips Bay Plaza. They now summoned decades of mastery to produce surfaces that, if not identical to adjoining marble, at least approximated its gleam.

Poured concrete, like Jell-O, duplicates the texture of its mold. Because every blemish produces a permanent flaw, cabinetmakers sanded, oiled and polished thousands of feet of clear-grained Douglas fir as painstakingly as if it were a parquet floor and fashioned it into molds. These exquisite vessels, with mitered corners and parallel grain, qualified as works of art in themselves. Most were discarded after a single use.

On pouring day the watercooler was removed to ensure that no paper cups contaminated the mix. Workers unfurled protective tarpaulins, cleaned their shoes and inspected the molds for stray coffee cups and cigarette butts. Mixing trucks then filled the molds with white cement blended with pink aggregate and marble dust in proportions carefully gauged to duplicate the color and texture of adjoining marble. As the mixture hardened, workers dislodged air bubbles by pounding the sides of the molds with wooden mallets and by inserting giant vibrators into the mixtures. To everyone's relief, glistening, luxurious pink surfaces emerged. (Ten years later Pei required the Louvre's contractors to match the quality of the East Building's concrete. At his insistence French foremen flew to Washington to inspect the handiwork.)

After six months of tinkering, Pei decided that the heavy coffered ceiling he had originally sketched was too claustrophobic for an almost windowless atrium of heavy lintels and uninflected walls, so he replaced it with a vast skylight—"a bunch of jackstraws thrown into the sky"—covering more than one-third of an acre. It was enormous, and enormously complex: hundreds of odd-shaped interlocking panes were suspended more than seventy feet above the floor. The space-frame itself was a major undertaking, requiring months of consultation between architects and engineers. Within this glazed canopy Pei embedded heating wires capable of melting the heaviest snowfalls and tiny neoprene gutters to lead rainwater into drains concealed behind walls.

To prevent ultraviolet light from damaging the art, Pei invented a sunscreen of tubular aluminum louvers which, unlike the ordinary flat variety, cast a consistently soft, undifferentiated shadow. A diffused light now bathed the pink walls from above and played across a canopy of potted trees, transforming the atrium into a continuation of the adjacent Mall. "Bringing the garden inside is very much an Eastern tradition," Pei said.

A smaller skylight would have emphasized the atrium's enormity by comparison. Pei paradoxically made the gargantuan space seem smaller by capping it with a skylight of vast proportions. "It was a problem to make the skylight look effortless and fit into that geometry as though it were born into it," said William Pedersen. "The sobriety of the exterior volume can be off-putting. The skylight lightens it up and switches the scale to the four ficus trees. The trees not only warm the room by populating it, they also perform the same role as the baldachin over the altar in Saint Peter's: they provide an intimacy within a much larger space."

Improvisations were under way at the bottom end of the building as well. Machines excavating the subterranean concourse burrowed among a forest of pilings supporting the old gallery and a tangle of utilities buried beneath Fourth Street, including a thirty-inch water main, telephone cables and a 33,000-volt electrical line, to connect with the lobby of the West Building.

With its auditorium, lecture hall, loading docks, storage rooms, cafeteria, gift shop and garage, the concourse was an entire two-story building embedded in the mucky remains of Tiber Creek, an old swamp at the foot of Capitol Hill. In fact, the water table was so high and the bedrock so deep that Pei was forced to design the entire East Building as a watertight vessel moored by forty-foot steel cables to prevent it from floating away in spring rains.

Because the sodden ground discouraged deep excavation, the concourse became a low-ceilinged tunnel. Pei originally planned to brighten it with skylights set within a circular reflecting pool. That idea fell by the wayside, and he searched for an alternative until, in 1974, junior designer J. Woodson Rainey proposed seven glass pyramids protruding from the plaza with water cascading down a rough slope to the cafeteria below. ("See what you started?" Weymouth kidded Rainey when Parisians attacked Pei's pyramid ten years later.)

Pei labored to make the whole intricate affair look simple. Fresh air, for example, inconspicuously entered between the wall and the atrium skylight and escaped through ducts tucked discreetly under the lip of each staircase tread. Four ficus trees occupied marble planters equipped with their own watering systems and drains. The top of the reception desk slid open and a closed-circuit TV camera rose like a periscope to scan for after-hours intruders.

"Is it Miesian?" the young designers asked of every innovation, referring, of course, to Mies van der Rohe, author of the famous adage, "God is in the details." To be Miesian, then, was to pursue the elegant imperatives of pure geometry down to the finest degree. The 19.5-degree angle on which Pei based the building made a difficult imperative to obey, and it was sometimes upheld at the cost of convenience, as in the diamond-shaped columns that ran through the offices. "You expect me to hire curators with triangular heads," Brown jokingly told Pei, "to fit into the triangular offices."

Brown urged Pei not to "crucify himself on a pattern nobody would understand." But for Pei, executing the geometry the right way, *all* the way, was a moral obligation. "Architecture must have integrity," Pei said, "like a friend."

"The design team was forever coming up with some bright new idea that set the whole construction back six months," said planning consultant David Scott. As a result, only about 30 percent of the building was completed by 1973, forcing the trustees to postpone the opening from 1975 to 1976 and, once more, to 1978. "If Damon Runyon thought watching America's Cup races was like watching grass grow, he never had the opportunity of watching, day-to-day, the seemingly immutable silhouette of anything as internally complex as the National Gallery's building project," Brown wrote in the gallery's annual report. "Using Pierre L'Enfant's eighteenth-century city-plan geometry as its leitmotif, the design of the new building, with its cubistically interlocking spaces, gradually began to take shape in a welter of rebars, forms, trusses and conduits that had the apparent logic of Kandinsky."

Building progressed despite what Brown called a "diabolically clever" succession of strikes staged in such a way that they hampered all but a few weeks of the seven-year construction period. Work nearly halted altogether in 1975 when waterproofers, cement mixers, operating engineers, field survey-ors, painters, building laborers and concrete-truck drivers all walked off the job when their contracts expired, followed by the stonemasons, bricklayers and marble setters. The strikes, combined with the princely materials and the militant Miesianism, contributed to a debilitating money crunch with one-third of the building still to go. Mellon was among the richest men in America, and he might have absorbed the prodigious overages had it not been a period of wildly escalating construction costs, raising to 40 percent the total increase since Mellon had broken ground in 1971.

Something had to be done. In 1974, Mellon hired Hurley Offenbacher, a construction manager who had built the Air and Space Museum across the Mall in just three years, to sort things out. Offenbacher arrived to find the East Building a leviathan adrift. Three years after groundbreaking, there was no schedule or coherent budget. "The initial estimate was based on so many unknowns," explained Bill Mann. "There were entire sections of specifica-tions that in effect said, 'You bid it and invent it and we'll pay you.' "

Offenbacher submitted a new budget based on his own estimates of un-written specifications. "I waited for the bomb to burst," he said, "because it was twenty-five million dollars more than expected, but they took it calmly— more calmly than I would have."

Nonetheless, Offenbacher's appraisal shocked the trustees into soliciting Pei's help in trimming costs, and he obliged by scaling back here and there: he laid a terrazzo floor in the concourse, for example, instead of marble, and he replaced stainless-steel trim in the study center with aluminum. Up until then, Pei had received a percentage of construction costs, an arrangement that theoretically discourages architects from curbing expenses. He now reluctantly agreed to a flat fee.

These incidental cutbacks failed to satisfy trustee Stoddard Stevens, a tough Wall Street lawyer and shrewd guardian of the bottom line to two generations of Mellons. Rather than shave nickels, Stevens wanted to postpone the study center until they knew how much money remained. Mellon uncharacteristically overruled his financial adviser and proceeded with Pei's original vision on the theory that spiraling costs would make the study center three or four times more expensive at some later date. "We were past the point of return," Brown recalled. "I.M. said, 'Let's do it right. This is for the ages.' " So Mellon persuaded the family foundation to provide the extra millions.

At $94.4 million, the East Building would be by far the National Gallery's priciest acquisition to date and one of America's costliest public buildings— far costlier on a square-foot basis than its Washington neighbors. The Hirshhorn, across the Mall, had cost a mere $16 million. Even the Air and Space Museum was a comparative bargain at $34 million. The new FBI building had cost $129 million, but it was four times the size. "With I.M.," went the inevitable joke, "you Pei and Pei and Pei."

"Ninety-five million dollars does seem like a lot of money," Mellon acknowledged. "But, after all, we're not building a resort hotel or high-rise office building that will be torn down in twenty years. We're building a *museum,* something intended to last forever."

So the project continued intact, but not without suffering a bout of public criticism for its extravagant price tag. The building would have to be sensational to justify its budget, even though it came from Mellon's pockets, and so far nobody could tell what lay behind its parapet of scaffolds. "During its seven years of construction many of us had misgivings about the East Building," wrote *Washington Post* critic Wolf Von Eckardt. "What had seemed so dazzlingly clever on the cardboard model grew to seemingly monstrous proportions. Had we been blinded by architect Pei's brilliant geometry? . . . In clear light there were moments when the huge stark pink Tennessee marble sculpture seemed threatening. It seemed abstract and alien, coldly unrelated to the familiar temples along the avenue and an insult to the picturesque majesty of the Capitol in the background."

After reading about the design in the *Washington Post,* one reader predicted that it would prove to be "the ugliest building in all history." Director Pontus Hulten of the brash new Pompidou Center in Paris pronounced it "too elegant," and editor Charles Peters of the *Washington Monthly* called it "the aesthetic crime of the century."

"Those of us who have watched it rise day by day during the past three years have had our moments of doubt," wrote the *New Republic.* "When it was half built, it seemed too heavy, squat, almost an affront."

On April 26, 1977, Pei's staff presented him with a sixtieth-birthday cake baked in the shape of the building's fused triangles. It was an apt gesture, for Pei remained confident that his geometry would prevail. "I.M. kept saying, 'It's like a teenage girl with braces on her teeth. Wait until the scaffolding comes off,' " remembered J. Carter Brown.

Sure enough, the rude noises gave way to gathering anticipation as the main silhouette of Pei's flying wedge took shape between Pennsylvania Avenue and the Mall and the horrifically complex construction wound down.

The telephone switchboard was the first new space to go into official use in May 1976, followed by the cafeteria, which served a menu planned in part by James Beard to more than 30,500 visitors on the bicentennial Fourth of July weekend. By year's end the exterior walls had risen to the roofline, and the following February workers cleared the site, allowing the first unobstructed view of the building's pink walls and knife-edged angles from all sides. Meanwhile, librarians boxed 300,000 books and a million photographic images in precise categories in preparation for "the move."

The East Building at last resembled a finished building, but it would not be a gallery until the art arrived. The transformative moment was of crucial importance to Pei, since art, particularly the postwar abstract art slated for permanent exhibit, was a subject close to his heart. No modern architect, with the exception of Philip Johnson, has involved himself in the visual arts more than Pei.

Almost every Saturday he and Eileen toured the New York galleries. When he was away or too busy to go, she went alone and reported what she had seen. Over the years they cultivated friendships with gallery owners Leo Castelli and Arne Glimcher, and such artists as Jacques Lipchitz, Louise Nevelson, Al Held and Isamu Noguchi. Barnett Newman's widow, Analee, has been described as a surrogate grandmother to Pei's four children.

Pei had gone out of his way to install works by Moore, Calder and Picasso beside his buildings long before every charmless corporate plaza contained the obligatory abstract sculpture. There was nothing perfunctory about Pei's impulse; he felt that abstract sculpture had the capacity to enrich large-scale modern architecture in a way that figurative sculpture could not: "Contemporary buildings have a very big scale, a scale that sculpture of Rodin's tradition can't satisfy. Take a sculpture like Rodin's *Burghers of Calais*. You can't blow it up to three or four times the size. It would look grotesque. There is a limit to the size of a human form. Even Michelangelo's *David* looks ungainly, almost grotesque in the Piazza della Signoria in Florence. . . . It's abstraction that makes the very large size possible, although it might have been inspired by the human figure or by the skull of an elephant, as in Henry Moore's case."

Pei believed that architecture needed art. They had, after all, enjoyed a cozy cohabitation for most of their history. Pei may also have sensed, consciously or not, that abstract sculpture counterbalanced his own geometric severities. In any case, it was natural for Pei to join Carter Brown in selecting a dozen large-scale works by the surviving masters of modern art to add incident to the East Building's vast expanse of stone.

As hard hats tore down the East Building's interior scaffolding in November 1977, twenty packing crates arrived containing pieces of a huge Alexander Calder mobile. After inspecting a model of the East Building in April 1972, Calder had pointed to a spot just inside the entrance. "I'd like to put something right here," he said. In a single evening he fashioned a delicate wire maquette of a mobile to dangle from the atrium ceiling. It was to be his largest such effort, three stories high and seventy-six feet wide.

But when Brown, Pei and consultant David Scott visited the Tours factory where workers were fabricating the piece from steel pipes, they discovered that it would weigh five thousand pounds and would therefore be too heavy to rotate in the internal air currents. "I was terribly disappointed," Pei said. "It almost looked heavy enough to support the building." Documentary filmmakers brought along to record the happy occasion captured instead worried glances and furtive consultation.

They decided to withdraw the project from the Tours factory and turn it over to Carter Brown's Harvard roommate, Paul Matisse, grandson of Henri and an artist in his own right, who lightened the piece to 980 pounds by replacing the steel with honeycombed aluminum. Calder approved a maquette based on Matisse's technique. At lunch afterward Calder gave David Scott a

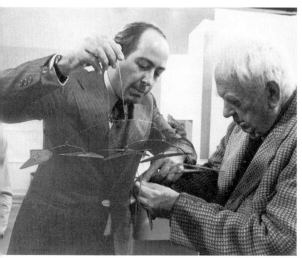

◄

Paul Matisse, LEFT, and Alexander Calder.

▶

Installation of Calder's mobile, November

18, 1977. "I can't imagine this space with-

out it," Pei said.

◄

Henry Moore and Pei discuss one of the

sculptor's reclining pieces.

long slow wink and a smile. Calder died of a heart attack eight days later, leaving Matisse to install his last and largest work. Matisse spent most of a day arranging the twenty crates in precise locations around the floor according to nineteen pages of handwritten notes while photographers and filmmakers documented the event. Matisse issued his final instructions to workmen late that afternoon. They hoisted the mobile's arms and wings to an aperture affixed to the skylight and adjusted air ducts to nudge its petals and arms into orbit for the first time. "I can't imagine this space without it," Pei said.

A few days later clouds of sparks burst forth from a ledge above the doorway leading to the study center as British sculptor Anthony Caro supervised welders affixing strips of straight and curved steel. "He was directing it like an orchestra conductor," said David Scott. "He was standing up in the mezzanine trying to adjust his sculpture to the building as this piece went here and that piece went there. . . . In one terribly dramatic moment he threw up his arms and said, 'Take it all down.' " Caro finished the *National Gallery Ledge Piece* ten days later, just before the opening.

Caro's welding sparks flew precariously close to Joan Miró's one-ton tapestry woven as a textural counterpoint to the high, stark south wall. Isamu Noguchi's twelve-foot obelisk of Japanese basalt, entitled *Great Rock of Inner Seeking*, assumed its sentinel position in the triangle's apex, and the building filled with other permanent pieces by Jean Arp, David Smith, James Rosati and Robert Motherwell.

Pei had a particular affinity for Jean Dubuffet, whose writhing, distorted sculptures counterbalanced his own cool geometry. He persuaded Brown to commission his artistic opposite to fill the prominent niche on the front alcove beside the entrance. Dubuffet, a natty figure with a shaved head and a precise manner, arrived from Paris to inspect a cardboard model of the building. "He looked and he looked and he looked," Pei said. "He crumpled some paper up and put it in front of the model. He looked again and measured the size. He said, 'All right.' And he left."

Pei and Brown visited Dubuffet's Paris studio a few months later to inspect half a dozen whimsically grotesque figures waving and gesticulating beside a mock-up of the gallery entrance. *The Welcome Parade* struck Pei as an inspired counterpoint to the solemn marble surroundings. "Washington was so staid, especially then," Pei said. "The building was also very restrained because it had to be a part of Washington. I thought it would be wonderful to have something light. . . . Sort of like a circus. 'Come one, come all.' "

Brown did not share Pei's enthusiasm, however, in part because he was responsible for upholding the gallery's image as a serious institution before the trustees and legislators who determined its day-to-day funding. "There's an acidic quality to Dubuffet's work," he said. "The entrance to a great national pavilion needs something uplifting, not these cynical personages. It gave the wrong vibes for that spot." The trustees agreed that this Dubuffet was too sardonic; in a closed-door meeting they voted it down. *The Welcome Parade* was never built, but its maquette stood for some years in a pool outside the building's north wall.

By the late 1970s every cultural institution in the country seemed to have a prominently displayed Henry Moore sculpture. Pei tried to avoid this cliché by diverting Moore's *Spindle Piece* to the Pennsylvania Avenue side of the building. Moore arrived to inspect the site with his daughter, *New York Times* art critic John Russell and Gordon Bunshaft while Pei was at the University of Virginia receiving the Thomas Jefferson Memorial Medal. "It will get no sun there," Moore complained to Pei associate Thomas Schmitt. "No piece of sculpture should be without sun." Sure enough, Moore's daughter suggested they walk around to examine the front of the building. "No, I should have the piece here," Moore said. That night Schmitt called Pei out of a dinner held in his honor at the University of Virginia to convey Moore's reaction. "To tell you the truth," Pei said, "we *have* been looking for something to anchor that side of the entrance." After combing through Moore's catalog, Pei asked the sculptor if he would be willing to produce a larger version of *Knife Edge Two Piece*, which sits in a park near the Houses of Parliament in London. "Why not!" Moore said. "Let's look at it."

At fifteen tons, the enlarged version, *Knife Edge Mirror Two Piece*, was Moore's largest sculpture. His foundry cast the slightly smaller half in bronze, crated it in molded Styrofoam and shipped it without mishap. Its plumper companion had to be trucked to the dock on the Sunday morning roads. By the time it reached Southampton, a dock strike had halted all shipping, so the movers trucked it to Liverpool instead, knocking down several streetlights and road signs along the way, and deposited it aboard a Baltimore-bound ship.

Workers were rigging the 27,998-pound piece in a girdle dangled from a blue crane in preparation for Moore's arrival when a taxi pulled up and Pei embraced the passengers. Photographers closed in, assuming Moore had arrived. The couple turned out to be concert pianist Byron Janis and his wife, Maria (Gary Cooper's daughter), whom Pei had invited to test the building's acoustics. Just then a sturdy figure with rolled-up sleeves and a walking stick strolled across the plaza. "Welcome, Henry!" Pei said.

Moore conferred with the crane operators and ducked inside where Janis was playing Moussorgsky's *Pictures at an Exhibition* on a Baldwin baby grand while Pei raced around sampling the acoustics. "I.M., I think you've built yourself a concert hall," Janis said.

"If so, it's just a fluke," Pei said. "It's probably because there are no parallel walls to make the sound bounce back and forth."

"I would call this building the perfect example of rubato," Janis said. "It's a musical term for 'give-and-take.' If you have one phrase with 1-2-3-4 and you do 1-2 quickly and 3-4 slowly but have them end in the same time, that is rubato."

"It means," Pei interjected, "freedom within discipline."

Meanwhile, Moore had taped the precise spot beside the entrance where his sculpture should land. The crane operators somehow maneuvered the mammoth piece into place while the sculptor bustled about brandishing his cane. They repeated the entire procedure the next day with the smaller piece.

All the commissioned artists were, like Pei, prestigious, costly and safely established. They nonetheless represented something of a departure from past policy, and their arrival did not pass unnoticed. Chief Justice Warren Burger, who chaired the gallery's board, recalled his reaction to Alexander Lieberman's *David:*

> Every morning as I came down to the Court I would have my driver slow the car a little bit so I could see what the status of the development was. I noticed that as we were finishing there was some abstract art on the Pennsylvania [Avenue] side of the building. I wrote a letter to Paul [Mellon] . . . and said, "Dear Paul, I know the building is almost finished and we'll soon be dedicating it to the public. Perhaps you don't see the side of the building that I do every morning as I pass, but the building contractor has left a pile of air-conditioning vents, and we ought to remove those before we go to the final."
>
> I knew of course that they weren't air-conditioning vents. This is some of this alleged art that the abstract people inflict on the public. . . . Paul wrote me and said that if I realized how much the donor of that piece of abstract sculpture had done otherwise for the gallery, and that he hoped would continue to be doing in the future, I would not press the matter too much!

All of Washington was by now waiting in suspenseful anticipation of the opening. The East Building claimed the covers of *Esquire, Smithsonian* and a special edition of the *Washington Post* magazine, which bragged that the new gallery would make Washington an "Athens on the Potomac."

The expectations swayed earlier skeptics, including Wolf Von Eckardt, who retracted his earlier reservations and published an outright rave less than a month before the opening. "I. M. Pei's architectural Hallelujah," he wrote, "reminds me of the joyful white and gold domed naves of Bavarian baroque churches, where swallows twitter and swoop through theatrical sunbeams. It is that evocative. . . . My guess is that in contrast to most modern buildings, Pei's East Building, like Verdi's operas, will be instantly popular."

Art critic Hilton Kramer of the *New York Times* added his voice to the gathering endorsements: "Entering the great hall of the East Wing one is made to feel a tremendous sense of confidence in the culture and the civilization it symbolizes. It is a thrilling experience, and I suspect that it will fill the hearts of all but the stoniest skeptics with a feeling of pleasure for a long time to come."

On the evening of May 30, 1978, Paul Mellon and his wife, Bunny, stood on a red carpet that had been unfurled across the atrium floor and welcomed two hundred artists, collectors and local luminaries to a black-tie dinner kicking off three days of celebratory parties and previews. The room filled up with famous names: Robert Motherwell, Willem de Kooning, Helen Frankenthaler, Betty Parsons, Katharine Graham, Joseph Alsop, the widows of Jackson Pollock and Barnett Newman, Walter Annenberg, Armand Hammer, Jacqueline Onassis, and, of course, Eileen Pei and I.M. himself, who received unrelenting rounds of congratulations. Hurricane lamps and candles cast shadows against the marble walls as white-gloved waiters served champagne and platters of pâté en croûte and filet of beef among twenty-five triangular tables decorated with small Calder sculptures. Pei sat grinning between Bunny Mellon and Jackie Onassis.

"Not the least of these great masters [on exhibit] is I. M. Pei," Mellon told his guests after dinner, "inside whose monumental contemporary sculpture you are all sitting at the moment—a very contemporary work of art indeed." Afterward, Pei jumped from his seat to introduce a mysterious "guest," who turned out to be Benny Goodman. The musician and his orchestra then played a dance concert arranged by Bunny Mellon as a surprise for her husband, who loves swing as passionately as he loves thoroughbreds and paintings.

Pei was the celebrity of the hour, and he returned the next day to eat a cannelloni lunch on the study center's fourth floor with one hundred fifty curators and collectors, then descended to the mezzanine to greet First Lady Rosalynn Carter who was hosting a tea for the wives of visiting NATO leaders. That night he attended a party for the inaugural exhibit, *The Splendor of Dresden,* featuring eight hundred rarely seen porcelains, suits of armor and paintings borrowed from East Germany. It was exactly the sort of blockbuster show Brown had envisioned for the East Building: a diplomatically sensitive loan deftly secured through social and political connections.

All of the preliminaries conferred an air of grand occasion on dedication day. On June 1, a standing crowd packed the plaza between the buildings and 2,500 invited guests sat in folding chairs fanning themselves with programs while the Marine Corps Band played a Sousa march. Mellon closed his brief remarks with the same words he had used to dedicate the West Building thirty-seven years earlier: "This building is the product of many minds intent on giving America their best, and we are happy to turn it over to you, Mr. President . . . to be dedicated forever to the use and enjoyment of the people of the United States."

President Jimmy Carter snipped the ceremonial ribbon that was stretched across the doorway and signed the guest book as the first official visitor. Af-

◄

The installation of Moore's KNIFE EDGE MIRROR TWO PIECE. LEFT TO RIGHT: J. Carter Brown, Eileen Pei, Henry Moore, I. M. Pei.

▼

Dedication Day. LEFT TO RIGHT: J. Carter Brown, Paul Mellon, Bunny Mellon, Jimmy Carter, Joan Mondale, I. M. Pei.

ter pausing to admire the gently gyrating Calder, the president took a twenty-minute tour. "First impressions are very important," Pei told him. "They should give visitors an enjoyable time, and then they will come back again."

After Carter's brief visit, guards flung open the doors and the waiting populace rushed inside. "In an instant, it seemed, visitors had thronged into the courtyard and up to the various levels, searching out all the perspectives and patterns, experiencing the spaciousness, savoring the works of art," said J. Carter Brown. "It was wonderful to see the caps thrown in the air, because we hadn't known what to expect."

Few buildings in history have courted such a reception. Its opening became a national event, like a space launch or a presidential inauguration, and people arrived in equivalent droves to walk among the building's odd vectors and rich effects. More than a million passed through its low vestibule in the first seven weeks to gaze up at the red-and-black Calder rotating playfully in that airy Piranesian space flooded with shifting daylight. Pei's choreography drew them in and led them up staircases and escalators, across the Romeo and Juliet balconies and in and out of the galleries.

The irony of it all was that the East Building pleased the public at a time when "modernism" had become a dirty word. Guards reported that visitors were reluctant to leave at closing time. In what became a ritual of visitation, people lined up to stroke the 11-degree marble prow, known as "the point," to the right of the entrance. After decades of unhappy resignation to monotonous slabs, the public jumped to celebrate an exuberant public building with an interesting shape. Philip Johnson explained it thus:

> As we have become impoverished in our external
> architecture by the lack of decorative motifs our
> forerunners could use—steeples, pointed and unpointed
> arches, and the like—we have turned to other modes of

expression. Since there are no structural limitations today like the lintels of Stonehenge or the Parthenon, we can warp or carve or tilt our buildings the way we will. A wonderful example comes to mind: the fantastic gouges and the slithering angles of I. M. Pei's National Gallery addition—majestic, playful, abstract sculptures.

The critics spouted a surprising flood of hosannas and hyperbole for a building that stood safely back from the advance guard of architectural thinking. Unlike the recent Pompidou Center and Yale Center for British Art, the East Building was deliberately unprogressive. "It does not break ground," acknowledged Ada Louise Huxtable, "it deals in established excellence." Its charm derived from a mature Pei bringing his geometries into sharp focus: they are massive yet gracefully proportioned, discreetly detailed with every advantage extravagant funding can provide. The result is a cool, somewhat distant institutional elegance with a hint of the Beaux-Arts exuberance of Pei's early schooling in its ceremonial sweep and powerful staircase. By humanizing modernism, Pei charted what appeared to be a stable path for the coming decade, and the critics greeted it as a welcome respite from the din and confusion of the sixties and seventies.

In a review headlined "Masterpiece on the Mall," *Time* critic Robert Hughes wrote: "I. M. Pei has produced, in the fullest sense of that hackneyed but unavoidable word, a masterpiece—a structure born of sustained and highly analytic thought, exquisitely attuned to its site and architectural surroundings, conveying a sense of grand occasion without the slightest sense of pomposity. It restores the sense of craftsmanship, as distinct from routine fabrication, without which major architecture cannot exist."

In the fickle kingdom of architecture, however, popularity often comes with a price. "Pei was a natural target because of the establishment, high-profile nature of his work," Philip Johnson said. "You can't be the respected senior citizen without being the target to shoot at."

Sure enough, the accolades did not continue unchallenged. By fall a gathering militia of critics had broken the euphoria with a backlash of doubts over the East Building's merits as a museum. Head counts don't prove a building's worth, they said, any more than box office measures a movie's quality. Pei's happy-making atmospherics were accused of upstaging the art, just as a spectacular set might distract attention from the play. "After the excitement of this space," Paul Goldberger wrote, "that building has given us its all, and the art itself is left to be squeezed into the corners."

Arbiters also maligned Pei for offering the architectural equivalent of easy gratification—a sugar rush in marble. In his zeal to popularize art, they said, Pei had turned a connoisseur's sanctuary into a consumer event. His gallery was variously described as "the poshest of suburban shopping malls," "a superluxurious transit-lounge" and "a collection of planes and masses in search of a building." *Architectural Review* called it an "artistic terminal building" in which "your baggage is not tumbling off the carousels when you reach the atrium, you are not in an airport or a shopping mall, but, believe it or not, in a space ostensibly intended for the quiet contemplation of works of art."

Like the Guggenheim and the Pompidou Center, the East Building was accused of indulging in gratuitous self-drama. "How will people think of that building fifty years from now?" asked architect Paul Rudolph. "Is it too much like an airport? In traditional architecture the flow of space is clear. In Gothic cathedrals, for example, it leads to the altar. In this case, there's lots of movement, but does it lead anywhere in a coherent fashion?"

In 1939 the Museum of Modern Art had opened its doors as a neutral, self-effacing container for art. "Forty years later," the architect and essayist Witold Rybczynski observed, "I. M. Pei relegated the world of art to the background and gave center stage to an unusual angular atrium with a huge glass roof and zigzagging escalators. It's no coincidence that the East Building has become one of the most popular tourist attractions in the capital. Museums now have an imperative other than pure aesthetics: in order to survive, they must attract greater and greater numbers of visitors, and flashy architecture is one of the draws."

The most caustic verdict of all came from Richard Hennessy, who, in a review published in *Artforum*, decried its "shocking fun-house atmosphere" and "deeply philistine unseriousness."

When Pei was at Harvard, Dean Hudnut derided the musty old West Building as "the last of the Romans." But now, with classical details returned to fashion, the pendulum of opinion swung back in its favor. Why, commentators asked, hadn't Pei learned more from its dignified procession of paneled rooms?

Nobody was more displeased than John Walker, the gallery director who had launched the entire affair before nursing a quiet regret in retirement. As an old-school curator, he deplored the vulgar pandering to tourist obligations and the bald betrayal of the scholarly standards that he held to be the art museum's most sacred trust. "As I write these words," he admitted on the last page of his memoir, "I beat my breast and say, 'Mea culpa, mea culpa, mea maxima culpa.' For it was I who proposed the enlargement of the National Gallery of Art. But museum directors are incorrigible. Once they begin spending Other People's Money they will never leave well enough alone."

11

VINDICATION

While Pei was pouring his energies into the East Building, architecture was undergoing a radical change induced in part by his rival Louis Kahn. Kahn never built anything as elaborately debated as the East Building. He lost that plum to Pei, and his pursuit of other big commissions proved similarly unavailing. Although revered by fellow architects, he never duplicated Pei's success at securing the blockbuster jobs that forge public reputations. As a result, he built surprisingly little until a late spate of work appeared in remote corners of the world. At an age when other architects lay down their pens, he embarked on grueling excursions to supervise projects in the Middle East and Asia.

In March 1974 he missed a flight home from India, where he had gone to lecture and inspect the construction of his India Institute of Management in Ahmadabad, and he was forced to fly to New York via Bombay, Kuwait, Rome and Paris and then return by train to Philadelphia in time to teach his Monday morning class at the University of Pennsylvania. Kahn went to the men's room in Penn Station that night and dropped dead of a heart attack. His family was unaware of his improvised itinerary, and his body lay unclaimed for two days. It was later revealed that he had died several hundred thousand dollars in debt. "Thus the end of a man whom many considered the world's greatest living architect was strangely anonymous and even martyrlike," wrote *Art in America*.

◄ **Pei seated in the Shizilin garden. His companions could only guess at the emotions at play beneath his mild demeanor.**

It was fitting that Kahn died en route to his students. He was a charismatic teacher, and his classes at Yale and Penn inspired a generation to explore new ways of thinking at a time when established architects purveyed zestless corporate modernism long after the style's original conviction had diminished to a faint glow. Kahn helped end that banal era and showed the way to postmodernism by guiding his cult of admiring students back into history. Although Pei would continue to espouse modernism, he too was indelibly influenced by Kahn. The East Building marked the arrival of a humanized modernism.

As a young professor, Kahn had traveled through Europe sketching ancient ruins in Rome, Pompeii, Athens and Delphi. At home he was an elfin figure who stood before his students in his rumpled suits and bow ties talking nonstop in a thin, reedy voice about the need to recapture the powerful variety of ancient forms grounded in the fundamental issues of shelter and light. He urged them to rethink architecture not from Volume One but from "Volume Zero," the edition that "precedes shape, it is the source."

"He broke the models," the Yale architectural historian Vince Scully once observed, "and set his strongest students free."

One former student, a then unknown Philadelphia architect named Robert Venturi, delivered the sharpest jolt the profession had absorbed in half a century by publishing, in 1966, an antimodernist manifesto entitled *Complexity and Contradiction in Architecture*. Venturi's ringing indictment unhatched a Pandora's box of suppressed grievances against a movement that had broken its promise to make the world beautiful. The early 1970s saw a spate of books, like Peter Blake's *Form Follows Fiasco*, chronicling the damage inflicted in the name of modernism. In 1975 the Museum of Modern Art mounted an exhibit of exquisite drawings and renderings produced at the Ecole des Beaux-Arts in Paris. It was as if the curators were recanting all the museum had done to popularize the modern movement.

Just as Pei's generation had rebelled against the Beaux-Arts, a new generation having been forced to kneel at the altar of Mies and Le Corbusier in turn rebelled against a landscape of second-rate modernist knockoffs and hastily constructed rectangular glass towers. "Architects can no longer afford to be intimidated by the puritanically moral language of orthodox modern architecture," Venturi wrote. "I am for messy vitality over obvious unity. . . . I am for richness of meaning rather than clarity of meaning."

The economic slump of the mid-seventies forced architects of Venturi's generation to support themselves by teaching until building resumed. The campus thus became the incubator of uninhibited alternatives to modernism. Liberated from the constraints of real building, young talents like Frank Gehry, Peter Eisenman, Robert A. M. Stern and Michael Graves dreamed up a campy hilarity on paper. From architecture's musty basement they disinterred forgotten details like plinths and mullions, and combined them in a glib pastiche that came to be known as postmodernism. "It starts from failure," explained Charles Jencks, its most ardent champion among the critics, "and then asks what is left to enjoy, to salvage." It wasn't long before barrel-vaulted entrances, stick-on columns, pedimented roofs and polychrome keystones sprouted from skylines like flowers in a time-lapse movie. A public long deprived of color and form welcomed the spectacle.

Postmodernism achieved its clearest measure of public legitimacy when *Time,* the arbiter of mainstream taste, put Philip Johnson on its January 7, 1979, cover after he adroitly abandoned modernism, the style he had introduced to America forty years earlier, and reinvented himself as the author of the first postmodern skyscraper, the controversial AT&T Building in New York. The cover photo showed Johnson holding a model of the building which, costumed with an arched entrance and a much-discussed Chippendale crown, symbolized the new appetite for the visually exciting. "We stand at an enormous watershed," Johnson said in accepting the AIA's Gold Medal in June 1978. "We stand at a place where maybe we haven't stood for fifty years, and that is a shift in sensibility so revolutionary that it is hard to grasp because we are right in the middle of it. It is the watershed between what we have all been brought up with as the modern, and something new, uncharted, uncertain and absolutely delightful."

If Johnson had nimbly maneuvered to the fashionable side of the watershed, Pei remained encamped on the other. Long after the ideological ground shifted beneath him, he maintained a quiet dedication to his restrained brand of institutional modernism, an aesthetic that might, in its mature form, be described as a rigorously engineered lyrical geometry. "Pei's approach was absolutely perfect for the corporate office building of the fifties through the seventies," said architect Robert A. M. Stern, "when the expectation was a chilly, imposing aesthetic. 'Cold' was an adjective of praise. 'Austere' was good. Then came postmodernism, when buildings were asked to be engaging, to charm people, to cuddle them. Pei is not professionally inclined to work that way. He rarely discusses human considerations."

The lone march was a familiar condition for Pei. He had always maintained a certain detachment. When Philip Johnson used to gather the leading practitioners at his glass house in New Canaan, for example, Pei played his cards conspicuously close to the vest. He volunteered nothing. "He never played ball," said Robert Stern. "He's aloof. He would never commit himself to any opinion that could be construed as controversial. One feels he's always sitting there plotting what he's going to do next."

Pei maintained a fastidious personal distance as well. He did not join Johnson, Frank Gehry, Richard Meier, Peter Eisenman, Robert Stern, Charles Gwathmey and Michael Graves at the all-male black-tie dinners held every few months in an upstairs library at the Century Club. Nor did he participate in the notoriously bitchy dialogue conducted over hundreds of luncheons at Johnson's corner table in the Four Seasons Grill Room, New York's premier power restaurant. "It never crossed our minds to invite Pei," Johnson said.

"He doesn't encourage you to include him in a discussion about architecture. Anyway, our group didn't consider him a design influence."

It would not be unusual at these events to hear the architectural gadflys bad-mouth Pei for purveying middlebrow corporate gift-wrapping, for advancing no movement save the perpetual refinement of conventional modernism and for avoiding campus discourse. "He has made a point of not declaring himself ideologically," said his partner Henry Cobb. "He has stood aside from it totally. For a major figure, the absence of theoretical statements or any kind of record other than his buildings is remarkable."

Pei, for his part, regarded Johnson and his protégés as couturiers of fashion. Their immoderate pronouncements, petty intrigues and turgid architectural blather offended his Chinese sense of modesty, discretion and continuity. "A truly understandable person does not have to explain himself," Lao-tzu once said. "A truly illustrious person does not have to publicize his fame, and a truly respected person does not have to praise himself."

Moreover, postmodernism's stylistic caprice revived all the old specters of Beaux-Arts tradition—faux historicism, pandering to a nouveau riche clientele, superficial packaging—that Pei's generation had struggled against. "After the First World War, there was a battle to break out of the nineteenth-century tradition," he told *Art in America*. "We have won that battle. I don't believe in constant, perpetual revolution. In the last several years, of course, we've had a recession. Not much building has been done. This has given architects, particularly young architects, a chance to think about these issues of modernism and postmodernism—to experiment—which is well and good. I think it's necessary. But I look at architecture, especially big movements such as modernism, as being like a tree. There are those who think that this tree is not going to last very long because it is built on rather weak stock. Others take the view that it's going to be a long time before it runs out of steam."

The East Building was Pei's rebuttal to all those who dismissed him as the last spasm of a desiccated movement, a throwback to the days of high-rise slabs and sweeping concrete plazas. By replacing modernism's biggest yawn—the glass box—with what he called "a passionate geometry" Pei showed that it was possible to provide a picturesque, sensuous experience without stooping to false nostalgia and historic schmaltz. The visitors who lined up outside the East Building seemed to vindicate him—here was modernism with a friendly human face, and it was a bull's-eye.

Meanwhile, postmodernism lost much of its luster when its highly publicized monuments, like Philip Johnson's AT&T Building and Michael Graves's Portland Public Services Building, spawned their own shoddy knockoffs. The eclectic mishmash of historical styles no longer seemed witty or inventive after developers burdened every mid-sized city with tacky crypto-Egyptian shopping malls and faux-Renaissance office towers. By the early 1980s the postmodern riffing began to fall flat and arbiters of taste slowly recoiled from its overrich displays. "Plain has been replaced by fussy, the bland by the tricky, and the merely dull has given way to the actively annoying," wrote Ada Louise Huxtable. "When modernism is bad, we have been told over and over, it is very, very bad; but when postmodernism is bad, as the nursery rhyme goes, it can be horrid."

As the wheel of architectural fashion turned once more, Pei emerged for the better for having resisted the seduction of decorative indulgence. His East Building has been called the first late modern building, and its clean, elegant abstraction helped promote a new appreciation of the maligned style. Modernism would never reclaim its position of central authority, but the disintegration of dogma allowed a more complex, mannered version to persist alongside other historical styles. It even regained a bit of bravado. "It does one thing that's good," Pei said of postmodernism. "It makes many architects look back and say, 'Now, let's not be so uptight. Let's have a little fun. That battle is won, now let's search further; let's relax a bit.' That's good. I'm certainly not one to belittle previous generations. I owe a great deal to them, just as the young today owe something to us."

Despite the critics, the East Building redeemed Pei's reputation. Six months after it opened, the American Academy and Institute of Arts and Letters elected him the first architect to serve as its chancellor, an appointment that signaled his acceptance as a cultural laureate. In June 1979 he received the AIA's Gold Medal, the highest accolade awarded by his peers. In his acceptance speech, Pei played the role of conciliatory elder statesman offering his colleagues—he specifically named Philip Johnson—an olive branch:

> Today the values which inspire those who have stood in this
> place before me seem to be in doubt, and architecture
> appears to be in two worlds. I do not mean the world of
> modern architecture, which I do not believe is dead. Nor do
> I mean the world of what is called postmodern architecture.
> Instead, there seems to be the world of practice and the
> world of ideas, each in alienation from the other. . . . Today
> the schism that exists between the two confuses and divides
> the profession. While I believe that ideas and practice are
> complementary, I reject the notion that the world of practice
> and the world of ideas require two different sets of skills,
> insights and temperament—indeed, two different kinds of
> people. They belong together in one world of architecture.

Twenty years after Frank Lloyd Wright's death and ten years after Gropius and Mies passed away, there was little doubt that Pei had assumed the role of America's most famous living architect. "When I went to architecture school in the 1960s architecture was dominated by three or four great masters, like Kahn, Le Corbusier and Saarinen," said Witold Rybczynski. "Then they all died or fell out of favor. Somebody from the next generation had to be elevated to their position, and Pei seems to be the one who has achieved that level. How that happened is a complex question."

The East Building secured Pei's place as a socially connected, politically adept architect favored by the establishment—a latter-day Stanford White. "It erased the stigma and opened a whole new era," said Eason Leonard. "We were standing toe to toe with our competition again. We were on the rise again. Pei became the number one seed." Johnson & Johnson bravely hired him to design its New Jersey headquarters even before the East Building proved to be a runaway success. Nine months after the gallery opened, New York state and city officials picked him to build a $375 million convention center on five dilapidated blocks beside the Hudson River, the largest municipal project since the World Trade Towers and a symbol of the city's recovery from the brink of bankruptcy. Corporate clients then returned to Pei in hordes; Arco, Pitney Bowes and IBM (which had summarily abandoned him a few years earlier) all commissioned major buildings. "Once the East Building opened, things were never difficult again," remembered designer Karen Van Lengen. "The office just blossomed. It carried I.M. into a different realm. It made him into a little god."

Pei restored himself just in time for the overheated 1980s, a decade in which the design field enjoyed a rush of popular attention far beyond its traditional upper-crust constituency. After Philip Johnson graced the cover of *Time* in 1979, some of his young protégés were transformed into celebrities by a flood of glossy new design magazines and galleries that displayed their paper architecture. Middle-class consumers who could not afford a "name" architect could at least participate vicariously by collecting Michael Graves renderings or Richard Meier coffeepots.

The rising tide of design consciousness buoyed Pei up along with the rest, but the shift in emphasis from buildings to personalities altered the alchemy of his fame. Architects have their own revolving lineup of deities, only a few of whom attract much notice outside the profession. Pei somehow transcended intramural recognition to become not just famous but publicly familiar in the manner of those inducted into *Vanity Fair*'s pantheon of celebrityhood. He beamed from the cover of the *New York Times Magazine* beside the headline, "The Winning Ways of I. M. Pei." His name appeared in boldface in gossip columns alongside mentions of Jacqueline Onassis, the Kempners, the Buckleys, the Kissingers and the rest. There came to dwell in the popular imagination an image of Pei the personality: a cultivated sprite swathed in the glamour of accomplishment warming famous clients on three continents with his thousand-watt smile.

Facilitated in part by their lasting friendship with Jacqueline Onassis and the Mellons, Pei and Eileen joined that small stylish circle of New Yorkers who were invited to Manhattan's A-list dinner parties. His admission into the top bracket of New York's social whirl added fresh layers of lacquer to his image, further boosting his stock among clients attracted to architects with social cachet. His presence was in demand everywhere. "He just glided in," said Philip Johnson, "perfectly naturally."

On a November evening in 1982, two hundred of Pei's friends, an assemblage that included Louis Auchincloss, Estée Lauder, Diane Sawyer, Marietta Tree, the Kennedy sisters and Leo Castelli, mingled in Lord & Taylor's ground-floor cosmetics department before setting their champagne glasses down on the Clinique counter and ascending to the roof garden for a "visual tribute" to Pei narrated by Tom Brokaw. Slides of Pei's work alternated with appearances by family members and friends. Even Betty Grable made a cameo—"I.M. *loved* her," Brokaw explained. When the *Star Wars* theme music swelled to a crescendo, the guests stood and applauded. After a candlelit dinner of smoked trout with caviar, medallions of veal and apple tart, Pei was asked to name his favorite buildings. "I can't compare them," he said. "They're all different; they're like children."

12
CHINA AGAIN

Henry Cobb once described I. M. Pei as a "cultural cross-dresser." Virtually every episode in his long career was informed by his ability to assimilate while maintaining his authentic mandarin character. "I have two worlds," he said. "It's difficult for me to practice architecture without occasionally looking back into my own background."

Pei's ethnicity may have been a drawback in the eyes of some building committees early in his career, but it usually helped distinguish him from the lily-white pack. His cultural inheritance added an authoritative weight to the considerable pull of his charm: here was a son of the world's oldest civilization, a man with a gentle certitude of behavior and a refined touch—a mandarin of modernism.

The extent to which Pei remains Chinese after living in the United States for more than half a century is the subject of avid speculation and gossip. Those who have seen him don his mandarin mask at propitious moments sometimes suspect him of posturing for professional gain. "Pei loves to give the impression that he's so cultured and above it all," the critic Martin Filler said after accompanying Pei to Japan and Hong Kong in 1989. "He has tapped into the Oriental stereotype of cleanliness, refinement and rationality. He cloaks himself in a mantle of cultural sanc-

◄ The *liu shui yin:* according to legend, poets floated wineglasses down the water maze in the moonlight.

tity: 'I'm this immensely refined mandarin that you barbarians will never fathom.' "

"He can talk about his ancestors and the stone gardens of Suzhou in the most aristocratic way," said Philip Johnson. "I would too if I were a Chinese gentleman. Why not? We all use what we can."

At other times Pei downplayed his ethnicity in order to integrate. For years he limited the number of Asian employees so as to avoid being labeled "the immigrant firm." But as his staff expanded, so too did the number of Asians. One day Pei stepped off the elevator, glanced across the studio and, without a hint of irony, asked his luncheon companion, "Have you noticed how many Orientals there are around here lately?"

Some immigrants fall between cultures and end up without any true home. As a graceful traverser of cultural crevasses, Pei gained a world without losing another. When the Chinese revolution stranded Pei in America, he and Eileen judiciously absorbed the best aspects of Western life. In the mid-1970s they moved to a town house overlooking a garden and, beyond it, the East River in the quiet Upper East Side enclave of Sutton Place. They furnished it with Mies chairs, fine French wines ("Wine stewards tremble," said William Walton, "when they see him entering their restaurant") and works by the established masters of postwar abstraction—Tworkov, Lipchitz, de Kooning, and Kline, with a group of small Dubuffet sculptures arranged on a stairway landing. "Great big abstract things," is how Jim Freed described Pei's home, "and funny little Chinese things." The sitting room was "all dark brown and stiff," wrote Jackie Onassis, "with nary a comfortable chair in sight. Both I.M. and Eileen admire the stiff hierarchical arrangement of old Chinese furniture." The bookcase in Pei's tidy study contains works on Magritte and Rembrandt, and monographs on Marcel Breuer and Le Corbusier. They raised their four children to speak only English and enrolled them in private schools.

There was a distinct European flavor to their casual elegance, particularly at their weekend home in Katonah, where languorous lunches on the screen porch stretched well into the afternoon and were followed by a siesta. In the evening there were informal candlelight dinner parties with plenty of wine. The Peis often took summer vacations in France or Italy.

Pei absorbed the West's finest offerings without relinquishing his own rich heritage. He stayed in touch with the old F. F. network, collected antique Yixing teaware and indulged his encyclopedic knowledge of Chinese cuisine with frequent, well-informed forays to Chinatown. "He never cared for the American sandwich," said his partner Eason Leonard. "Those of us who traveled [with Pei] to Singapore and Hong Kong received an education in Chinese food and how to eat it. When you had dinner with Pei it was always special. He loved the unusual. Hairy crabs, chicken-feet stew, sea slugs, ducks tongues, snake meat. Plus a few things you wouldn't want to know about until the next day. But it was all good."

Even as a New Yorker, Pei read Chinese classics by writers like Lao-tzu, who taught that contentment and inner strength are found by cultivating a relationship with the Tao, the mystical force that unites all things. "When I was in college, I really did not have the wisdom to read Lao-tzu, although I did read it when I was a child," Pei said. "I forgot it as quickly as I read it. But I have read Lao-tzu a great deal since then and I think that his writing probably has more effect on my architectural thinking than anything else. I think perhaps that many modern architects would tell you the same. I would certainly recommend it. It's a very difficult book to read. I can only take about one page at a time. You are sort of exhausted when you get through that page. It's not the kind of book that you would really want to read in your light moments."

When asked what part of Pei's personality remains unreconstructedly Chinese, intimates usually refer to his thought process. He weighs all options with serene watchfulness before declaring his opinion. "Dad is extremely shrewd," said his daughter, Liane. "He's charming in a seductive way, but he's much harder to read than my mother. Her way of thinking is more Westernized; she can be very direct with people she feels comfortable with. Dad is good at sizing people up—his mind is always steps ahead of the conversation—but he's never demonstrative. He's always thinking without revealing his thoughts. . . . In certain ways he considers himself an American. He is, after all, the classic American success story. He didn't arrive a penniless immigrant, of course, but America provided him with an outlet, with the opportunity to make his own name. But he remains very Chinese in the way he thinks about his personal life and his family. . . . My mom and dad think of us as completely American, but they don't see that we've maintained a certain Chineseness."

The Chinese by tradition value family above all other allegiances, and the Peis manifested that closeness in New York. After Katonah weekends, they could be seen dining together at a favorite Italian or Chinese restaurant before dispersing for the week. Because Didi and Sandi worked in their father's firm, they saw him daily. Pei tried to visit his own father every Sunday at his Park Avenue apartment. It is a closeness marked by Confucian filial respect; unlike the typical American family, there was very little bickering or back talk. They gave each other a certain formal distance.

How far one was invited into the halls and courtyards of an acquaintance's home was to the Chinese of Pei's childhood an important indicator of status. Pei's private life is similarly sealed against all but an intimate inner circle. Few of his many friendships penetrate the walls within walls, sanctums within sanctums. He submits to countless interviews but rarely reveals much of himself, even to his closest associates. "I have to confess, I don't know *anything* about I.M.," said his partner Jim Freed, "even though I've known him for more than thirty years."

Pei's inner self remains as elusive as a distant, mist-draped temple glimpsed in a scroll painting. "He's absolutely hermetic," said Philip Johnson. "We have lunch and we're very polite to each other. I like him, but one never really gets to know him." This inner withholding is the crux of his enigma.

Pei's private domain is guarded by his wife, Eileen, a woman of such discretion that she refused to be photographed for *Vanity Fair*'s 1989 profile of her husband. "She's a Nancy Reagan type," said the author, Martin Filler, "who feels her nice husband is constantly being set upon by people, which is baloney. She feels nothing good can come of publicity." He agreed to appear on Charlie Rose's talk show, for example, only if Rose refrained from asking personal questions. Pei also asked that the interview take place in Paris, the scene of his greatest triumph.

"Sure, I'm very Westernized," Pei once told his friend William Walton, "but it's far from complete. I understand so much about people on both sides and feel very much at home with them. But finally, between me and Westerners there is a curtain, not as thick as a Bamboo Curtain, but a thin curtain that sets us off from one another in the final analysis. . . . The differences between Orientals and Westerners are far deeper than the differences between most other people of the world, such as Russians or people of the Middle East. Perhaps it is because we are so old, our civilization goes back so far, farther than anyone's."

Walton responded that he did not think of Pei as Chinese or alien in any sense. "Oh, but I'm much more Chinese than you think," Pei quickly replied. "I don't show it to you, I guess. I don't know whether that's on purpose."

■　■　■　■

The I-Ching states: "All creatures return to their roots, return to their destiny." That seemed unlikely for Pei, however. The Bamboo Curtain dropped with a resounding thud shortly after Mao established the People's Republic in 1949. His anti-Western policies barred correspondence with the outside world. Pei could only imagine the deprivations suffered by friends and family, including his uncle Tsuyuan, who were subjected to "reeducation." Stories leaked out about terrible punishments inflicted on intellectuals and members of well-to-do families, about cherished belongings burned or confiscated, about imprisonment, beatings and suicide.

Chinese civilization has survived endless cycles of rebellion and war, and Pei expected China to recover from Maoism as well, but not in his lifetime. "You don't look at China in five years," he said. "You look at China in five hundred years. You have to look at it in the long, long range." Just as Suzhou gardeners placed rocks in swirling waters for their grandsons to retrieve, Pei foresaw the day, perhaps generations hence, when China would emerge from darkness.

That day arrived sooner than expected. In April 1971, China invited the U.S. table-tennis team to Beijing, a development that Pei astutely read as a portentous signal. After hearing the news, he fluttered through the studio in a state of excitement. "Do you know what this means?" he asked. "In a couple of years you'll be able to go to China!"

"What about you?" one designer asked.

"Well," Pei said, "that's another question."

Pei didn't have to wait long for an answer. It was customary for outgoing presidents of the American Institute of Architects to lead foreign excursions, usually to picturesque settings like Italy or Greece. Shortly after Nixon visited China in February 1972, however, AIA president Max Urbahn told the trustees he wanted to go to China. They laughed. China might have yielded to Nixon, but it repelled every other delegation, save for a few doctors and archaeologists. Urbahn nonetheless mailed a letter addressed to the President, Chinese Society of Architects, Peking, People's Republic of China. He had no idea if such a group even existed. But in August of 1973 he received a cordial invitation to come to China.

Traveling with a professional delegation was the most inconspicuous way for Pei to return. The Chinese government might have construed a private homecoming as an endorsement or capitulation. By traveling under the AIA's auspices, Pei prevented the government from using his visit for propaganda purposes.

In April 1974 a group of fifteen architects, including the Peis, traveled from the Hong Kong train station aboard the so-called gin and tonic express to the Chinese border, where British guards stamped their passports "departed." They then filed through a green doorway below a hand-painted sign that said, "To China," and walked across a wooden railroad bridge spanning a shallow river to a stucco border house where young guards in khaki Mao suits and caps with red stars greeted them with green tea and cigarettes. They passed customs without incident, except for Walt Meisen who, as chief architect of the U.S. General Services Administration, carried a government passport. Armed guards led him to a booth and inspected his list of declared belongings. "What's a mouth organ?" they demanded. Meisen pulled out his harmonica and played "My Country 'Tis of Thee."

The Chinese treated the architects like visiting dignitaries. They traveled by plane and in first-class ("soft-seat") train compartments among eleven cities, escorted by translators and government agents. A delegation of architects met them at every stop—in one case, at 3:00 A.M. After offering the ritual tea and cigarettes, along with effusive accolades, their hosts showed them the local sites—schools, kindergartens, housing projects, factories and communal farms.

At night they lodged as guests of the government in hotels reserved for foreigners, and ate in private dining rooms gazed upon by the obligatory Mao portrait, save for two evenings when, at Pei's urging, they took their chaperons out to restaurants off the tourist route. Banquets ended with elaborate toasts, both solemn and satirical, and shouts of *"Gan bei"*—"Empty the cup!"

Walt Meisen noticed the Chinese taking only shallow sips after the third or fourth round. "Each according to his own ability," they told him.

Foreigners were still rare in China, particularly in the north, and parting crowds broke into spontaneous applause as they entered train stations. Giggling children trailed them for blocks. Walt Meisen and William Marshall attracted thousands of onlookers while walking around the central square in the northern city of Shenyang. "We were like creatures from outer space," said Marshall. "I'd go into one of their department stores, and they'd see the hair on my arm and reach out and pull it."

Robert Madison, a black architect from Cleveland, was the object of particular curiosity, but nobody drew more attention than Eileen. People accustomed to enforced plainness could not take their eyes off her. "She was absolutely elegant," Meisen remembered. "She wore long conservative dresses with a spot of color. The women especially were overwhelmed by her appearance and how she carried herself. Everywhere we went the women just died. They *drooled*."

The Peis helped reveal to their traveling companions the unrehearsed China that lay behind the tightly scripted version routinely shown to foreigners. They made sure the itinerary included historical attractions Americans would not otherwise have seen, like the 1,500-year-old Buddhist cave sculptures outside Luoyang and the army of life-size terra-cotta soldiers and horses discovered buried in eastward-facing battle formation outside the tomb of Emperor Qin Shihuang. Between them, the Peis spoke several Chinese dialects, and they corrected translations and bantered with people on the street. They waded in among gawkers, offering children the traditional Chinese greeting (*"ni hao"*) and shaking hands with the parents.

Throughout the trip, Pei anticipated a reunion with his uncle, Tsuyuan Pei, whom he hadn't seen since he sailed for America in 1935. While Pei attended MIT and Harvard, Tsuyuan had sold Chinese goods in Southeast Asia in exchange for arms to be used in the war against the Japanese. When Mao overthrew Chiang Kai-shek in 1949, Tsuyuan was forced to give up his comfortable Shanghai residence owned by the Bank of China and move to a small house in a modest neighborhood. His humbled life was tolerable until the upheaval known as the Cultural Revolution began in August of 1966. In one of the darkest passages of modern Chinese history, paramilitary bands of teenagers known as the Red Guards stirred up by Mao—he called them his "little generals"—waged a campaign of terror against the "four olds": old ideas, old habits, old customs and old culture. The inquisitions and abuses have been eloquently documented: Children denounced their parents. Intellectuals died in labor camps. Universities were closed and classic books burned indiscriminately. Architecture was all but extinguished. The Red Guards closed design schools and ground their professors into submission. Anyone suspected of admiring the past was hauled before revolutionary inquisitors. Meanwhile, the old and the beautiful were systematically disfigured: Gardens hundreds of years old were destroyed. Temples were converted to factories. Commemorative arches toppled. Work crews razed Beijing's magnificent city wall, with its towers and monumental gates guarded by stone lions. "It was as if my own flesh was being torn off, as if my skin was being peeled off," wrote architectural historian Liang Sicheng.

Tsuyuan's privileged background made him an obvious target. The Red Guards searched his house and locked his prized belongings in one room. They burned or confiscated family photos, paintings, calligraphy, a cache of poems written by I.M.'s mother, and I.M.'s letters. They forced him to attend indoctrination classes and demoted him to coolie. He spent the rest of his career doing manual labor in a warehouse. For many years it was impossible for him to contact anyone outside China. Amid the political relaxations of 1974, however, Tsuyuan sent a letter through his work unit which eventually made its way to I.M. via the Chinese delegation to the United Nations.

▲

Pei chats with a passerby in China.

"Dear Uncle Yong," Pei answered in a postcard mailed from Hong Kong. "Although we have not seen each other for half a century, after reading your letter, I felt that things had not changed in forty years. I am going on a business trip to Singapore via Hong Kong and so would like to take this opportunity to send my regards to stepgrandmother and all the other relatives. Meanwhile, I have very good news. . . . [We] will be in Shanghai around mid-April, and then we will have the opportunity to meet and have long talks. Reflecting on the past, it is a long story that is hard to say in a few words."

Meanwhile, the Party cadre in charge of Tsuyuan's neighborhood informed him that an important figure from America was coming to see him. By the way, the Party leader asked, did Tsuyuan need anything? It was the first time the neighborhood cadre had offered him assistance. To Tsuyuan's bitter amusement, twenty or so carpenters showed up the next day to replace his worn wooden floor. Pei and Eileen split from their group shortly before noon on the appointed day to meet Tsuyuan at Shanghai's Jinjiang Hotel, where Nixon and Premier Zhou Enlai had signed the Shanghai Communiqué two years earlier. After a long teary embrace and a brief chat, they joined a cousin and three Party officials for lunch. Afterward Tsuyuan took I.M. and Eileen to see his home since the revolution, a small-roomed dwelling in a modest neighborhood.

Pei invited Tsuyuan to attend a reunion banquet the following night at the Park Hotel, the same Art Deco edifice that had aroused Pei's early interest in architecture. The thirty or so guests included J. D. Woo, the friend who had accompanied Pei to MIT, and assorted relatives from Shanghai and Suzhou. Tsuyuan stood and sang "White Christmas" in memory of the Bing Crosby movies he and I.M. had attended long ago at the Grand Theatre next door.

Other signs of Shanghai's glory days were still evident. The Union Jack no longer snapped in the breeze above the Bund, of course, but the crumbling remnants of colonial grandeur endured beneath a scruffy overlay of Communist usage. The exclusive Shanghai Club had been transformed into a hostel for seamen. Laundry lines and mattresses cluttered the smoking room where old China hands had once snoozed over the London *Times*. The opulent Cathay Hotel had become the "Peace Hotel." The British embassy was a "friendship" store, and the former Pei home on Ferguson Road was now a hospital.

The city that had once throbbed with jazz and gin had become a model of puritanical industriousness. Sweepers patrolled the streets at dawn, followed by workers in uniform khaki garb pedaling fleets of identical black bicycles to work in eerie silence. The ubiquitous Mao portrait gazed down on charmless gray streets. At night the city fell silent and dark. Families turned their lights out by 10:00 P.M. Shanghai was so moribund, in fact, that the visitors celebrated one companion's first wedding anniversary by sitting around a hotel room sipping whiskey. "Well," someone joked, "Saturday night in Shanghai!"

The Americans found current Chinese architecture similarly uninspiring. At every stopover they saw the deadly dull concrete slabs that had been inflicted on the landscape by Soviet "advisers" in the 1960s and anonymous three- and four-story blocks where families occupied single rooms without bathrooms or kitchens. A republic struggling to shelter a quarter of the world's population, they were told, had no time for the finer elements of design. "Be frugal," Mao exhorted, "and build the country."

Marxist sloganeering, it seemed, could dim the light of the world's oldest continuous civilization, but could not extinguish it. By 1974, Communism's war against traditional Chinese culture had given way to an awakening pride in the bygone landmarks of the Ming and Ching dynasties. Unlike Eastern Europe, China valued its heritage enough to maintain workshops, some of which Pei visited, where apprentices practiced the arts of pottery, jade and ivory carving and silk embroidery under the tutelage of masters. "Beauty is a craving of Chinese culture," the correspondent Theodore White observed, "and the leadership has been restoring it. Each major city, each minor county seat, cherishes its own local beauties—gardens with green gnarled trees, ancient pavilions with reflecting pools, refurbished monuments with poetry scrolls."

Few places preserved the past more vigilantly than Suzhou, Pei's ancestral home, where farsighted officials had safeguarded a dozen or so luxuriant gardens from rampaging Red Guards. (It has been reported that Premier Zhou Enlai personally arranged for their protection.) Upon arrival, Pei's group visited the Shizilin, his family enclave, by then reopened as a heavily trafficked "people's park." They were received by more than a hundred Pei relatives dressed in baggy tunics, a chastened clan gathered to greet an illustrious son who was, as the Chinese say, "returning in silk." But for an accident of history, he might have stood among them. Pei was surprisingly impassive for so poignant a reunion, but his companions could guess at the emotions at play beneath his mild manner—distress at the garden's deterioration, embarrassment at his own prosperity, wonder at how fortuitously he had escaped their fate and frustration at his inability to help them. He also felt an obvious pride in the garden itself. He seated himself on a rock and explained to his American friends how it evolved through the generations, how gardeners had deposited rocks in the scouring waters for their grandsons to retrieve.

. . . .

The China Pei visited in 1974 was on the verge of one of its periodic mood swings. The following year, the reform-minded pragmatist Deng Xiaoping returned from political exile to become "paramount leader" of China's Politburo and a patron of post-Mao reforms that swung the country back toward modern development. Almost overnight China veered from Mao's xenophobic isolation to uncritical acceptance of all things Western. "To be rich," Deng declared, "is glorious."

Deng's China came to see prominent émigrés like Pei as a valuable source of professional help. In 1978, Deng's regime put aside any lingering enmity over Pei's political pedigree and invited him back to advise them on development and city planning. Pei, the unreconstructed modernist, now found himself espousing tradition to revolutionaries. He worried that the influx of affluent foreigners would encourage China to forsake what little precious heritage survived in order to become thoroughly modern. He had already seen developing countries like Iran and Egypt blindly import the bad along with the good. Over endless cups of tea he cautioned his Chinese hosts not to erect the world's newest civilization at the expense of its oldest. Above all, he voiced concern for Beijing's yellow-tiled Forbidden City, the splendorous 250-acre Great Within where thousands of concubines and courtiers had attended successive emperors. The Forbidden City's vast courts and palaces had survived as the best-preserved cluster of ancient buildings in all of China. An imperial edict had once barred buildings taller than its thirty-five-foot walls; Pei now urged a similar moratorium in order to protect the azure sky above its yellow roofs from development.

But Pei's warnings fell on deaf ears. A country yearning for its first taste of forbidden fruit—television, T-shirts, Coca-Cola, high heels and hamburgers—was not inclined to worry about preservation. Architecture students in particular were intent on duplicating the glistening emblems of Western prosperity they admired in glossy design magazines. "The students were all very disappointed in my talks," Pei said. "They expected me to tell them about glass curtain walls, about the latest in forms and high-rise buildings and so on. Instead, I . . . told them not to forget about their past."

Pei returned to the United States in November of 1978 and immediately boarded a twin-engine plane for a turbulent flight to the tip of Cape Cod so that he could head a design competition for the Provincetown Playhouse, the theater that had launched Eugene O'Neill. The next day he flew to Dallas to supervise the installation of Henry Moore's reclining *Dallas Piece* in the sprawling plaza outside his anvil-shaped city hall. "You know," Pei told a fellow passenger, "I haven't slept in three days."

Chinese officials invited him to make a third visit a few weeks later, in December 1978. He declined, explaining that he planned to spend the holidays with his family. In that case, the Chinese said, why not bring them along? So the Peis; their three sons, T'ing, Didi and Sandi; their daughter, Liane; and two grandchildren, Alyssa, age six, and Stephen, just five months old, embarked for Christmas in Beijing, their suitcases stuffed with Pampers. In China they attended one banquet after another (Stephen was said to be the youngest guest ever presented at a state dinner at the Hall of the People).

The Chinese did not know what to make of the Pei children. They *looked* Chinese, of course, but they spoke English. "At the time, everybody in China wore blue cotton jackets," said T'ing. "We were dressed in colorful ski parkas. People followed us around out of curiosity. They couldn't figure out if we were Chinese or what. Once, we were driving through a town during market day when a horse-drawn wagon loaded with hay collapsed in front of us. We were stuck. In an instant a hundred noses were pressed to the windows. It was as if we were aliens from outer space."

Their own relatives were no less quizzical. "They were horrified that we couldn't speak Chinese," said Liane. "We could only smile stupidly at them; we couldn't communicate. We actually didn't feel that much connection with them. We had grown up in entirely different circumstances. We couldn't begin to understand what they'd gone through."

Having chosen the path of modern development, the Party was anticipating an influx of business and tourism, but it had no decent accommodations. Even the simplest amenities like potable water and clean sheets were a rarity. Ignoring Pei's earlier advice, a vice premier invited him to design ten modern hotels of one thousand rooms apiece, including a massive high-rise near the Forbidden City. Pei politely refused. "I just couldn't do it," he said. "My conscience wouldn't let me. If you look over the walls of the Forbidden City you see the golden tiles on the roofs, and beyond that you see just sky, except for Coal Hill where the Lama Temple is. That's what gives the Forbidden City its character. If you destroy that sense of being alone, of being an object by itself, then you destroy the artifact. I can't imagine a tall building looking over the Forbidden City as the Hilton Hotel does over Buckingham Palace. . . . I just didn't want to be party to it."

The People's Republic was eager to show the world that I. M. Pei was helping to build a new China, so they barred high-rise buildings within a certain radius of the Forbidden City as he had advised and offered him a series of alternative sites. None worked until Beijing's tourist agency, the First Service Bureau, asked if he would consider doing a low-rise hotel in a park it managed outside the city. Two days before Christmas, officials took Pei and his son Didi twenty-five miles northwest of Beijing to a former imperial hunting preserve called Fragrant Hill where the picturesque ruins of a walled park of pavilions and pagodas lay under a light snow cover. They climbed a rough path in a bitter north wind to a pavilion halfway up the hill. From there the park looked like a scene from a scroll painting.

The steep valley below resonated with historic associations. It was created by Qianlong, the eighteenth-century emperor who had snubbed the British emissary at the nearby Summer Palace. That rebuff had started a chain of events leading to foreign incursions which, in turn, nearly reduced Fragrant Hill to ruins in 1860 and again in 1900. And it was here that another isolationist, Chairman Mao, negotiated the surrender of Beijing in 1949 with a Kuomintang general. "When that site was shown to me," Pei said, "I didn't even hesitate. I said, 'Let's build here.' "

A low-rise hotel of 325 rooms was a modest venture by Pei's standards. But it offered one unique virtue: it allowed Pei to resume the search for a modern

Chinese style that had begun when the first wave of foreign-trained architects returned in the 1920s to blend Western building techniques with the ancient Chinese vernacular. Pei had drafted his own contribution when he submitted the Shanghai art museum as his graduate thesis at Harvard. Fragrant Hill was his chance to resume the experiment thirty years later. His ambition was to forge a new architectural language for a new China. It was to be a hybrid of old and new—"a third way"—for young Chinese designers to follow. Like the Georgian style of eighteenth- and early nineteenth-century England, it could be applied to both grand public buildings and private homes.

"Chinese architecture is at a dead end, totally," Pei said. "There is no way for them to go. Chinese architects will agree with me on that. They couldn't go back to the old way. The days of the temples and the palaces are not only economically out of reach but ideologically unacceptable to them. They've tried the Russian way, and they hate those buildings. They are trying now to take the Western way. I am afraid that will be equally unacceptable. I would like in a small way to pay a debt to a culture from which I came, to try to help them search for a new way. . . . It's an approach that can be replicated by architects all over the country in a hundred and one ways. And I think that's the only way to begin a new vernacular in architecture. This is how the Renaissance started."

Pei's search for a new style began with his own past. In gardens and courtyards once inhabited by families like his own in the Yangtze Valley cities of Suzhou, Hangzhou, Yangzhou and Wuxi he reacquainted himself with aspects of his former life—upturned eaves, moon gates, accented windows and trickling waters. He was convinced that, despite political upheaval, this vocabulary still had meaning to most Chinese. He wanted to revive those stylistic traits that still spoke to the average person—not the red pillars and golden roofs of obsolete palaces and temples but the white walls and gray bricks of ordinary residences. "Architecture has to come out of people's homes," he said. "I would not look for Italian roots in Michelangelo's work in the Vatican. I would go to Florence to look at the houses where people live."

After conveying his concept to deputy designers, Pei usually moved on to other responsibilities, returning periodically to evaluate their progress and present it to clients. But Fragrant Hill was his personal expression of a new China and, as such, commanded his intimate attention. Employees were surprised to see him, pencil in hand, worrying over drafting tables in the open studio. "This was *his* project for a couple of years," said designer Karen Van Lengen. "Every two hours he'd come to my desk with drawings and elevations. We worked extremely long hours. He was *obsessed*."

Unlike Western edifices, which tend to present themselves in a single frontal announcement, Fragrant Hill unfolds in teasing succession. As Pei envisioned it, visitors would pass under a commemorative gate topped with five scarlet flags to a formal, intricately tiled forecourt facing a white stucco facade pierced by traditional diamond and plum-blossom windows. From there they would enter a spacious four-story lobby enclosed by Pei's signature space-frame skylight. The Four Seasons Courtyard, as Pei called it, was a cross between a Suzhou garden and the East Building atrium, a place in which to admire goldfish and stands of bamboo while sipping tea in the shifting shadows. From this sunlit court, corridors snake outward among four low-lying wings with carefully calculated views of the surrounding gardens. "In the West, a window is a window," Pei said. "It lets in light and fresh air. But to the Chinese, it's a picture frame. And the garden is always there."

The Chinese hinted that they might build directly from the presentation model, so Pei's team incorporated as many details as possible before shipping it to Beijing on Easter 1979. If the fifty officials gathered to see Pei unveil his model anticipated a glittering badge of sophistication, they got instead a history lesson. An organized sprawl of silk-white wings no more than four stories high and accented by latticework and diamond-shaped win-

◄

Fragrant Hill: Pei wanted to establish
a new architectural language—"a third
way"—for young Chinese architects
to follow.

▼   Eleven courtyards contain ancient trees and
meandering pebble paths. One of the trees
is said to have shaded Mao himself on the
eve of the Communist takover.

dows snaked around courtyards in the manner once said to deter wandering ghosts. This airy, serene pavilion with romantic motifs culled from history looked both familiar and strange to sons of the revolution—all the stranger since the flat roof and white walls Pei had borrowed from Suzhou looked out of place in the north. Most of all, the officials were confounded by Pei's deliberate simplicity. "Pei wanted it to express real beauty," explained associate Fred Fang, "like a young maiden with no lipstick."

The Chinese had no choice but to accept a design submitted by their most esteemed émigré, but they did impose one condition: Pei had to save as many trees as possible. A zealous campaign was under way to reforest a countryside stripped of firewood and lumber. Tiny saplings dotted the denuded landscape. Freshly planted willows and sycamores lined roads and parks. No trees in the country were more valued than those in Fragrant Hill, one of Beijing's most popular parks. Hordes arrived by bus each year to view its autumn foliage. So it was unthinkable for a Western architect to sacrifice any of its beautiful old cypresses, chestnuts, cedars and pines—one of which supposedly shaded Mao himself.

They could scarcely have found an architect more inclined to respect the site's natural beauty. Practically every space in Pei's portfolio contains at least one thoughtfully landscaped tree, dating back to the gnarled pine planted on the terrace of Webb & Knapp's office. "All you need to know about I.M.," said Henry Cobb, "lies in that pine tree."

Pei was, if anything, more concerned than his client about preserving Fragrant Hill's gnarled old trees. In fact, he based the entire hotel's alignment around two 800-year-old ginkgo trees, and he zigzagged rambling wings so that the most valuable trees were saved, and "in the end, the trees came back to bless us," he said. "The whole site became an instant garden."

Pei's point man in the Far East, Kellogg Wong, was about to return to America when Pei phoned him from New York. A crisis had arisen at Fragrant Hill. Could Wong stop at the site on his way home? A last-minute excursion into mainland China was the last thing Wong wanted to undertake after a long trip abroad, but he dutifully obliged. "I've always thought my role was similar to [that of] the scouts dispatched by an army," he said. "We're expected to throw ourselves across barbed wire so that Mr. Pei can proceed unencumbered."

The Chinese wanted to show Wong an outline of the building they had traced on the ground in lime ash which, to their alarm, indicated that Pei's plan would claim more than one hundred trees. Wong scrambled over boulders and underbrush in the rain accompanied by forty functionaries. "By golly, they were right!" Wong said. "We'd eliminated many trees we thought we preserved." Closer examination revealed that the surveyors had begun from the wrong starting point; the entire outline was off by six feet. Even the corrected contour threatened more trees than necessary; Wong labored through the night drafting additional zigs and zags. From then on, the Chinese called him "Save-the-Tree Mr. Wong."

The job of coaxing a five-star hotel into existence on the far side of the world fell to Preston Moore, an associate partner who had studied under Pei at Harvard and joined his staff in 1953. Moore already had a vague familiarity with the site: he had eaten lunch there in 1931 while traveling with his parents from Honolulu to Boston. By 1979, Moore, a tall, mustached sixty-year-old with a shock of white hair, looked eminently eligible for the respect Chinese traditionally accord elders. He was astonished when a woman on a public bus offered him her seat. The workers gave him his own honorific nickname, "the White Fungus."

While Moore commuted between New York and Beijing, another associate of long duration, Fred Fang, stayed on the site for two full years. Having grown up in China before the revolution, Fang knew how to court bureaucrats and cajole idle workers. He understood, as no American could, when to push and when to conciliate. Although Fang was conversant with the Chinese code of proper behavior, he was nonetheless ill at ease as the son of a prominent Nationalist family living among Communist cadres. In fact, his family made Pei personally guarantee his safety.

Fang found that what the Chinese lacked in technology, they often recouped in limitless manpower. The Communists knew how to mobilize the workers, and they attacked the site with an impressive labor force. Boulders torn from the ground by mules were hauled away on bamboo slings and donkey carts. Two thousand workers dug the foundation by hand; in fact, they dug two stories too deep. An entry road that would have taken a month or more to build in the United States took less than a week. Rotating shifts poured a vast concrete basement in a single night. "It was a miracle," said Fang, who rewarded workers with a banquet of beer and chicken cooked on the site. "To this day, I don't think it would be possible to do in America."

Manpower alone could not compensate for generations of backwardness and institutionalized indifference, however. Deliveries were erratic. Light bulbs, scraps of hardware, even cardboard boxes vanished in a plague of petty thievery. Workmen loitered about chatting and drinking tea. "I think Pei backed into a project that he wanted very badly," said architectural historian Ron Knapp, author of *Gardens of Longevity,* "but he had no sense of China's inability to carry it off. Skills had atrophied over the years. Communism isolated the country from the whole idea of creating artistic spaces."

Unlike the intellectuals who had aroused the Russian Revolution, Mao's Long Marchers were for the most part coarse, uneducated peasants. These unsophisticated Party hacks, now in control of China's vast bureaucracy, had no understanding of Pei's intentions. The man who led them to power had denounced the comfort and beauty Pei now asked them to facilitate. Mao "would have forbidden everything we have done," Pei said.

Worst of all, the Cultural Revolution had stripped architects of authority.

They were expected to advise rather than instruct the workers. Some Chinese architects even lived at the site in order to enact changes "suggested" by workers. As a result, Fang found his every decision subject to debate. "Sometimes I was so bitter and frustrated that tears came to my eyes," he said. Fang's constant adversary was an intransigent named Captain Yang, head of Beijing's Number Six Construction Team. Like many bureaucrats atop private fiefdoms, Yang was accustomed to running things his way, and he resented the sheaf of translated specifications Fang toted around like Mao's little red book. The two men nearly came to blows.

One day, Fang offered Captain Yang lunch as a peace offering. After two drinks, his guest erupted in a bilious rage. "Fred, you are the only person who talks back to me," he said. "Who the hell do you think you are?"

"Normally, if someone talked to me like that I would blow my top," Fang said. "I was mad as anything, but I just sat back and laughed. 'Are you finished, Captain?' I said. Then I opened the window to show that his words had passed right outside. I said, 'You are one hundred percent wrong. I *always* consult you, but I'm here to represent Mr. Pei. And this building will be implemented according to his specifications.' "

Fang gradually found ways of exerting control. He befriended Beijing's deputy mayor in charge of construction who, as a member of the postrevolutionary generation, was anxious to show that joint ventures could work. He invited Fang to air grievances on his direct phone line.

Fang also roused listless workers with merit pay and promises carefully recorded in a notebook so that he might hold officials and foremen to their word. "You can do things your way out there," he told them. "Within the property line, let's try something new."

Fang, meanwhile, waded into Beijing's Byzantine politics in search of help. Decorum prohibited him from directly soliciting aid from agencies in charge of sewage, water and other key services. He could ask for their help only after preliminary get-acquainted meetings arranged by a third party. Chinese civility required Fang to make conciliatory remarks over tea before alluding to the issue at hand. Bureaucrats seated around enormous tables offered interminable niceties without ever reaching a decision. They rarely even mentioned schedules. Some requests evaporated altogether in a cloud of politesse. "I've never been to so many meetings at which nothing was accomplished," said Preston Moore.

Pei could have saved time by importing materials and know-how from Hong Kong, but he mandated the use of traditional Chinese methods whenever possible. Graphic designer Tracy Turner, for example, resurrected half-forgotten arts and crafts such as silk embroidery for menu jackets and cut-paper motifs for menus. There were no Beijing Yellow Pages, so she found the craftsmen herself, venturing alone into manufacturing plants equipped with sketches and a rudimentary grasp of Mandarin gleaned from preparatory classes in New York.

Pei hoped to trim the windows with old-fashioned tiles like those in the Beijing city wall. Craftsmen had contrived to give the tiles a distinctive dark gray sheen by sprinkling them with oil as they emerged from the kiln. It was Pei's kind of material—humble but elegant. By coincidence, Suzhou craftsmen were using similar tiles in a replica garden installed in New York's Metropolitan Museum of Art. The craftsmen had baked the hand-cut terra-cotta tiles in kilns last used in the construction of Qianlong's Imperial Palace and had brought them to New York along with bricks, carved wooden posts, lintels and a chef who cooked their meals in a spare office.

One might think that a Chinese tile brought all the way to the Met would also be available at Fragrant Hill, but intercity bureaucracy prevented Beijing from importing materials from Suzhou. Beijing officials insisted they could no longer make their own tiles because the kilns were closed. Pei's staff was by now accustomed to fending for itself. They found a sympathetic artisan in his seventies who happily replicated the tiles in a surviving kiln on the city's outskirts.

Part of Pei's self-appointed mission was to remind China that nature was once to architecture what yin was to yang. "The indoors and the outdoors are always one," Pei said. "A study for a scholar without a small garden in front of it is not a study. You have to talk of the two as one." In a similar fashion, Pei's Western-style guest rooms gave onto eleven serene courtyards inhabited by exotic flowers and ancient trees. The meandering garden paths were inlaid with exquisite bamboo and plum-blossom patterns composed of colored pebbles that Calvin Tsao, a trusted design associate, had collected from a remote riverbed near the Vietnam border. The villagers near the river had never seen a foreigner, and they were slaughtering a pig in Tsao's honor when he arrived by mule. "There was blood everywhere," he said. "I thought, 'My God, they're going to kill me.' . . . They were astounded that this foreigner was going to give them thousands of dollars for pebbles. All the grandmothers and kids descended on the stream."

Just as the East Building's corner galleries duplicated the intimacy of house museums within a vast public gallery, Pei wanted to evoke the compact beauty of Suzhou's private gardens inside Fragrant Hill's roomy, rambling grounds. But how? The rock gardens of Pei's childhood were far too small in scale. While flying from Paris to Beijing one day, Pei happened to read a travel article about a maze of weathered limestone pillars in the Stone Forest of Yunnan, an isolated province near China's southern border. According to myth, the Gods had created the labyrinth by smashing a mountain into pieces to accommodate lovers seeking privacy. The resulting formations had a brooding, otherworldly power, and they conveniently matched the gray hotel tiles. The discovery so excited Pei that he shouted to Fred Fang before clearing customs that he needed the Yunnan pillars. "Now that you're here in person," Fang replied, "we can get the moon."

Workers prepare the Four Seasons Courtyard. A mad scramble was
required to finish the hotel in time
for its October opening.
◄

▶

Pei discusses plans with Chinese officials.

▲

The Four Seasons Courtyard: a cross be-

tween a Suzhou garden and the

East Building atrium

Actually, Fang knew how hard it would be to persuade middle-level bureaucrats to transport rocks halfway across the country when they saw the
need for nothing more elaborate than a concrete plaza. A short time later, Pei
and Fang, along with Pei's son Didi and Calvin Tsao, attended a small banquet at the Hall of the People given by two vice premiers in honor of Pei's
sixty-fifth birthday. The Americans conspired to use the occasion to sell their
idea at the top. It would be cheaper to import rocks from Yunnan, they argued, than to carve rocks on the site. Besides, it would promote the Stone
Forest as a tourist destination. After a discussion that persisted through many
courses, the vice premiers nodded. Yes, they would consider the idea. Fang
pulled out his notebook. "Can I put down that we will at least try?" he asked.

It was, of course, impossible for them to allow foreigners to remove rock
formations from a valued park, but after a full year of negotiation, Tsao was
permitted to walk around a pasture owned by a minority tribe just outside the
Stone Forest. He sketched and photographed the twenty-foot formations from
all angles and marked his choices with paint. Laborers then severed the pin-
nacles from their bases and loaded them—230 tons in all—aboard forty
flatbed train cars for the 1,500-mile trip to Fragrant Hill. One-third of the
cargo fractured in transit, but the surviving pieces confer an eerie primordial
air on the eleven landscaped gardens.

The relics left on the Fragrant Hill site included a gray marble platform,
known as a *liu shui yin*, carved with a serpentine channel. According to legend, poets floated wineglasses down the water maze in the moonlight. They
were permitted to drink only if they could compose a poem in the seven or so
minutes it took the slow-moving current to carry a glass to the end of the 165-
foot passage. This particular *liu shui yin*, one of five left in all of China, was
damaged by workmen mixing cement, so Pei ordered a replica cut from a
thousand-year-old quarry outside Beijing. He positioned it as an island in an
ornamental pond inhabited by goldfish, the traditional Chinese beacon of

nourishment and prosperity. When forty workers finished carving its channels, Pres Moore tested the flow of the water by launching crumpled balls of paper.

At the hotel site, the Number Six Construction Team muscled through the heavy labor, but a generation raised in isolation from the industrialized world was ill prepared for the carefully sequenced finish work required of a Western tourist hotel. Pei's staff grew more and more exasperated as workers accustomed to dirt floors and outhouses fumbled through final preparations, mopping rugs with kerosene, dripping paint on carpets and in some cases plastering the walls before installing electrical wiring. They even connected the bathroom exhaust to the air-conditioning ducts. "It stunk to high heaven," said Tsao.

Instead of hiring Hyatt to manage the hotel, as planned, the First Service Bureau installed an illiterate veteran of Mao's Long March, a toothless bureaucrat whose only qualification was loyal service to the Party. As a result, the young people assigned to staff the hotel received no training. They dutifully arrived for work and spent the day chatting or knitting on the atrium floor. Eventually, Tracy Turner, who had designed the tableware, and David Martin, an associate responsible for all the technical drawings, took it upon themselves to explain the twenty-five place-setting items used in a formal Western dining room. They demonstrated how a fork goes to the left and the knife to the right; how a folded napkin sits atop a plate; how the small plate to the left is for bread; how one glass is used for water, another for wine. The Chinese listened with mounting incredulity: their banquets entailed more food, not more utensils. "The more we explained," Martin said, "the more absurd we sounded. By the end, we were convulsed with laughter."

It had become clear by the summer of 1982 that a mad scramble would be required to finish the hotel in time for its October opening, an event Pei had scheduled to coincide with Fragrant Hill's autumn burst of fiery red foliage. Fang was "like an ant crawling over everything. This wasn't finished. That wasn't finished. All I could do was get on the phone and ask the deputy mayor for assurances that everything would be done."

In June, Pei celebrated his fortieth wedding anniversary in Venice. Shortly after his return to New York, Pres Moore sent him a telex informing him of the delays. Pei arrived at Fragrant Hill several weeks before the opening to apply his finishing touches and attend endless rambling meetings with Chinese bureaucrats, including one at which it was suggested that he had been overpaid. That charge did not stick, of course. On the contrary, the word in Pei's office was that the project had cost him dearly. In the company of the local cadre, Pei adopted the Chinese custom of bowing and eating with one's mouth open. "I was appalled," recalled David Martin, "to see the world's most elegant man with food flying in and out of his mouth."

Ironically, Pei probably never felt more American. At one meeting he uncharacteristically abandoned all politesse and pounded the table with his fist, the same Western mannerism that had struck eighteenth-century mandarins as the epitome of foreign coarseness. "The Chinese bureaucrats were aghast," Pei said. "But suddenly I got what I wanted. I guess I'm not as completely Chinese as I thought."

Pei always worried that Americans saw China as backward and crude. When acquaintances joined him for a Chinese meal he carefully explained the menu and warned them not to be offended by table manners, which permitted slurping of glutinous noodles from bowls lifted to mouth level. Fragrant Hill's disorder aroused similar anxieties, particularly since Pei's guest list for the opening ceremonies included some of his most distinguished American friends—Jacqueline Onassis, Marietta Tree, Evangeline Bruce, William Walton and Thomas and Nancy Hoving. Hoving, who was by then editor of *Connoisseur*, wasn't the only one taking notes. William Walton was on assignment for *House & Garden*, and Jackie Onassis was considering a book. It would be an international embarrassment for such illustrious guests to see Pei's hotel in a state of unpreparedness. The prospect thrust Pei into a rare state of exasperation. "In emotional energy, this has to be the most difficult and the most tortuous thing I've ever done," he said, "because I have to deal with a system I don't understand."

Pei concluded after a few enervating days that there was nothing more he could do. He and Eileen decamped to sculptor Isamu Noguchi's rustic retreat, a restored samurai dwelling near a stonecutters' village on the Japanese island of Shikoku. If anyone could share Pei's bicultural anxiety it was the American-born Noguchi, who spent half of each year in Japan until his death in 1988. "I am the fusion of two worlds," he once said, "the East and the West."

The Peis returned to China in time to join their American friends in Suzhou where an old Saint John's classmate, Jing Shu-ping, whom Pei had not seen in forty years, held a fifteen-course banquet in his honor consisting of spiced livers, roast duck, bamboo shoots, curried crab and candied banana. By coincidence, Pei's American entourage stayed at a guesthouse one day after Henry Kissinger had checked out. The Hovings found his black sock under their bed.

On a hot morning, while holding his granddaughter Alyssa's hand, Pei led his friends through the waterside pavilions and rockeries of the Shizilin garden. With surprising dispassion, he showed them the rigid-backed chairs where he had sat motionless facing his grandfather, and the rockeries where he'd played hide-and-seek. He compared the rocks to Dubuffet sculptures. At one point he picked up a particular rock and palmed it, as if embracing an old friend.

Pei registered shock at the intrusive hordes scattering candy wrappers and posing for snapshots in what had once been a private sanctuary designed for quiet contemplation. "You must see a Chinese garden alone," he said. "It is not possible to get an idea of it with so many people in it, but that is the only way you can see it today." He covered his face in mock horror when confronted with his granduncle's more questionable additions, most conspicuously a boat-shaped pavilion built out over the pond. "Tell the truth," Pei told a tour guide, "my family ruined the garden. It was all rocks and water. They added too many structures."

Jackie Onassis recorded everything about the visit in her notebook. "Old Chinese houses have carvings on the walls—calligraphy, sayings," Pei remembered. "She was particularly taken with two panels. One said, 'See Fragrance.' The other said, 'Read Paintings.' Of course, she thought this was fascinating, and she wrote the sayings down. After we returned, she painted a picture for me in Chinese style, with black ink. It said, 'See Fragrance and Read Paintings.' She was a lady of great sensitivity."

Throughout the trip Mrs. Onassis enjoyed a rare anonymity; the Chinese simply left her alone. The only thing they noticed about her, one companion said, was the size of her feet. The Chinese were far more interested in Pei's family. "The Chinese couldn't take their eyes off Pei's children and grandchildren," remembered Evangeline Bruce. "They were clearly Chinese, and yet their clothes and gestures were foreign. Huge crowds gathered around, and all eyes were on them."

"I *don't* speak Chinese," one grandchild announced to approaching strangers.

Suzhou was part of a cultural mystery tour Pei arranged for his friends with hidden clues to China, old and new, and hints at his own relation to them. "Only in looking backward after we had reached Beijing and seen his new Fragrant Hill hotel did I realize how subtle had been his travel schedule for us," Walton wrote in his travel diary. "Hong Kong, Canton, Kweilin, and, finally, to Suzhou. Each had a lesson for us—negative as well as positive."

While Pei's friends continued to the Great Wall and the Ming Tombs, Pei returned to Fragrant Hill refreshed and ready for the final push. Upon his direction, a stand of bamboo was moved three inches to the right and the forty-foot entry wall was redesigned in a day to afford approaching guests an unobstructed view of the bone-white facade. There was no plumbing until a week before the opening, and yet every toilet had been fouled. David Martin scoured them out by hand. Pres Moore cleaned windows and collected garbage that had been dumped down a back staircase. Calvin Tsao ironed curtains. Eileen made the beds and vacuumed hallways. Pei himself was on his knees chipping paint from the marble floor. It was, of course, too late to set things right. The Hovings arrived to find a young Chinese couple smooching in their bed. Their shower curtain collapsed, and the toilet backed up.

Meanwhile, Jackie Onassis and Evangeline Bruce were riding to the opening when their chauffeured car bogged down in one of Beijing's impassable traffic jams. It looked as if they might miss the event altogether until their interpreter leaned out a window and exchanged a few words with a policeman who obligingly cleared their way. "What did you say?" they asked. "Mandarins," she replied.

Twenty miles later they pulled up to Fragrant Hill's serene white-and-gray facade nestled among crimson foliage billowing up and down the surrounding hills. "It was the lightest, whitest thing I've ever seen," said Bruce. "I was open-mouthed at the beauty. I gazed and gazed out of my hotel window until it was time to go downstairs for the ceremony."

Gongs sounded at seventeen minutes past four as a procession of dignitaries dressed in uniform blues and grays, including the minister of commerce, Liu Yi, and the mayor of Beijing, Jiao Ruoyu, entered the banquet hall for a reception of sweet Chinese wines, dim sum and assorted canapés. It was the world's most implausible congregation: Jackie Onassis in a chic black dress mingled with coarse Party bureaucrats in Mao suits. "They were all lowlifes smoking and spitting on the floor," said Thomas Hoving. "The contrast was amazing. Here was this light, delicate structure filled with thugs. It was clear they had no clue."

There were, of course, the obligatory mutual congratulations and toasts. "The roots of Chinese culture are deep," Pei said in Chinese, "and it is possible to graft the new onto the old." When the VIPs filed out to admire the gardens, the uninvited engineers and foremen rushed inside to devour leftovers from dirty plates.

The Chinese expressed only tepid enthusiasm for Fragrant Hill; the gulf of understanding was simply too great for them to appreciate what Pei had achieved on their behalf. "I've seen this before," one baffled official told Pei. "This looks . . . *Chinese*."

"The Fragrant Hill Hotel initially seems unimpressive," wrote *Renmin Ribao,* Beijing's daily newspaper. "It even appears a little strange. . . . This type of building is quite unusual in north China. Some people even think it is too bland. If you look inside, you will think you are somewhere else."

Pei's team had brought the project to fruition by sheer force of will, but it was up to the Chinese to maintain it until that day, perhaps decades hence, when it might serve as the stylistic example Pei envisioned. "The hotel was like an orphan," Fang said, "we didn't know if anyone would bring it up to be a useful person." When Evangeline Bruce left for the airport at dawn the morning after the opening she passed workers asleep on lobby couches, their dirty boots resting on new upholstery. Six months later, Pei began hearing complaints of bathrooms infested with flies, missing baggage and interminable dining room delays. Fang returned after one year to find cigarette burns in the carpet, a layer of paint slopped across the tiles and hairline cracks in the facade. Pei now publicly discourages people from visiting the hotel. "A work of architecture is not finished when it opens," Pei said. "It's just the beginning. That's why it's so important to me to find the right clients. Hopefully it will have a second life; hopefully it will come back."

Until then Pei considers the abolition of tall buildings near the Forbidden City his main contribution. "That to me is my greatest achievement," he said, "and the greatest satisfaction."

Fragrant Hill may have had a bigger impact in America where postmodernists interpreted it as Pei's capitulation: the high priest of late modernism, they gloated, had at last adopted historic references and ornament. "Not at all," Pei responded. "I am still on the same highway as twenty years ago. Modernism has not run out of steam, not at all. Of course it has changed, for the better. It's much freer now."

Once again, Pei had obliquely incorporated the best new ideas without overtly joining any group. "He denounced postmodernism while pleading for historicism within China," said Calvin Tsao. "This dichotomy in his philosophy mystified everyone, but he's a mandarin. He likes to surprise people. He's abstruse. He loves to alter people's perceptions of him. He's many things to many people."

Seven months after Fragrant Hill's debut, a six-person jury, including J. Carter Brown and Thomas Watson Jr., chairman emeritus of IBM, awarded Pei the Pritzker Prize, the architectural equivalent of a Pulitzer, for which he received $100,000 and a Henry Moore sculpture. If anything, Fragrant Hill demonstrated the value of continuity in culture—of not denouncing the past. Pei took this opportunity to confirm his bedrock faith in modernism as an evolving, vital idiom:

> You may be amused to know, although it was not amusing
> to me at the time, that a house designed for a friend in
> Cambridge in the early 1940s was denied a mortgage
> because it looked modern. I belong to that generation
> of American architects who built upon the pioneering
> perceptions of the modern movement, with an unwavering

> conviction in its significant achievements. . . . I believe
> in the continuity of this tradition, for it is by no means
> a relic of the past but a living force that animates and
> informs the present.

Pei used the $100,000 to establish a scholarship fund to allow Chinese students to study in America. He made the donation with one stipulation: students could tour the United States for one summer following their studies, but they had to return to China to apply what they learned—as he once intended to do.

◄

Thomas Hoving interviews Pei

for CONNOISSEUR.

Pei and Jackie Onassis greet a Chinese

guest at the opening, October 17, 1992.

▼

13
BAD FÊNG SHUI

When the time came at last to abandon Fragrant Hill to its uncertain fate, Pei retreated to the Mandarin Hotel in Hong Kong where he informed associates over drinks that his next project would be a monumental tower for the Bank of China to go up just blocks away, on the edge of Hong Kong's business district. He had rejected an invitation to replan Suzhou—"I want out of China," he told William Walton on his final vexing day at Fragrant Hill—but the Hong Kong branch of the Bank of China was a commission he could not turn down. China's top bankers were a worldly, Western-educated lot, so he would not have to contend with the heedless cadres that had impaired Fragrant Hill. Plus, Hong Kong's contractors and engineers were as sophisticated as any in the world.

Pei had a sentimental motive for accepting the job, as well. His father, Tsuyee Pei, had founded the Bank of China's Hong Kong branch in 1918, when I.M. was one year old. In a historical twist, the Communists who had seized the Bank of China from Tsuyee now wanted his son to build a commanding new Hong Kong branch building that would impart an aura of optimism and reconciliation.

In 1982 bank officials contacted Tsuyee, then eighty-nine, in New York and sought his blessing. "That is Chinese," Pei said. "Very respectful even though they were politically at

The Hong Kong branch of the Bank of China:
A symbol of China's future?

odds. So with one hand my father wanted to have nothing more to do with it and with the other he thought it important for me to do it. I accepted."

Pei's brother Y.K. was at that time preparing to move to Beijing after a long career as a materials engineer for Corning Glass in Ohio. Unlike I.M., he still considered China home, and he proposed to take their aged, senile father along. Tsuyee would have to leave his second wife, I.M.'s stepmother, but their lives had long since diverged. "He was sitting in his apartment staring at his four walls," said Y.K. "His wife was much younger and still full of life. She had different interests. So there was no one for him to talk to. That's no life for an old man. I thought it would be a good idea to take him back to China so that he could enjoy the rest of his life with his people. We could live together in a house. I would take care of him. He could talk to old friends and watch Chinese television."

Y.K.'s siblings approved of the plan—even their stepmother agreed—except for I.M. who, according to his brother, worried that it might appear unkind to send his father back to China, with its backward medical care, while he enjoyed a comfortable New York life. As the eldest sibling, I.M. prevailed. His father died in New York a few months later.

Hong Kong would seem a natural place for Pei to work. More than any other city, Hong Kong, like Pei himself, combines old and new, East and West. It is the hub of an émigré network and the cultural as well as physical gateway to the motherland. Its most prominent Chinese families faxed invitations to Pei's New York office in advance of his periodic layovers en route to Singapore or Beijing. "Once they know he's in town, he's inundated," Sandi said. "He has what appear to be endless social demands. He leaves a standing order at the Mandarin Hotel to hold all calls. For him, it's a place to have a suit made and eat well."

As a teenager, Pei had toted a bottle of wine through the streets of Shanghai with his uncle Tsuyuan, pausing as they walked among tea houses and mah-jongg counters to sample bubbling cauldrons of crab soup, sizzling wok-fried seafood and dim sum piled in wicker baskets. A similar gastronomic street party flourished in Hong Kong, where Chinese immigrants purveyed their regional cuisines from canopied stalls erected in the shadow of office towers. Pei led his partner Eason Leonard on a walking feast one day while waiting for a flight to Singapore. "We had about three hours to kill," Leonard remembered. "It was midday, so we agreed we would have lunch. We moved up the hillside behind the central district and had noodle soup at the first stop, hacked chicken and pork at the next, paper-thin abalone, crab, shrimp, duck, and on up the hill, enjoying something different at each one. Though we had not brought a bottle of wine, we'd reenacted one of his favorite experiences."

For all of Hong Kong's sentimental attractions, Pei had contributed just one ordinary glass box to its continuous building boom. He abstained from further participation because Hong Kong rarely provided the kind of enlightened patronage he found elsewhere. Hong Kong's British establishment favored Commonwealth architects, and the prosperous Asian bankers and shipping tycoons were content to erect a drab palisade of metal and glass.

Hong Kong's architectural reputation improved in the late 1980s when Norman Foster designed an audaciously high-tech headquarters for the Hongkong & Shanghai Bank, a powerful British establishment known throughout Asia simply as "the Bank." It was as if Foster had landed a spaceship on a prominent harbor-front site. Its innovations include columnless floors suspended like bridges from an exoskeleton, sixty-two crisscrossed escalators with mechanics encased in glass, mirrors that deflect sunlight into work areas, a vertical track that distributes documents among floors and elevators that blink the latest stock quotes. This futuristic assemblage of trusses and pipes was one of the most advanced—and expensive—buildings in the world, and it made Hong Kong a city the architectural community looked to for advanced thinking.

Foster's Hongkong Bank was the latest installment in an architectural rivalry with the Bank of China dating back to the Shanghai Bund. Banks were important institutions in laissez-faire boomtowns, and for decades the two banks leapfrogged over each other with ever grander edifices. The bank Foster replaced, for example, was once the tallest building between San Francisco and Cairo, and the first in Asia equipped with air conditioning. It had a squash court inside its imposing granite tower. Mosaics depicting the glories of commerce, transport and profit covered the ceiling of a grandly scaled banking hall. The bank had asked the architects to "please build us the best bank in the world." At its 1935 inauguration, a top official predicted that "generations yet unborn will gaze at it with something of the same gasp of admiration that we today bestow on, let us say, Durham Cathedral."

The Bank of China had answered with a slightly taller building which, in Communist hands, displayed Maoist slogans in illuminated Chinese characters above the adjacent cricket field. Also installed was a larger, more ferocious pair of lions than those guarding the Hongkong Bank.

Since Margaret Thatcher had agreed to transfer control of the colony to the mainland in 1997, in accordance with a treaty signed in 1898, Pei's new branch would inevitably symbolize Hong Kong's future under Communist rule. It had to dwarf Foster's bank and other emblems of colonial rule while announcing Communism's arrival in Asia's bastion of capitalism. It would also have to reassure the established old firms that Hong Kong would continue to prosper under Chinese sovereignty. It should, Pei said, represent "the aspirations of the Chinese people."

Pei also welcomed the chance, at age sixty-five, to add a distinguished skyscraper to his portfolio, especially since it would allow him to answer the postmodern high-rises topped with party-hat roofs arising in every American city. "I think [postmodernists] are missing the point," Pei said. "There's so much to be accomplished by staying very close to being pure—pure in the structural sense—which, in turn, will also be pure aesthetically."

Pei's firm was known for glass towers, but most were handled by his partners Henry Cobb and Jim Freed, while Pei concentrated on institutional plums. Pei dismissed those few he designed himself as inconsequential. "None was particularly memorable," he said, "but they were necessary to keep the office going." (His renunciation offended former clients, particularly the Singaporeans who valued his contributions as emblems of their struggle to overcome colonial backwardness.)

While Foster had built his landmark with an extravagant $1 billion budget on a prominent harbor-front site, Pei enjoyed no such advantages. He received a modest $130 million and a small, inhospitable plot hemmed in on three sides by elevated highways. To make matters worse, a Japanese military headquarters had occupied the site during the Second World War, and many Hong Kong residents believed it was haunted by the ghosts of tortured prisoners.

Pei would have to build to a prodigious height on this disadvantaged site if he was to stand out among the dense cluster of forty- and fifty-story skyscrapers squeezed between harbor and hills. A statement based on sheer verticality was, he acknowledged, a "180-degree shift" from the deliberate modesty of Fragrant Hill, but Hong Kong already contained more skyscrapers per block than any other city in the world. The bank, he promised, would be as "Western as any building. Hong Kong is the crossroads of the world, and it has the technique and means to do a modern building."

In conventional high-rises, weight accumulates with every floor: the taller the building, the thicker the columns. Lateral bracing is affixed to the rectangular frame holding the building's weight to steady sideways wobbling. Because Hong Kong suffers frequent typhoons, the standards for lateral bracing are twice as rigorous as New York's. A less audacious architect encumbered by this added burden and a slim budget might have been content to build the standard fifty-story box. But the implicit competition with Norman Foster's highly acclaimed bank located just two blocks away drove Pei to test the limits of structural possibility.

One weekend at his Katonah home shortly after returning from Fragrant Hill, Pei asked Sandi to slice a square wooden shaft lengthwise into four triangular quadrants, chamfer the ends and bind them together with a rubber band. As Pei slid the shafts out of alignment with one another, a pylon of incrementally diminishing masses emerged with a setback one-quarter of the way up, another halfway up and a third at the three-quarter point. A single stalk ascended to a pyramidal peak. "My father has a way of working in isolation before summoning any associates," Sandi said. "I sensed that it was an idea he already had fully formed in his mind."

Pei showed drawings and a model extrapolated from the bundle of sticks to Leslie Robertson, a structural engineer whose tall-building credits include the World Trade Towers. Robertson recognized in Pei's sculptural impulse the seed of a concept that could replace the costly agglomeration of I-beams that burdened conventional high-rises with the economy of a vertical spaceframe. "I.M. has a wonderful intuition," Robertson said. "He has a fundamental sense of buildings and people and all sorts of things. He is often unable to articulate it, but you can rely without question on his feeling for structure."

One way to make a tall building stable is to shift the weight out to the edges so that it withstands winds like a sailor with his feet spread apart. Robertson accomplished this by cross-bracing Pei's tower in thirteen-story modules, like a radio antenna. The diagonals transferred all building loads, both vertical and lateral, to four corner columns. Steel that otherwise would have gone into redundant lateral bracing could instead be applied skyward. "It represented a new way of building," Robertson said. "It opened people's

Pei's family home in Suzhou as it appeared

about the time of his return.

▼

minds to the importance of structure in architecture. It raised the height of the bar."

To emphasize that what works structurally also works aesthetically, Pei highlighted in red the diagonal members and horizontal trusses bracing the tower in thirteen-story intervals. "If we don't express the structure," Pei said, "the building will not look comfortable."

Pei recessed from his most high-tech undertaking long enough to honor an ancient influence. In 1985 he returned to China to attend the 2,500th anniversary of Suzhou's founding. For four days, the city's most illustrious son lingered in the Shizilin, attended traditional Chinese opera and storytelling in the Suzhou dialect, and was reunited with relatives. He obtained a copy of the family genealogy, which he would distribute to his children so that they could know their family history. Since the Pei family tombs were destroyed during the Cultural Revolution, Pei arranged for a memorial tomb for his mother, father and grandparents to be erected in a cemetery on the outskirts of Suzhou.

Pei showed a proper Confucian respect for history, but he did not always welcome its intrusions on his professional life. He used to joke that he failed the site-planning portion of the New York State licensing exam for architects because he applied the principles of *fêng shui*, an ancient Chinese discipline which, like a cosmic building code, dictates the luckiest position for towns, buildings, walls, furniture and even graves in relation to the invisible energy—the "breath of life"—pulsing through the landscape. Like the art of acupuncture, *fêng shui* is about finding the spot where energy will be most beneficial. An unobstructed view of an ocean or stream, for example, is thought to enhance "positive energy flow." Hills situated to the north ward off evil, but houses south of graveyards attract malevolent spirits. Triangular plots of real estate suffer calamities. Violation of these principles invites problems, even catastrophe. In some cases, entire villages have been abandoned when nearby construction upset their *fêng shui*.

Fêng shui holds great sway in Hong Kong, where arcane mystical practices and rites designed to placate the spirit world thrive incongruously alongside high-tech financial institutions monitoring the world's markets. When the Regent Hotel was being built, for example, adherents worried that the nine dragons of Kowloon, symbolized by the surrounding hills, would be unable to find their favorite bathing spot. The problem was considered grave enough to require the addition of forty-foot atrium windows so the dragons could find their way to the water.

On the advice of an eminent *fêng shui* master, Norman Foster repositioned escalators within his bank and ordered potted plants to ward off the malignant effects of interior cross bracing. Before the bankers could move into their new headquarters, the *fêng shui* masters decreed that the recumbent bronze lions, named Stephen and Stitt after early managers, should be moved to their sentinel position flanking the entrance at 4:00 A.M. on a Sunday. Furthermore, they must be transported simultaneously so that neither lion would become jealous. The bank directors had to be there to ceremoniously greet them.

Pei has variously declared and denied his belief in *fêng shui*. On the one hand, it is an ancient art encoded with cultural meaning and wisdom; on the other hand, its irrational aspects contribute to the Western view of China as a land of backward mysticism. "How can I believe those things?" Pei said. "All the same, *fêng shui* is part of my training. It is part of architecture." In any case, Pei was able to suspend his own ambiguities long enough to ask his Far East clients if they subscribed to it.

While at work on the Bank of China, Pei gave an associate a book on *fêng shui* and asked him to evaluate the design according to its principles. After careful research, the associate reported a few transgressions. "Oh, those Chinese," Pei scoffed. "They're so superstitious!"

"The Hong Kong Chinese are the most superstitious bunch you could ever find," Pei explained on a later occasion. "*Fêng shui* is a big business there. *Fêng shui* masters are like lawyers here: they're everywhere and you cannot make a move without consulting them. I knew I'd have trouble, but I didn't know what kind of trouble to expect."

The Bank of China was one client that could not subscribe to *fêng shui* principles, at least not publicly, since Communist dogma officially rejected spirituality. Nonetheless, with technical drawings under way, the bank sent Pei a telegram expressing concern about the giant boxed X's expressed by cross bracing and horizontal bands visible on the facade. In China the X signifies damnation, in part because condemned prisoners wear placards with their names crossed out. China's top bankers might not have accepted *fêng shui* themselves, but they feared that it might upset depositors and tenants. More than a few Hong Kong real-estate deals had unraveled over bad *fêng shui*. "They politely suggested to me that I might want to look at those X's again," Pei said. "I told them X's were the most important part of the design. They were holding up the building."

After much deliberation, Pei concealed the horizontal trusses separating each thirteen-story module, leaving what he shrewdly described as a series of interlocking diamonds—a propitious image that pleased the bankers. He also compared the tower to a bamboo shoot aspiring upward after a spring rain, a traditional Chinese symbol of renewal and hope. "There is an ancient Chinese proverb that speaks of the lotus rising from the muddy bottom of the pond to flower pure and unscathed on the water's surface," Pei said. "We wanted the building to have this same quality about it."

Pei spoke in symbols that Hong Kong understood. In addition to diamonds and bamboo, he invoked the solidity of impenetrable colonial-era banks by embedding his shiny obelisk in a three-story granite base enclosing a vast banking hall. It was a clunky postmodern pedestal awkwardly related to the lithe pylon above, but it served its purpose by expressing dignity and weight. "A bank," Pei's father once told him, "has to look secure." Pei originally wanted to exploit the steep site by channeling fountain water into the building at one end and out the other, but this, according to *fêng shui*, signaled departing wealth, so he settled for flanking the monumental base with two sloped waterfalls, which muffle the noise of the surrounding traffic.

Pei was able to build the tallest structure in the world outside of New York and Chicago on a modest budget because of the efficiency of his skeletal system. Even with the additional typhoon bracing, it required 40 percent less steel than conventional buildings and one-quarter of the welded joints. Following the groundbreaking in mid-1985, the Bank of China arose at a pace of one floor every four days. The entire superstructure went up in just sixteen months. A topping-out ceremony marking the completion of upward progress was held on August 8, 1988. Two hundred guests donned plastic helmets and rode wire-meshed construction elevators seventy stories to a rough concrete floor where a beam inscribed with the names of one hundred workmen was lifted into place and secured with ceremonial gold bolts. Colored balloons were released as VIPs lifted symbolic spadefuls of cement with red-ribboned shovels. They drank a barrel of sake, lit incense and ate roast pig. Jokes were made at the expense of Norman Foster's Hongkong Bank which, from this aerie, looked like an ornament on a toy city far below.

It was a carefully timed celebration: because the number eight—*baat*—sounds like the Cantonese word for prosperity—*faat*—some residents believed the eighth day of the eighth month of 1988 to be the luckiest day of the century. But even these bows to Chinese tradition could not extinguish the persistent conviction among neighbors that Pei's tower would cast bad luck. *Fêng shui* masters, shunned by architect and client, gave their prognosis to the press: what Pei poetically compared to an aspiring bamboo shoot was to them a flashing knife blade with pointy triangular edges threatening to unleash malevolent spirits from the underworld. "If an angle is pointing at you, it's like a knife pointing at you. It could cause bad health or economic damage," said *fêng shui* master Sung Siu-kwong. "Some of the angles are pointing into the center of the building, like knives at the stomach." Nervous neighbors hung *ghat gwa* mirrors outside their windows and balconies to deflect the forces of ill fortune emanating from Pei's tower.

Some of the sharp angles were said to be aimed at the governor's residence and, by extension, at the government itself. Shortly after newspapers printed these reports, the Peis ran into Governor David Wilson and his wife on a flight from Paris, where Pei's pyramid was provoking its own outrage. The Wilsons invited the Peis to Government House the next day. Before sitting down to lunch, their hosts showed them an ironic addition to their garden. "Since, to many people, Government House symbolized the government of Hong Kong, we took protective action by planting two willow trees in direct line between the sharp angle of the bank and the center of Government House," Wilson explained. "The soft, rounded shape of the willows counteracted the sharp, knifelike angle of the building. Thus, the problem was solved and everybody was happy."

The bad *fêng shui* was soon eclipsed by a greater calamity. During the predawn hours of June 4, 1989, Deng Xiaoping sent tanks and troops through barricades to fire on thousands of pro-democracy demonstrators assembled in Beijing's Tiananmen Square, the symbolic heart of Chinese state power. Pei was by coincidence traveling to mainland China at the time to select rocks for the bank tower's water garden. He entered the country as planned on the assumption that his stature would protect him, but he advised an accompanying journalist, Martin Filler, to stay behind in the safety of Hong Kong.

In the following weeks elderly hard-liners arrested tens of thousands. Once again a nightfall of repression and fear overtook China. Pei understood far better than most Americans the misery China faced under martial law. "I've never heard I.M. speak so frankly," remembered Calvin Tsao. "He went on and on about how disappointed he was. I never realized he cared that much about China."

The crackdown shattered Hong Kong's fragile faith in a stable and prosperous future under Communist rule. The fearful realization that as of 1997 it too would stand in the line of fire prompted a rare political awakening in a trading enclave normally concerned only with earning, producing, consuming and spending. Hundreds of thousands of Hong Kongers wearing black armbands and funeral garb marched through the streets in orderly protest.

The building Pei had conceived as a totem of hope in a united future now stood before the world as a reminder that Deng was poised to inherit Hong Kong. Depositors lined up at the Bank of China to withdraw their money. Workmen erecting the glass facade unfurled an enormous black banner bearing a message in Chinese characters: "Blood for Blood. Long Live Democracy."

Like most observers encouraged by Deng's relaxations, Pei felt betrayed by the crackdown. For all its talk about reform, China had not changed at all. "It hurt me very deeply," he said, "because doing this building was an expression of confidence in this country. When Tiananmen happened, I looked at the building and I felt terrible."

Pei received a deluge of calls soliciting his reaction, but he declined to speak publicly. Aside from signing petitions opposing alterations to two modernist landmarks—Marcel Breuer's Whitney Museum and Gordon Bunshaft's Lever House—Pei avoided overt political gestures. "Bobby Kennedy's assassination turned my parents off politics," said their daughter, Liane. "His death was a turning point for them. They maintained their convictions, but they no longer attended fund-raisers or lent their name to causes."

Pei was, in fact, notoriously shy of such efforts. A group of architects participating in an antinuclear protest march down Fifth Avenue, for example, spotted the Peis window-shopping. "Pei has always been politically progressive in an understated way," said architect James Polshek, "but he would never have marched. That would have been too demonstrative."

In the case of Tiananmen, Pei was especially wary, since his younger brother Y.K. had returned to China and was, by coincidence, living in an apartment near the square. Whatever Pei said could be used against his brother.

Tiananmen nonetheless incited Pei to abandon his ingrained sense of discretion and guardedness in favor of a quiet activism. In a rare public gesture, he published an op-ed piece in the *New York Times:*

> More than fifty years ago, my wife and I came to this
> wonderful country from China. For forty of those years, we
> dreamed that one day it would be possible to work in our
> native land. More than anything we wanted to combine our
> love of the nation that had become our own with our desire
> to do something for the land of our birth and heritage.
>
> In 1978, thanks to Deng Xiaoping's remarkable
> economic reforms, we were given the chance to work in
> China. As I worked with a new generation of Chinese, my
> hopes for the future of China were ever more optimistic.
> We believed that China was gradually emerging from its
> long nightmare of war and repression. . . . Today, those
> dreams are dashed by the horrible events at Tiananmen
> Square. We were shocked beyond measure. . . . It was

always easier to work in the United States, but we worked
in China, despite many frustrations, out of a love of that
country, out of a sense that things were getting better. . . .
Will we ever be able to work in China again? I am not sure.
In any case, I cannot accept the thought that all the blood
was shed in vain that Saturday night, June 3, 1989, at
Tiananmen Square.

Pei had no satisfactory answer for reporters seeking the Chinese-
American community's reaction to Tiananmen because there was no consensus. It was balkanized into too many fractious contingents—Hong Kongers,
mainlanders, Taiwanese, backers of Communists and Nationalists, privileged
uptown Chinese like Pei and recent immigrants toiling in restaurants and
sweatshops. These divisions, along with the traditional Chinese reluctance to
organize outside the family, inhibited the formation of a representative group
like the Anti-Defamation League or the NAACP. Chinese-Americans, the
"silent minority" as they were sometimes called, were conspicuously absent
during Tiananmen as network anchors interviewed Caucasian sinologists associated with universities and think tanks. "There was no organization to turn
to," Pei said. "There isn't any spokesman for Chinese-Americans. That
seemed a pity."

For more than a decade, Chinese friends had urged Pei to adopt a political role in the belief that, as the most widely known Asian in the world next
to Deng himself, he was uniquely qualified to provide the political voice
Chinese-Americans have traditionally lacked. Pei resisted until, about a
week after Tiananmen, he invited to his office a handful of prominent
Chinese-American acquaintances, including General Motors vice president
Shirley Young, investment banker Oscar Tang and the Nobel laureate physi-
cist T. D. Lee of Columbia University. We no longer consider China our home,

Pei said, but shouldn't we discuss our concerns for its welfare and try to express them together?

"Like many of us, he was horrified at the killing and repression, particularly in contrast to the optimism the pro-democracy movement had inspired in previous months," said Oscar Tang, who, like Pei, grew up in Shanghai's French Concession. "We had all watched the rationalization of China with phenomenal hope that finally, after 150 years of turmoil and domination, China would absorb new ideas and move forward. Tiananmen Square threatened to reverse all that. China looked as if it were falling back into chaos."

Over the course of the summer, the original nucleus enlisted a wider circle, including the cellist Yo-Yo Ma, playwright David Henry Hwang, software entrepreneur David Lam, San Francisco developer Leslie Schilling, novelist Bette Bao Lord, U.S. District Court Judge Ronald Lew, Astronaut Taylor Wang, and Chang-Lin Tien, chancellor of UC Berkeley.

It was an unlikely congregation. "Chinese generally don't understand affiliations with nonfamily causes," said Shirley Young, the committee's chairperson. "Joining goes against their natural grain."

Nonetheless, they straggled into Pei's conference room on periodic afternoons, wilted from the heat and bleary from late-night CNN. They convened in crisis, and, at first, there were raised voices and pounded fists as China's most accomplished expatriates contemplated a swift, public condemnation of the PRC. Gradually, though, over the course of the summer, the old mandarin circumspection reasserted itself. "These were highly sophisticated people who had been through a lot," said Shirley Young, who came to America after the Japanese executed her father, a Chinese consul general posted in the Philippines during World War II. "Unlike the ad hoc committees collecting signatures and donations around the country, this was a thoughtful, big-picture group. As we spoke it became clear that Tiananmen was by no means the only reason we should be getting together. We focused on the greater implication: what could we do to be helpful when the immediate crisis died down."

By September, the Committee of One Hundred, as they by now called themselves, had drafted a mission statement for an unaligned enterprise capable of promoting "the inherent dignity and inalienable rights of Chinese-Americans and Chinese everywhere." (The membership falls short of its title: there are some eighty members to date.)

At the committee's first annual meeting, an all-day affair held at New York's Century Association, an imposing McKim, Mead & White club on Fifth Avenue, Pei's friend Ambassador Richard Holbrooke helped set their sights beyond Tiananmen by emphasizing the influence such a group could have as a resource for Washington policymakers who only dimly perceive a cultural history so removed from their own. "The American way of doing things is not the Asian way," observed Pei's daughter, Liane, a lawyer. "Western diplomats don't understand the distinct nature of the Chinese personality. The more the United States pushes, the less likely it is to get anywhere. . . . My father views all this with tremendous regret. There have been so many missed opportunities."

The committee's first formal meeting convened in March 1991 at the Mandarin Oriental Hotel in San Francisco. At the time, the Bush administration was trying to repair its relations with Beijing, and its ambassador to China, James Lilley, traveled to San Francisco to encourage the committee. ("It's not every day that I receive a letter signed by I. M. Pei," he said.) Beijing also signaled its support by sending its ambassador to the United States, Zhu Qizhen.

Lofty endorsements did not stop grassroots Asian groups from criticizing the committee's members for presuming to speak for all Chinese-Americans. The elitism implied in its name also rankled. "How can Yo-Yo Ma, whom I respect very much as a musician, represent me on social issues?" Dr. Rolland

Lowe, chairman of the Chinese Democracy Education Foundation, complained at the time to Fox Butterfield of the *New York Times*. "And the same for I. M. Pei. . . . We have a Chinese saying: Leadership is what people accord you, not what you declare for yourself."

Critics also faulted the group for its reluctance to endorse specific causes. "That's typical Chinese-rooted caution," said one Asian-American political organizer. "You know, 'The reed in the wind bends but does not break.' " A San Francisco–based newspaper, *Asian Week*, compared the committee to "a high school student without a date, all dressed up with no place to go."

The committee found a more specific role for itself as Sino-American relations soured in the early 1990s. Mindful of the precipitous collapse of Communism in Eastern Europe, Deng allowed entrepreneurial ventures to flourish with unprecedented freedom from official control while resisting political openness. A few years after Tiananmen, the Chinese were too busy making money to worry about political reform. As China's vast populace accumulated wealth faster than that of any other major country in the world, billboards once devoted to Maoist slogans began advertising cameras and computers. Stores sold soft drinks and color television sets. A Kentucky Fried Chicken franchise operated within sight of Mao's mausoleum. A stock market opened in Shanghai. Streets were brightened by Western business suits, fashionable hairstyles, makeup and high heels.

"When China wakes," Napoleon Bonaparte once predicted, "it will shake the world." China seemed to fulfill his prophecy as a galloping economy aroused the spirit of nationalist strength and, along with it, a fresh cycle of popular resentment toward the West. China is now a legitimate power with nuclear weapons, a seat on the U.N. Security Council, the world's largest army, and a growing military arsenal capable of reclaiming territories China feels it unfairly lost over the last century.

Not surprisingly, China's nationalist vigor has unsettled its trade partners. In mid-March 1994, President Clinton sent Secretary of State Warren Christopher to Beijing to convey the administration's reluctance to renew the low tariffs on exports to the United States, known as most-favored-nation trading status, unless China improved its human rights record and curbed unfair trade practices and trademark violations. Christopher's hosts flaunted their contempt by detaining dissidents on the eve of his arrival. "It is futile to apply pressure against China," Premier Li Peng told American reporters.

The Committee of One Hundred had, by coincidence, arranged to send a twenty-two-person delegation to Beijing just weeks after Christopher's misbegotten mission for a week of consultations facilitated by Pei's childhood friend Jing Shu-ping, now a high-ranking Party economist. It was the perfect chance to play the role of unaligned intermediary. "The two sides seemed to be speaking past one another," said Shirley Young. "Since we are bicultural, we could explain each side's position in a personal and emotional way."

Pei assumed the ceremonial role of chief delegate: he entered meetings first, occupied the seat of honor in the club chair beside his Chinese counterpart and offered the first toast. By speaking in Mandarin, he attained an empathy and subtle coloration of meaning beyond the reach of U.S. diplomats dependent on translators.

Under these sympathetic conditions, Pei conveyed to Deng's heir apparent, President Jiang Zemin, and other Politburo members an inkling of the human sentiment behind American policy. He shared the results of a survey conducted among 1,300 Americans that showed divergent impressions of China—from the approval expressed by companies doing business there to harsh denunciations voiced by Congressional leaders and their staffs. The committee warned officials accustomed to a single party line not to be confused by the cacophonous sound of American democracy; congressional outbursts and newspaper editorials, they explained, do not reflect administration policy.

The surest way to improve their own press coverage, Pei advised, was to make life easier for Western correspondents, an embattled lot whose simple requests for information routinely encounter infuriating bureaucratic obstruction and harassment. Restricted travel encourages them to interview Beijing-based dissidents which, in turn, provokes police surveillance and wiretaps. The best way to convey *your* side of an issue, the committee told their hosts, is to provide more information, not less.

President Jiang, in turn, warned that America could no longer impose its own trade and human rights rules on a country governed by different cultural principles. He repeated the PRC's persistent claim that the term *human rights* has a separate meaning in China, where Confucian thinking values the society's welfare—the food, housing and medical care Americans take for granted—above individual rights. Clearly, Beijing's top priority is maintaining stability (i.e., the Party's authority) during the transition to a market economy that had unraveled other Communist regimes. Jiang also appealed to their ethnic pride by recounting childhood visits to Shanghai's foreign concessions, the self-governed Western enclaves where Pei grew up. Having seen those symbols of China's semicolonial subjugation, Jiang said, he resolved to fight foreign intrusion. His comments contained an undertone not lost on his Chinese-born guests: how dare the United States, with its homelessness and race crimes, admonish China, a sovereign nation of ancient distinction, as if it were some developing country. By all accounts, it was a most persuasive discourse. "I've arrived at a more balanced understanding," Pei told a committee colleague.

"To them—stability, stability, stability—that's it," Pei told Western reporters. "If you allow 1.2 billion voices, you are liable to get drowned. I think we have to begin to understand their dilemma. I've done that."

The committee reported their observations to Robert Rubin, then director of Clinton's National Economic Council and a guiding hand in White House trade policy. In a letter to the president, they urged policymakers not to cancel the MFN status, but to encourage trade and cultural exchange that would open China to the outside world while allowing its leaders to save face. Sustained growth of China's economy, they promised, would inevitably lead to openness and reform.

President Clinton agreed. Three days after receiving the committee's letter, he announced that improved human rights was no longer a condition for China's trade privileges with the United States. Since then, American companies have barnstormed China, but more trade has not led to the political freedoms Pei and others anticipated. On the contrary, correspondents and human rights groups have reported a relentless crackdown over the last year. China's most famous dissident, Wei Jingsheng, returned to jail in April. On November 24, police detained the poet Bei Dao as he arrived at the Beijing airport; he flew back to the United States after an all-night interrogation. A week later, five men looted the Beijing apartment of Liu Zaifu, a prominent literary scholar and pro-democracy activist living in the United States. A State Department report issued last January reported no progress on human rights. "Frankly, in the human rights front, the situation has deteriorated," acknowledged Winston Lord, the State Department's top diplomat for Asian affairs and husband of committee member Bette Bao Lord. "They're rounding up dissidents, harassing them more."

Meanwhile, the committee has tried to use its credibility and influence to promote Chinese-American interests without endorsing specific causes, as lobby organizations for other ethnic groups do. For example, the committee supports Chinese-American candidates of both parties by bringing them together with its wealthy and influential members. Beneficiaries include former L.A. mayoral candidate Michael Woo, California State Treasurer Matt

Fong and Cheryl Lau who, after a failed gubernatorial bid in Nevada, was appointed general counsel to the U.S. House of Representatives. "We're well-wired on both sides of the aisle," said one committee official. "We had friends in the Bush era; we have friends in the Clinton era."

The committee is also guarding against defamation. On May 19, 1994, Connie Chung aired an interview with national security expert Nicholas Eftimiades on the *CBS Evening News* suggesting that Beijing forces Chinese-Americans to perform acts of espionage on its behalf by threatening their relatives in China. "Every day planeloads of Chinese citizens arrive legally in the United States," she reported. "Ordinary people. But to the Chinese government, some of them may be future spies who a few years down the road will be activated to steal America's military and technological secrets, whether they want to or not."

In June, the committee asked the U.S. Commission on Civil Rights to investigate what it characterized as a reckless, one-sided report that unjustly caused hundreds of thousands of Chinese-Americans to be viewed by their neighbors and colleagues as untrustworthy. "These broad-based generalizations virtually instruct the American public to view Chinese-Americans and Chinese visitors as spies," their letter said. "We believe that this broadcast implants a stereotype of Chinese-Americans as being crafty and devious. . . ."

The Commission on Civil Rights, in turn, sent CBS News president Eric Ober a letter stating its concern that the segment "may have sown the seeds of suspicion that large numbers of Chinese-Americans and Chinese nationals in the United States are potential foreign agents. . . . The First Amendment rightly protects the free press, even when its reporting is unfair or sensational. However, news organizations have a responsibility to report with special sensitivity when the subject matter could exacerbate existing racial and ethnic tensions."

A week later, Ober invited a delegation of Chinese-Americans to air their grievances at CBS headquarters. "I was quite surprised by their reaction," Connie Chung said. "I don't believe in any way that our report cast aspersions on anyone living here in the United States. I thought people would be glad that we were exposing what the Chinese government was doing. I thought this would focus attention on it and put the Chinese on notice that they couldn't get away with that kind of pressure."

Five months after airing the segment, Chung issued a rare "clarification" on the *CBS Evening News.*

The irony, of course, is that Connie Chung is one of the most prominent Chinese-American of all. The group solicited her participation early on, and she might well have signed on had CBS policy not discouraged affiliations that could be construed as a conflict of interest. In lieu of her personal involvement, she donated an undisclosed sum.

Just as Max Urbahn's AIA excursion had afforded Pei an unobtrusive homecoming, the Committee of One Hundred allows him the kind of inconspicuous means of political influence he has always wanted. "Mr. Pei was the godfather and guiding spirit," said Shirley Young. "He is a refined and elegant mandarin. He wants to have the facility to guide, but he doesn't want to put himself in the fore."

14
A CERTAIN AGE

Chinese civilization endured by accepting foreign influences—Buddhism from India, Bolshevism from Russia—and enfolding them into its own culture. It made them its own.

Pei survived at the top of the architectural world in a similar way: his alert antennae scanned the cultural horizon, and he judiciously incorporated what he liked best. Unlike the mercurial gadfly Philip Johnson, who remade himself according to each emerging fashion, Pei absorbed the best of current sensibilities without debasing his consistent commitment to refined, gentlemanly geometries. "Architecture really is the need to synthesize the best out of life, out of history," he said. "Whatever is still valid, I do not care how old it is, use it. And what is not valid, abandon it."

By shrewdly discarding and consolidating, Pei moved his enlarged kind of modernism beyond the boring box to inhabit new realms, new moods. "He's blown modernist functionalism out of the water," Paul Goldberger said. "He's shown that there's room for civic grandeur, monumentality and buildings with great presence."

Pei was able to extend his range as he got older in part because he knew how to cultivate great clients. Part of his genius was his ability to inspire in them a collaborative pursuit of something finer and more ambitious than was originally imagined, no matter the cost. "He leads them, subtly and

◄ **The Shinji Shumeikai bell tower.**

351

marvelously, to a high level of judgment," his friend William Walton once said, "explaining why they don't want what they just said they wanted."

"It's a mutual challenge," Pei said. "I challenge the client, of course. You have to. But they challenge me. . . . If I count all the projects I have a fondness for, behind them are great clients."

．　．　．　．

Stanley Marcus, the former head of Neiman-Marcus department stores, called Pei "the best salesman, in the best sense." Marcus chaired the committee that hired Pei after the Kennedy assassination to build a new city hall as part of a wide-ranging campaign to help Dallas overcome its reputation as the redneck city of hate. Pei prescribed an assertive Le Corbusian edifice with a concrete facade leaning outward at 34 degrees toward a plaza enlivened by indigenous oaks and a Henry Moore sculpture Pei insisted they could not do without. It was a conspicuous case of modernism trying to convey the civic authority normally associated with classicism.

The rehabilitation of Dallas continued for two decades after the assassination with plans for an exuberant symphony hall capable of enhancing the city's stature. It was hoped that a new hall, combined with an art museum designed by Edward Larrabee Barnes, would excite an arts district animated by galleries and cafés in the underutilized northeastern fringe of a city dominated by high-rises and highways.

Once again Stanley Marcus led the search for an architect. He summoned nine worthies one by one to a conference room at Ross Perot's Electronic Data Systems offices and asked them why they wanted the job. All answered suitably: It would be an honor. It would be a unique opportunity. All except the incorrigible Philip Johnson who said, "Well, I don't know that I *want* to do your building."

When no clear favorite emerged, Marcus asked Pei to fly down for an interview. Pei had initially eliminated himself from consideration. His firm had done several conspicuous buildings since the city hall, provoking some complaint that Dallas was becoming Pei City. Nonetheless, when summoned, Pei arrived, the *Dallas Morning News* reported, "like an ambassador on a high-level mission." While his competitors toted monographs, slides and models, Pei arrived unencumbered, bathed in his own elegant aura. He was impeccably dressed in a gray suit with a subtle wine-colored tie and a single pen tucked in an inside pocket. He recalled frequent evenings spent listening to Mozart, Beethoven and Bach at Lincoln Center and Carnegie Hall. "I don't know much about the design of a concert hall," he told them, "but I've made up my mind that I must do one great concert hall before I die."

Afterward Stanley Marcus asked members of the search committee to submit their first three choices. The symphony's executive director, Leonard Stone, wrote "I. M. Pei. I. M. Pei. I. M. Pei."

"There was no haggling over the choice," Stone recalled. "Pei took control of the committee right away. He captivated us with his charm and understatement." Marcus called during Pei's office Christmas party to tell him he had the job. "This is a wonderful New Year's present," Pei said.

Pei was to have renovated New York's Vivian Beaumont Theater, but he resigned from that job in 1982 after disagreements with acoustician Cyril Harris. Good architecture does not necessarily make good sound, and vice versa. To discourage Pei from following an architect's natural inclination to favor design at the expense of sound, the Dallas symphony hired Russell Johnson, an esteemed and uncompromising acoustician, and asked him to report directly to them, thereby putting acoustician and architect on equal footing.

Most auditoriums built in this century are fan-shaped with low ceilings that slope down to the stage, a configuration that has produced a succession of well-publicized sonic fiascoes. Johnson preferred the intimate shoebox dimensions of the classical nineteenth-century halls like Vienna's Musikvereinsaal and New York's Carnegie Hall. Based on their precedent, Johnson advocated a relatively long, narrow, high-sided hall ringed with balconies. He would fine-tune the acoustics with sound-absorbing drapes, reverberation chambers equipped with concrete shutters above the balconies and an adjustable forty-two-ton acoustical canopy suspended over the orchestra. Most important, he wanted the room to be small—just 2,066 seats—to preserve the best possible acoustics and sight lines.

Symphony officials knowingly pitted Pei and Johnson against each other and, inevitably, a disputatious tug-of-war ensued between two strong-minded perfectionists working at cross purposes. "The man has a good pair of ears," Pei said, "but no eyes." Johnson countered that Pei cared only about appearance, not sound. Even their personalities clashed: unlike the blithe, engaging Pei, Johnson is a rumpled man of brooding professional rectitude. Dallas newspapers chronicled their run-ins with uninhibited relish. It was widely reported that both men threatened to resign, a charge both deny.

Building committee chairman Mort Meyerson welcomed a dose of discord. His experience shepherding fragile egos through complicated projects as president of Ross Perot's Electronic Data Systems told him that conflict often extracts the best results. "The press indicated that this was destructive," he said. "To me, it's part of the creative process."

When the standoffs degenerated into protracted delays, however, Meyerson vowed to "knock their two heads together until I get a sound I like." He flew to New York and reportedly threatened to fire one or both if they failed to resolve their differences and get on with the job.

In the end, Johnson was able to satisfy most of his demands: he dictated the shape of the room and positioned its seating; he installed his acoustical wizardry; and he specified thick walls constructed of concrete, plaster and heavy wood to deflect low frequencies. Johnson himself tapped the walls with a mallet and listened for air pockets that might trap sound.

"Russell has imposed an acoustic girdle on me," Pei complained, but he too won key concessions. He replaced a hulking U-shaped soffit over the stage (he compared it to the underside of a boat) with an array of canopies, framed the stage with two immense pillars and masked the reverberation chambers with a scrim and a decorative grid.

After these testy negotiations, Pei was free to beautify the room as he liked. He delegated most of the interior decisions to Charles Young, an associate conversant with the great halls of Europe, who steered a shrewd middle course between modern rigor and the sumptuous appointment of traditional music chambers. The walls were paneled in a grid pattern of African makore, American cherry and inlaid brass with softly backlit onyx affixed to balcony fronts. The seats were upholstered in rust-colored mohair with makore backs and cherry trim. Violinist Isaac Stern said it was "not a building but a musical instrument."

Pei recognized that symphony officials wanted an auditorium of international distinction but they also wanted a place to party. He obliged by rotating the building diagonally on its site to make room for a sweeping crescent-shaped lobby full of processional drama where Dallas society could gather at intermission to see and be seen. It was Pei's signature atrium crossed with Charles Garnier's Paris Opéra: an exuberant space designed to draw people in and guide them up swelling staircases watched over by long, rounded balconies. Pei gave Dallas a Texas-sized social stage on which a dress-up crowd of high-rolling patrons and grandes dames could survey one another before filing into the respectful hush of the inner hall.

Pei was not content to encase Johnson's rectangular hall within the predictable limestone box. He wanted to show that late modernism was capable of Beaux-Arts exuberance and civic grandeur. So he encircled the auditorium with swirling Piranesian curves illuminated by three intricately glazed skylights that envelop the lobby like a crystalline circus tent. "Anyone who

has seen some of the Baroque churches in Germany and Austria will understand the magic quality of an undulating space," Pei said. "This building is
our attempt to explore the possibility of undulating spaces. It is not exactly
like the Baroque, but nonetheless it achieves much of the same purpose."

The gardens of Suzhou surprised the visitor at every twist in the path. The
triangular East Building, with its three vanishing points, suggested the same
disorientation for effect. Now, a decade later, Pei played with the continuously shifting perspectives of curvilinear form. "His geometry puts us in an
exploratory mood by not revealing everything at once," wrote the *Dallas
Morning News*. "As we wander through the lobby we wonder what's around
this corner, or at the top of that stair. Levels change, lines dissolve. Concert-
goers will doubtless arrive early just to hobnob and survey the passing scene
from a balcony or staircase."

In one of his first meetings with symphony officials, Pei warned that he
would try to persuade them to exceed their original expectations. He succeeded: Dallas's bid for cultural advancement cost about twice what voters
had anticipated when they approved a bond issue to amass the estimated
$50 million, of which donors would pay 40 percent.

For starters, the original budget did not cover the limestone exterior the
building committee had admired on presentation models. So they found a
benefactor who agreed to give $1.5 million if the symphony found other funds
for a marble floor in the lobby. "Pei strategically sketched a bare-bones concert hall," said *Dallas Morning News* architecture critic David Dillon, "and
then worked on individual donors to add things. His constant line was
'You've built this wonderful hall, why stop now? Didn't you say you wanted
the best in the world?' They tried to get a handle on the budget, but they were
overmatched."

Pei is a master at getting his way without confrontation. He gently coaxed
the "burghers of Dallas," as he called them, toward an uncompromised hall

►

The Meyerson Symphony Center in Dallas. Pei warned that he would try to exceed the original expectations.

A place to see and be seen: the grand stairwell of the Meyerson Symphony Center.

▼

without being haughty or intimidating in the manner of many big-name New York architects. "He never puts anyone in a situation in which they're demeaned or lose face," said Ralph Heisel, who contributed to the early concept. "He always listens and brings out the best in clients."

Many benefactors were loosely connected with Ross Perot and his circle of hard-nosed Texas businessmen—a tough bunch to seduce with pleasing pictures. Still, they found themselves powerless to resist Pei's entreaties. "Let's take a blood oath," Mort Meyerson suggested to symphony executive director Leonard Stone one day in anticipation of Pei's latest proposal. "We're going to look him straight in the eye and say no." But sure enough, they relented before Pei's gorgeous rendering. "The guy did it to us again," Meyerson said. "How in hell did he do it?"

By the mid-1980s the budget for what the *Dallas Morning News* called a "rhapsody in red" had swollen to embarrassing proportions just as oil prices slumped and Texas banks dried up. Oil had cost more than $30-a-barrel when Pei unveiled his design in 1982; it dipped below $10-a-barrel on groundbreaking day. How could such wealth be squandered on a symbol of opulence, came the inevitable murmurs of resentment, while the rest of Dallas suffered? Disparate cultural groups carped at the symphony for milking the city of its philanthropic dollars. To this day, the city council is wary of arts spending.

Pei was not afraid to push for improvements late in the game, however. In 1989, with the project more than $30 million over budget, he unveiled a cardboard mock-up of a pair of long-stemmed lamps topped with translucent onyx panels, which he proposed to place on either side of the grand staircase. The lighting funds were already depleted, and there was much rolling of eyeballs when he said they were to be made in Italy at a cost of $12,000 apiece, but Pei's elegant lamps would contribute a colorful fin de siècle flourish to the vast neutral lobby. "My God," one benefactress said, "they look as if they were created by Frank Lloyd Wright." In the end, Pei secured not two but eleven lamps at a total cost of $250,000 by selling them as illuminated sculpture.

The whole venture might have choked to death on its own bills had Ross Perot not donated $10 million to see it through on the condition that it be named after Mort Meyerson, his friend and closest business associate. Perot gave another $2 million, contingent upon a matching donation, to pay for the makore wood, cherry and brass for the interior hall.

Meanwhile, the symphony nervously prepared for the September opening. After all the dollars and delays, anything short of unqualified success would be a civic embarrassment. Two weeks before the gala debut, a Russian-born cellist walked onto the unfinished stage for a private sound test. "I heard what I heard," Leonard Stone recalled, "and I said *yes!* It sounded so rich and throaty. I knew we'd gotten it."

Project manager Ted Amberg recalled the final round-the-clock preparations as "the most exciting days of my career. There was so much energy. There were hundreds of people on the site." Conductor Eduardo Mata reluctantly admitted crews during rehearsals to install railings, light fixtures and chairs on the condition that they work quietly. "The noise level slowly rose," remembered Amberg, "until somebody dropped a plank. Then Mata would stop and insist on silence. He'd get it for another half hour, then he'd stop again." Pei himself sallied about in shirtsleeves and sneakers attending to the freshly planted oaks in the plaza, supervising the installation of an Ellsworth Kelly painting at one end of the lobby, and imploring workers not to scratch the woodwork.

Pei held an opening-day press conference at a downtown hotel for two hundred journalists assembled from as far away as Vienna and Singapore. The first question came from a British reporter who asked about Pei's stormy collaboration with Russell Johnson. "Why focus on the ten percent of disagreement?" Pei retorted. "Why not celebrate that we agreed on ninety percent?" Johnson stood up with a smile and said, "I'm not sure that we agreed on ninety percent. I think it was more like eighty-five percent."

When Texas native Van Cliburn performed Tchaikovsky's First Piano Concerto that evening, symphony officials heaved a collective sigh: the music resounded clear and bright. Critics agreed that with some fine-tuning the room could rank among the century's best. "The tone of the Dallas Symphony reached out easily, smoothly, even and warm," reported Robert Commanday, music critic for the *San Francisco Chronicle*. "There was that special wished-for reverberance that sustains the chord an ideal micro-instant past the musicians' release of it. . . . The notes glistened distinctly, all the way back at the rear of the hall in the third or dress-circle tier."

After the maestro and soloists took their bows, Pei and Johnson stepped onstage. Each deferred to the other at the conductor's podium. They raised clasped hands and embraced in the spotlight as the applause rose to a crescendo. "It was glorious," said Leonard Stone. "This building had been the battlefield on which these two warriors had fought each other for years."

Although the envisioned arts district for Dallas fell victim to unchecked development, Pei gave a spiritual lift to a proud city laid low by hard times. "I hope the audiences of the twenty-first century, when they leave the warmth of our symphony hall on a cold and starlit night after a particularly brilliant performance, will recall that we did not lose our nerve," Mort Meyerson wrote at the time. "I hope that they, in turn, will resolve not to lose theirs as they face the future of Dallas."

■ ■ ■ ■

Pei plied his mature gifts at both ends of the cultural spectrum that year. A few months after Tchaikovsky and Mahler christened the Meyerson Symphony Center, Pei opened a jewellike Beverly Hills office for Michael Ovitz and his powerful movie agency.

Ovitz practically owned Hollywood by the 1980s. His Creative Artists Agency had eclipsed the studios by packaging the biggest producers, actors, directors and screenwriters. His all-star client list included Kevin Costner, Robert De Niro, Michael Douglas, Tom Hanks, Michael Keaton, Bill Murray, Robin Williams, Steven Spielberg, Barbra Streisand, Michael Jackson and Madonna.

Ovitz was not content to be a modern-day Thalberg or Goldwyn. He wanted to extend his reach beyond show-business boundaries into other, loftier business realms. In 1990 he advised Matsushita Electric, the world's largest consumer electronics firm, on its $7 billion purchase of MCA. He also brokered the $3.5 billion sale of Columbia Pictures to Sony. These and other deals helped secure his reputation as a fixer on equal footing with Wall Street biggies like Felix Rohatyn and Henry Kravis.

Along the way, Ovitz decided to build a high-toned Beverly Hills head-quarters befitting his expanding empire. Unlike Michael Eisner of Disney, who hired architects like Robert Stern and Michael Graves, Ovitz wanted to use architecture's image-making powers to distinguish himself from L.A.'s slick, of-the-moment culture. He sought a masterpiece of conservative good taste that would demonstrate that he belonged to a higher corporate caste than the abrasive showbiz hustlers.

After a two-year search, Ovitz chose Pei over the rising breed of innovative young California architects like Frank Gehry. "I did a lot of research," Ovitz told the *Los Angeles Times,* "and I decided I.M. was my man. I love the style of the classic period of modernism, especially the 1930s German Bauhaus, and I feel Pei is the purest inheritor of that tradition. . . . The last thing I wanted for this agency was a trendy L.A.-style building that would date in a decade. I wanted an I. M. Pei signature design straight from his own hands. I got exactly what I was after."

Ovitz approached Pei through a mutual friend, Arne Glimcher, owner of New York's Pace Gallery and a filmmaker (he produced *Gorillas in the Mist* and directed *Mambo Kings*). Pei was at first reluctant to take on a small job in a city far removed from his cultivated realm; he had not been to L.A. in a decade. But Ovitz pursued him as relentlessly as any movie star. "Ovitz was determined to get my father to do his building," said Sandi Pei, "and my father was impressed with his determination. He continuously sought an audience with my father. He refused to accept no for an answer."

Ovitz was not Paul Mellon, but he had established himself as a patron of unimpeachable taste with a prodigious collection of Picassos, Dubuffets and Lichtensteins—the exact genre of postwar abstraction Pei liked best. "He came across as someone who genuinely wanted to do something important," Pei said. "I was persuaded that I could work for him because he would back quality. That is very rare in Hollywood." With his alertness to change, Pei may also have sensed a shift in power and patronage from the old eastern establishment to a new breed of communications and entertainment moguls like Ovitz. Pei is a restless assimilator, and Hollywood was a rich kingdom he had yet to penetrate. There was, as well, a neat closure about the affair: movies had helped draw the adolescent Ieoh Ming to America fifty years earlier. In the end, Pei signed on.

Pei had to accommodate a corporate culture influenced by Ovitz's interest in Eastern disciplines. Ovitz is famous in Hollywood for practicing aikido at dawn and urging his agents to study Sun Tzu's *Art of War*. On his desk sat a vase that, in the Japanese style, contained bright-yellow flower petals floating in water. The agency itself has been compared to a Maoist camp where devoted young agents—the L.A. press likes to call them "ninja agents"—and their assistants work fifteen-hour days in collective effort without formal titles.

Ovitz wanted a Buddhist groundbreaking ceremony to ensure harmony and prosperity within his realm, so Sandi Pei referred him to Lin Yun, a *fêng shui* master and a distinguished teacher of Black Sect Tantric Buddhism who arrived from Berkeley with an entourage of twenty students. Speaking through a translator, Professor Lin told Ovitz how to position his desk in his existing office at Century City. Then he examined Pei's plans and indicated where plants should be positioned to resolve energy imbalances. Afterward all the agents and their assistants stood around the site with cigars and champagne as Professor Lin released white doves to spread news of the groundbreaking and sprinkled a mixture of rice, alcohol and red cinnabar powder to lay the seeds of prosperity and feed the bad spirits so they would leave. All the while he envisioned millions of Buddhas shining a light of power and compassion upon the site.

At the Bank of China in Hong Kong, Pei had frowned on what he considered an outmoded superstition, perhaps because it reinforced the image of Chinese backwardness. He was similarly standoffish in Los Angeles. He did not attend the groundbreaking, nor did he meet with Professor Lin.

Pei installed Ovitz and his top agents behind a curved three-story curtain wall of tinted glass overlooking the busy intersection of Santa Monica and Wilshire boulevards with the cool detachment of a limousine window. The supporting staff resides in a travertine-clad wing pierced by recessed windows with dark postmodern lintels. The two wings are united by a disproportionately large semicircular reception hall comprising Pei's signature atrium ingredients—creamy travertine walls, bridges, balconies and ornamental trees. Like other Pei atriums, the reception hall is dominated by large-scale artworks—in this case a bronze sculpture by Joel Shapiro and a 26-foot-high

Roy Lichtenstein mural based on Oskar Schlemmer's 1932 painting *Bauhaus Stair.*

The building has a formal street entrance rarely used in car-crazy L.A. Most visitors enter through an underground garage where a valet parks their car and a concierge escorts them to an elevator. Pei could have whisked Ovitz's celebrity clientele to upstairs meetings in immaculate privacy, but in consideration of the agency's air of openness and exchange, he evicted them from the elevator at ground level so that even the biggest stars, like Barbra Streisand and Michael Jackson, had to traverse the reception hall in full view of the offices encircling the upper atrium.

The atrium addresses the Creative Artists Agency's collaborative culture by celebrating interaction and contact within a central organizing space. Expensively enrobed in Italian travertine, tinted glass and elegant curves, Pei's urbane statement in corporate grandeur is a strangely formal environment for brash young agents who supposedly thrive on casual interaction. What's more, it is out of sync with L.A.'s air of playfulness and funk. Generations of cross-breeding between architects and stage designers had produced in L.A. a richly tawdry compote of Hollywood castles, Mayan theaters, Moorish apartment buildings and Aztec hotels. Camp is the city's absurdly wonderful heritage, and Pei was criticized for ignoring it. Nor does CAA's formal bearing respond to its immediate neighbors: it stands in comical contrast to the Budget Rent-A-Car and Wilson's House of Suede and Leather across the street. One commentator compared the building to an elegant woman who refuses to let her hair down. The *New York Times* called it "a Chanel suit among polyester jumpsuits, a BMW amid Hyundais, a Mont Blanc amid Bics." Critic Martin Filler wrote that it "could well be the capitol building of a small but prosperous monarchy, which in some ways CAA is."

"It has the air," the critic Leon Whiteson observed in the *Los Angeles Times,* "of a man from Manhattan who, hailing a cab on Park Avenue, to his astonishment, ends up at this corner of Beverly Hills." Ovitz is famously thin-skinned, and he reportedly complained about the tepid reviews to friends in the executive offices at the L.A. *Times*. Having spent $15 million—twice the price of most comparably sized offices—he had expected all-out raves.

Still, the building fulfilled Ovitz's ambitions: it is an unambiguous edifice of conservative good taste authored by the acknowledged master of institutional modern. It makes just the right statement about Ovitz's place in the corporate world—it is stylish but discreet, sumptuous but refined. "Hollywood is essentially a feudal society," the art critic Adam Gopnik once observed in the *New Yorker*, "and in a feudal society what matters most is that the feudal powers never put themselves in even a mildly ambiguous situation—that they never run the risk of looking ridiculous. Hollywood people, this argument goes on, like to build their own, indubitably serious establishments as soon as they can—I. M. Pei's CAA building is an example of this compulsion."

. . . .

With the exception of Tiananmen, 1989 was a charmed year. Pei seemed to be everywhere at once, the world over, attending one prestigious inauguration after another. His symphony hall in Dallas opened in September, followed by ribbon cuttings for a science building at the Choate Rosemary Hall School in Connecticut given by his friend Paul Mellon; the sleek CAA headquarters; and finally the Bank of China. In addition, the already medal-heavy Pei received, along with Willem de Kooning and David Hockney, the first Praemium Imperiale, a lifetime achievement award conferred by the Japanese Arts Association in five fields not covered by the Nobel Prizes.

More than any other building inaugurated during 1989's giddy spree, the Louvre bestowed a final benediction upon Pei's ascent. It was the crowning

▲

A Mont Blanc amid Bics: The Creative

Artists Agency in Beverly Hills.

► Changing of the guard: FROM LEFT,
Jim Freed, Henry Cobb, Eason Leonard,
I. M. Pei.

At the Four Seasons Hotel in New York, Pei
tried to revive the bygone notion of the
grand hotel as an exciting destination.

▼

achievement of an adventurous career, during which Pei had personally directed more than forty major commissions, and the culmination of a lifelong gravitation to power and prominence. "He parlayed that pyramid into an invincible aura," said Philip Johnson. If a single scene encapsulates Pei's final triumph, it is the gala dinner held beneath the pyramid days after François Mitterrand snipped the inaugural tricolor ribbon. Pei stood beaming at the foot of the escalator that night and embraced a spangled entourage of friends and patrons as they descended one by one to congratulate him—Henry and Nancy Kissinger, Mica and Ahmet Ertegun, Michael Eisner, Pamela Harriman, J. Carter Brown, Amyn Aga Khan, Isaac Stern, Philippe de Montebello and Claude Lévi-Strauss. After dinner, Minister of Culture Jack Lang offered a toast to the architect, and this rare congregation raised their glasses. *"A Pei!"* they said. Pei was urged to the microphone, where he uttered a few words in his broken French. In a quavering voice, he said, *"Merci pour tout."*

Thirty-five years after escaping the corporate captivity of Webb & Knapp, and fifteen years after Hancock, Pei was an ardently celebrated author of artistic spaces and, by some estimates, the world's most famous living architect. "He was terribly fearful of being dismissed as a commercial architect," said Paul Goldberger. "Above all, he wanted to be remembered as a serious aesthetic presence—a builder of great monuments. He deliberately brought himself to a point where he stood at the apex of his profession."

While other second-generation modernists fell into disfavor and obscurity, Pei sailed gracefully onward, swathed in an unassailable mystique. He flourished long after the world had rejected the modern aesthetic, according to architectural historian Vince Scully, because his pleasing, serene geometries contained an ingrained sense of balance. In a review of what it called "the Year of Pei," the *New York Times* labeled him "the high priest of modernism" and the only practicing architect "to achieve a viable modernist monumentality." *Newsweek* called him "a Mercedes among hot rods and Cadillacs" and a survey of peers named him the architect who had exerted "the most posi-tive influence on current design."

Pei is not, however, universally admired. For all his accomplishments, he will never attain that uppermost register reserved for first-magnitude form-givers like Richardson, Mies, Le Corbusier, Wright and his old rival, Louis Kahn, because he never subjected his ideas to campus discourse and be-cause, to theory-bound architects, his buildings represent no more than dis-creet refinements of what has gone before. He's a consolidator, not a pioneer. There is no groundbreaking Pei style that inspires imitators. "He's irrele-vant," said Ralph Lerner, dean of Princeton's architecture school. "There's no body of theory that goes along with his work. The forms seem more often than not gratuitous. His strength is that his buildings are usually technical tours de force. I'm always struck by the fabulous technique; I'm never struck by the ideas."

"He's not a design influence," Philip Johnson concurred. "He's just Mr. Success. He was always simpler and cleaner than anyone else. Too bad one can't grasp the man himself."

Pei's own prognosis is typically understated. He wants to be remembered "not as a late modernist, because modernism will continue long after I'm gone, but for giving new life to modernism, taking it a notch beyond where it was."

．　．　．　．

Pei has a gift for the impeccably timed exit. Consciously or not, he chose just the right moment to leave China for MIT, MIT for Harvard, Harvard for Webb & Knapp, Webb & Knapp for private practice. Now, in 1989, at the high point of his trajectory, Pei withdrew from the extraordinary institution he had fa-thered. In September, I. M. Pei & Partners changed its name to Pei Cobb Freed & Partners to reflect the transition to his long-term design partners.

Two months later, Pei posted an unassuming note announcing that he and his administrative partner, Eason Leonard, would retire altogether. "I no longer want to practice as I have," he later said. "I want to enjoy life a bit more—and I want to do better work. I want to take on projects that were too small for the firm in the past. My physical capacities are receding; they must. To do my best work, I can no longer work at that pace."

The firm Pei left was an enduring creation. All but one of his original partners were still there, and many associates had spent their entire careers on the staff. Pei profoundly influenced all those who worked with him. One of his overlooked legacies is the training he provided for the thousands of designers who passed through his office. New York's architectural community amounts to an extended I. M. Pei alumni society, and its graduates converge at professional functions to gossip about the firm. A generation of architects, including James Polshek, William Pedersen and Bart Voorsanger, learned from Pei how to think about projects, how to handle clients and assemble buildings with technical finesse. Many modeled their own firms after his.

The familial atmosphere endured as long as the firm contained sixty or so people working on a handful of jobs. The collective effort that saw them through the dark days of Hancock dissipated when prosperity inflated the payroll to three hundred. Then the creative exchange among teammates increasingly gave way to petty hierarchical concerns and internecine jostling. As the firm grew throughout the 1980s, Pei, Cobb and Freed balkanized into distinct principalities. The partners no longer knew their employees' names. There were too many shoulders to look over. Instead of circulating from desk to desk, they made decisions behind closed doors and communicated with their staffs through lieutenants. "It's a highly competitive, unfriendly place," said one employee. "You can go for months without anyone even acknowledging you." One designer who lived in China during the completion of Fragrant Hill recognized the office upon returning as a mandarin court on

Madison Avenue, an arena of intrigue and subtext, princelings and facto-
tums, entangled rivalries and devious ministers competing for the patriarch's
favor.

Pei himself grew increasingly distracted by the burdens of celebrity. He
was obliged to travel far and wide perpetuating his own public image—to
Katharine Graham's birthday party, to White House receptions for distinguished immigrants, to National Gallery openings, to a Fourth of July celebration aboard Mario Cuomo's chartered yacht and to endless award
ceremonies. "It really got to the point," said associate partner Kellogg Wong,
"where we became pretty blasé about Mr. Pei and his awards. Honestly, we
just couldn't keep up. I have no idea how many honorary degrees he's received, and he's turned down a lot more."

A Chinese proverb states that when two men sit astride a horse, one must
always sit behind. All the Confucian classics emphasize loyalty to a single
authority, a patriarch or son of heaven. So it was at 600 Madison, where for
many years Cobb and Freed built the projects that Pei handed them, but they
were never allowed to emerge as creative personalities in their own right.
They were forced to swallow their pride when clients solicited attention from
the firm's famous front man. "What does Mr. Pei think?" they asked. "Would
you run that idea by Mr. Pei?" "Will Mr. Pei attend the opening?"

"Whenever there was a problem they trotted Pei into a meeting," said one
designer. "He said a few words and smoothed things out. Everyone left smiling." Too often, employees say, Pei took credit without acknowledging his
partners. As far as the public was concerned, these were Pei's buildings.
"Harry wanted to be Henry James," said one office wag. "Jim wanted to be
I.M. and I.M. wanted to be the Emperor of China."

Like any mandarin family, I. M. Pei & Partners assumed a serene unified
front, but Pei's tendency to reserve the public role for himself did incite quiet
resentment. Employees sensed a certain coolness among the partners. "The

tension was never overt," said Karen Van Lengen, "but we felt it." Pei and Cobb, in particular, were said to be uneasy in each other's company. "Pei is such an egotist," said office veteran Preston Moore. "He doesn't want anyone to get any credit. He's the one who gets the awards—everyone else is second. Cobb and Freed had their little babies and I.M. always had the plums. He never gave them any identity but 'partners.' He never put their names on the door. It was sad. He never treated them as equals. *He* was the one who established the firm. *He* was the one with the concepts. *He* was running the show. I.M. has the nicest personality, but he is really not a gracious man."

Colleagues wondered why Cobb and Freed, two of the best architectural minds of their generation, languished so long in the shadow of Pei's commanding personality. They were reluctant to leave because they could never duplicate the talent and expertise amassed on Pei's payroll. Nor could they hope to match his caliber of commissions. They accepted relative anonymity on the assumption that their own names would eventually emerge. The partnership became a convenient form of subjugation, especially for Cobb, an excruciatingly shy Yankee gentleman with a deliberate, ponderous manner, which did not serve him well in the company of clients. "Harry is a quiet patrician Boston type," said the architect Robert Stern. "He's unable to go out there and wow clients. He's not the galvanizing type. He probably likes to go home in the evening and read an intelligent book and have an intelligent conversation with his wife. He's a bit dry, and his buildings, with some exceptions, tend not to be dazzlers."

Cobb is also temperamentally averse to self-promotion and glad-handing. Pei's mastery of architecture's retail chores—charming trustees, assuaging disgruntled community groups and performing other assorted ministrations required to lubricate the machinery—released Cobb to concentrate on design. "My relationship with I.M. required a certain suppression of ego," Cobb acknowledged, "which wasn't difficult for me because of who I am. It made it possible for us to build the firm we built. I'm a conservative in that I believe if you make an investment it should not be thrown away. I believe in the mode of practice we developed. I didn't want to abandon it. At the same time it seemed to me that the consequences of the suppression of my own identity were life-threatening to the firm. The dilemma was how to establish my own identity in a more definitive way without separating myself from the practice."

The first sign of change came in 1980 when, despite Pei's objections, Cobb became chairman of the department of architecture at Harvard's Graduate School of Design, a commitment that kept him away from the office several days a week. "I.M. didn't think it was good for the firm," Cobb said. "He was thinking about the fact that it wasn't going to do anything for the practice. It would deprive the firm of my presence and was therefore weakening. . . . He was thinking about tomorrow. I was thinking about the day after tomorrow. The long-range importance of it was that it established me as an individual in a way that no amount of work at I. M. Pei & Partners could and therefore strengthened the firm by ensuring that it would have a life after Pei."

At a surprise party for Pei's sixty-second birthday, Kellogg Wong and Fred Fang gave him a translation from Confucius advising that at age fifteen you should dedicate yourself to learning and studying; at thirty you should work independently; at fifty you should be successful in your chosen field; at sixty you should receive accolades for your accomplishments; and at seventy you should do what you want.

Pei turned seventy-two in April 1989, two weeks after his pyramid opened in Paris. His firm was by now a ravenous machine requiring a constant supply of work. As the sovereign partner and acknowledged front man, Pei had overseen the whole operation for four decades. He routinely evaluated his partners' work and courted as many as eight or so prospective clients at once while still finding time to refine his own projects. You do what you have to do

70 percent of your time, he often said, in order to do what you enjoy during the remaining 30 percent. The time had come for Pei to consider a change in the equation. What a relief it would be to shed the day-to-day administrative burdens and the endless traveling. Eileen complained that she never saw him. At home he was too often distracted by unresolved designs. If you don't get up and worry about a problem at 3:00 A.M., Pei sometimes said, you're not doing your best. "He's really impossible," Eileen once told a reporter. "He doesn't hear anything. I can't get through to him. You have to write out messages to him. He gets up in the middle of the night."

Pei had left the question of succession deliberately hazy. His two sons Didi and Sandi had risen to associate partner and senior associate. An unvoiced suggestion arose that, in the end, they might inherit the reins from their father. The way to save face all around was for Pei to retire from the partnership. Cobb and Freed would assume control, and Didi and Sandi would start their own office. Released from administrative burdens, Pei would pursue small plums selected for "personal or philosophical reasons, without having to worry how many designers the work can keep busy." In China the elderly often amuse themselves by making miniature replicas of fruits and vegetables. Kellogg Wong jokingly suggested to Pei that he could now devote himself to the architectural equivalent: small exquisite buildings fashioned for pleasure. "I passed by those enviable experiences that most architects have," Pei said. "To do a house is really a great joy. It's something I missed altogether."

"The party line is that he retired so he could do what he wanted," said Harold Fredenburgh, an associate partner who left during the reshuffling. "The truth is, he always did what he wanted."

It has not gone unnoticed that Pei extricated himself in time to avoid the economic downturn of the early 1990s. To make matters worse, prospective clients were reluctant to engage the firm if Pei himself were no longer involved. Many passed them over, forcing a rare round of layoffs. "I returned to the office for the first time after three or four months," said one victim, former senior associate Marek Zamdmer. "As I approached, I wondered who I'd see first. I opened the lobby door and there was I.M. 'Look at this,' I said to myself. 'God himself.'

"He said, 'I haven't seen you around. What project are you working on?'

" 'I *am* working on a project,' I replied, 'but it's not in your office.' He said, 'Oh, I didn't know.' Then his face lit up and he said, 'You know, I'm not working in my old job either!' "

Pei had been the consummate rainmaker, and his personality was the unifying core around which I. M. Pei & Partners revolved. "I.M. spreads his humor and enthusiasm throughout the office," said Kellogg Wong. "It's contagious. You can sense the pace pick up when he's here. The switchboard lights up." When Pei left, the office lost its prime energizer, its enabler. It looked for a while as if Jim Freed might sustain the firm's momentum with a string of top-tier commissions. His Holocaust Memorial, which opened in 1993 on a prominent site beside the Washington Mall, was one of the most celebrated buildings of recent years and among the strongest the Pei firm ever produced. Tragically, however, Freed suffers the degenerative effects of Parkinson's disease as he approaches his professional prime. Despite a nearly incapacitating loss of motor control, he bravely continues to work on high-visibility jobs, including the San Francisco Public Library, a federal courthouse in Omaha and the completion of Washington's Federal Triangle, an office complex between Pennsylvania and Constitution avenues that was curtailed by the Depression. When finished, Federal Triangle will be the second-largest government building after the Pentagon. "Freed's working harder than he ever has, and he's always been a terribly hard worker," said architect Richard Meier.

Parkinson's has left Freed's intellect intact, but imparting his ideas grows ever harder. His speech slurs and his head wags involuntarily. He cannot dress without help. Associates can only guess how long he will be able to sustain his demanding regimen of client meetings and travel.

Freed's condition compounds Cobb's burden. If the firm is to survive, Cobb will have to develop Pei's uncanny echolocation for blockbuster jobs. Cobb seemed to have landed the commission that would boost him into the realm of high-profile institutional projects when, in 1985, his conservative neoclassical scheme, as self-effacing as the architect himself, emerged as the favored finalist for an addition to the National Gallery of Art on Trafalgar Square in London. The Pei office was the undisputed master of museum additions, so the project was presumably Cobb's to lose. The gallery surprised everyone by choosing Robert Venturi, author of *Learning from Las Vegas,* to house the world's finest collection of early Renaissance art. Cobb suffered another setback when his vast overhaul of New York's JFK Airport, featuring a domed central hall designed as a symbolic gateway to the city, was abruptly abandoned in 1990. He is now at work on a massive new federal courthouse on the Boston waterfront initiated by Stephen Breyer before his appointment to the Supreme Court.

Pei's departure has had little effect on everyday life at 600 Madison. He still walks to work from Sutton Place every morning and occupies the same sparse corner office, now on loan from his former partners. The first project Pei enacted under these new circumstances was a bell tower for a Japanese Shinto sect known as Shinji Shumeikai. Pei had told the sect's spiritual leader, an elderly priestess named Kaishu Koyama—the Kaishusama to her followers—that his firm was unable to take on such a small, specialized job when she visited his office accompanied by a translator in 1987.

At that time, Pei was unaware of her significance and distracted by his heavy burdens around the world. Nor did he understand that she had flown all the way from Tokyo just to see him. In any case, he dismissed her with a promise to visit her temple in Japan the following year. What he saw on that trip made him reconsider: in the rolling, forested countryside east of Kyoto, he walked up a flagstone path leading to a sacred fountain designed by sculptor Masayuki Nagare where followers rinse their hands and mouths with cold mineral water. Beyond it lay a slope-roofed sanctuary and a vast travertine plaza, expansive enough to hold 30,000 followers, designed by Minoru Yamasaki, architect of the World Trade Center towers. Here the Kaishusama hoped to build a bell tower. The partnership could not accept such a job, but Pei decided that he could, and should, do it on his own, as a private tribute to his mother.

Pei then experienced what he called an "almost mystical" impulse: he would model the bell tower after an ivory object called a *bachi,* which is used to pluck an ancient stringed instrument. Pei had bought one in Kyoto in 1954. One side had cracked off in storage, an accident that Pei considered an improvement in form. With the help of his associate Christopher Rand, he translated the broken curio into a 200-foot tower flaring outward from a narrow base. It was the closest Pei ever came to pure sculpture.

The Kaishusama baptized the bell tower "the Joy of the Angels" after an image of an angel playing the *bachi* found in a Kyoto temple. The fifteen thousand faithful who gathered for its December 1990 opening considered it a sacred place and removed their shoes before entering as if it were a temple.

Shinji Shumeikai is dedicated to beauty in nature and art, wherever its origin. Its founder, Mokichi Okada, built two art museums. Before the bell tower was completed, his successor, the Kaishusama, commissioned Pei to design a third museum less than a mile from the sanctuary to house the sect's growing art collection. When the Miho Museum of Art opens in June 1996, visitors will arrive at a reception pavilion, then ride an electric car across a bridge and through a tunnel. The conveyance was necessitated by the hilly terrain, but it also imparts a sense of transit into a special realm. It should be like a Chinese painting, Pei told Rand. One makes a pilgrimage through the mountains to encounter enlightenment.

Japan was one of half a dozen countries in which Pei worked, but his hand was oddly absent from New York City. His firm had, of course, done Kips Bay Plaza, a handful of office towers and the disappointing Jacob Javits Convention Center, which, for all its promise as a grand civic commission, ended as an ungainly and unloved glass behemoth on a disreputable stretch of riverfront acreage. Like almost every convention center in the country, it is a deadening box without any relation to the surrounding city.

Pei had yet to make the grand statement expected of him in his adopted home. Some years ago, senior associate Marek Zamdmer put his arm around Pei during an office party and offered some encouragement. "We were looking out the window at the skyline," Zamdmer remembered, "and I said, 'You're the world champion. Where are you? We've got to get out there before we're through.' I guess he took me seriously. He said, 'Yes, but now is not the time.' And he started talking about the economic climate."

In his late valedictory phase, Pei had the luxury of applying himself in the most selective way. His most conspicuous New York building came with the 1993 opening of his $360 million Four Seasons Hotel on Fifty-seventh Street. Half a block from his office, Pei revived the bygone notion of a grand hotel as an elegant and exciting destination. Like the Park Hotel in Shanghai that had aroused Pei's childhood interest in architecture, the Four Seasons is a landmark of Art Deco glamour on a fashionable street. French limestone walls—the same material he used at the Louvre—and octagonal columns soar thirty-three feet to a backlit onyx ceiling. Six steps lead up to an altarlike reception desk. Le Corbusier prints hang beside Art Deco armchairs. Within days after it opened, Midtown media types were converging there for power breakfasts. Two spacious lounges flanking the grand foyer filled with shoppers. So many curious passersby ducked inside that the hotel stationed ten employees to conduct impromptu tours.

At fifty-two stories, it is New York's tallest hotel, and among its most expensive. The 367 rooms are beyond the reach of all but the wealthiest travelers—between $290 and $3,000 a night—but in the monumental lobby Pei tried to create the kind of grandly inviting public space New York has not seen since the days of McKim, Mead & White, a cross between Pei's serious corporate modernism and the Art Deco scenery of urbane old movies. Interior design critic Marilyn Bethany called it "a love song for New York."

Detractors characterized it as a self-conscious assertion of ego. "This was Pei's attempt to make a big urban skyscraper," said Robert Stern, "like Philip Johnson's AT&T building, the Waldorf-Astoria and the Chrysler Building, but it comes off as overbearing. A hotel should be a delightful place, not an exalting experience. It's just vulgar in my view with all those cheap jewellike lights."

Of all the unusual modernist mood pieces Pei executed late in his career, none was more unlikely than the Rock and Roll Hall of Fame. Annual inductions were held at the Grand Ballroom in New York's Waldorf-Astoria, but organizers felt the pantheon needed a permanent temple in Cleveland, where disk jockey Alan Freed had popularized the term "rock and roll" and, in 1952, organized its first concert, the Moon Dog Coronation Ball. Organizers invited Pei to design what the music industry envisioned as a memorabilia-filled shrine on the banks of the Cuyahoga River that would indulge rock's sentimental streak, a place to ogle Buddy Holly's glasses and Jimi Hendrix's guitars. "When the committee from the Rock and Roll Hall of Fame Foundation came and asked me to design the building, I was taken aback," Pei said. "I told them, 'You know, I'm not a fan. I'm really not.' When I thought of rock and roll, all I thought of was my kids, and with me it was always 'Kids, turn it down. Turn it *down*.' But the people on the committee said that it didn't matter that I wasn't yet a fan, and I was greatly encouraged. And so I started my musical education."

The job of persuading Pei to apply his decorous geometries on behalf of the raunchiest art form fell to Ahmet Ertegun, the bald, heavy-lidded founder of Atlantic Records. If anyone could interest Pei in rock's down-and-dirty demimonde it was Ertegun, an immigrant endowed with similar powers of assimilation. The son of a Turkish diplomat, Ertegun had listened to American jazz and blues as a child in Paris. He founded Atlantic Records in 1947 and, over the ensuing years, recorded Ray Charles, Otis Redding, Aretha Franklin, the Rolling Stones and Led Zeppelin, among many others.

Like Pei, Ertegun traveled in many orbits. For years he was an improbably debonair figure in the eye of rock and roll riotousness while moving with equal ease in the New York society of Bill Blass, Malcolm Forbes and Henry Kissinger. A uniquely American tableau ensued: the son of a Turkish diplomat educated the son of a Chinese banker about Elvis Presley and the Delta blues.

"American music to me is like a tree," Pei said, "and I wondered if rock and roll was just a branch or part of the trunk of the tree. If rock and roll was just a branch, I wasn't interested."

To convince Pei that rock had a lasting place in popular culture, Ertegun and *Rolling Stone* publisher Jann Wenner sent him to a Paul Simon concert at Radio City Music Hall and to a Genesis concert at the Meadowlands. The remedial rock primer continued with excursions to Graceland in Memphis and to Preservation Hall in New Orleans. He also listened to tapes of the Beatles, the Grateful Dead, Elvis Presley and the Sex Pistols.

The implausible image of I. M. Pei donning headphones to sample some down-and-dirty riffs amused associates down the hall, but Pei surprised them—surprised everyone—by accepting the job. After the Beatles, Bob Dylan and the Beach Boys were inducted at the third annual black-tie party and jam session, Pei unveiled a model of a glass pyramid propped against a square tower. Fund-raising and disorganization delayed the groundbreaking to 1990, by which time uncertainties had arisen over the site. The project bogged down so intractably that Mick Jagger dubbed it "the Phantom Temple of Rock." A modified design opened in September 1995 at a new site on Lake Erie.

Pei once said that his dream was to design an ocean liner. That will not happen, but the final chapter of his career is unfolding with a freshet of carefully selected work that fills his schedule to the brink of the next century. There will be a private museum in Athens to house the Goulandris family's Cycladic art collection, a research center on aging in Marin County, a home for Barcelona's La Caixa savings bank and a United Nations mission for South Korea located in Midtown Manhattan. "I think he's enjoying what he's doing now a great deal," said Henry Cobb. "I suspect the pleasure of it will show up in the finished work."

Pei has never indulged in regrets or postmortems. Even now, as his career unfolds in its final chapter, he is focused not on the past but on the present—and the near future. He has more time for his family, his grandchildren, and his friends, but he continues to scout for small, intimate projects distinguished by exceptional clients with elevated ambitions. "He has slowed only a little bit," said Jim Freed. "He says that he considers every morning that he wakes up a gift because it means another day to work. He does only those things that he considers beautiful—a beauty without shock effect. A beauty that you can't explain."

"I am at a certain age where I am aware of my mortality," Pei concurred. "I want to spend whatever time I have left working."

So far Pei has escaped what Charles de Gaulle called the shipwreck of age. He has maintained unslackened vigor and a playful, adventuresome spirit. Like Picasso and Frank Lloyd Wright, his creative flame may burn undiminished into late old age. It seems as if the mandarin child raised in a Western city built on Chinese soil could go on forever assimilating new realms, penetrating the inner circles of cities, forging new friendships, filling whatever blank spots remain on his personal map. In a rare forthcoming moment, Pei shared his inner thoughts on the balanced realms, the yins and yangs, that enriched his full life—Shanghai and Suzhou, East and West, old and new:

> When you think about the history of human feelings,
> which is what the history of architecture is, you will notice
> that the most fruitfully imaginative developments almost
> always take place when two or more very contrasting lines
> of thought or feeling come together. They may be rooted
> in very contrasting cultural soils, but if they do come
> together . . . then an unexpectedly rich relationship can
> emerge. Perhaps the developments that I've had a hand in
> building over the years are not as new and useful and
> inspiring as the developments that I have felt in these
> ways, as the contrasts of my life gradually attained a kind
> of complementarity. It is similar to sowing and reaping, the
> cycling of the seasons and sentiments, the movement of
> light and insights. You never quite know when something
> that you have planted is going to be harvested. The yield
> may be once or recurrent. You may forget that something
> was planted—an experience, a perception, a relationship
> to a person or to a philosophy or to a tradition. And then
> there is suddenly this bloom, called up by circumstances
> that are completely different. Such blooms can breach
> walls and whole epochs.

The Confucian philosopher Mencius once said, "The great man is the man who hasn't lost the heart he had when he was a little child." A former associate stepped from his office one evening and spotted the Peis dashing as nimbly as teenagers across Fifty-seventh Street, that great axis of art and power leading to their Sutton Place home. "I.M. is ageless," said Kellogg Wong. "His bearing. His posture. His energy. His manner. His charm. The twinkle in his eye. It's all still there."

According to Lao-tzu, a deep serenity comes to those who are attuned to the intangible forces astir in the natural world. Pei has largely ceded the Katonah house to his children and grandchildren, but he returns periodically to walk its wooded grounds. What he undertakes there is not gardening so much as an enlightened form of landscaping, the benefits of which will outlive him. The Pei children laughed among themselves one spring weekend as their father began clearing a patch of undergrowth. "We all thought, What is Dad doing?" said his daughter, Liane, "but his labor revealed a stand of beautiful trees in a sunlit glade. It was a revelation. It made perfect sense, but he was the only one who had seen it."

NOTES

Page CHAPTER 1: THE BATTLE OF THE PYRAMID

7   "When Mitterrand first": Pei address, Committee of One Hundred, Los Angeles, Feb. 25, 1995.

7   "I would not have accepted it": Wiseman, p. 234.

11   "In this case, I think being a Chinese-American": Interview with *Sixty Minutes* correspondent Diane Sawyer, Feb. 22, 1987.

12   "The center of gravity": *New York Times*, Nov. 24, 1985.

12   "a natural solution": *Newsweek*, Mar. 27, 1989.

14   "One after another": *New York Times*, Nov. 24, 1985.

16   "It is a great help": *House & Garden*, June 1985.

22   "Nobody would question Einstein": Pei address, Asia Society, New York, Sept. 24, 1991.

25   "That was the moment": Ibid.

30   "It is a story": Michel Laclotte at National Gallery Symposium, Washington, D.C., Mar. 13, 1994.

CHAPTER 2: SHANGHAI AND SUZHOU

37   "Little boy, are you trying": Tsuyee Pei interview with *Time* correspondent Marjorie Severyns.

50   "My father was": Pei address, Committee of One Hundred, Los Angeles, Feb. 25, 1995.

50   "She could only have me there": *Vanity Fair*, Aug. 1989.

50   "As the oldest son, I was supposed to": Wiseman, p. 32.

50   "was not the sort of man to pat a son on the back": Ibid., p. 31.

57   "How such gardens are made": *Christian Science Monitor*, Mar. 16, 1978.

58   "I had already sensed that the life of a banker": Ibid.

59   "I did not know what architecture": *New York Post*, May 20, 1967.

CHAPTER 3: A CHINESE STUDENT IN CAMBRIDGE

64   "What really determined": Diamonstein, 1979, p. 279.

65   "So I was able to enter Boston society": *Pan Am Clipper,* Nov. 1984.

69   "the two most important days": Pei address, MIT, Mar. 1, 1985.

69   "I drove into the compound": *Washington Post,* May 14, 1978.

73   "I was aware that something was happening": Wiseman, p. 37.

75   "When I decided": *AIA Journal,* June, 1979.

76   "I would be brought photographs": *Time,* Aug. 22, 1960.

78   "From Breuer": Ibid.

79   "It was a very exciting period": *ARTnews,* Summer 1978.

81   "As students we did many studies": Diamonstein, 1983, p. 44.

83   "It was so easy to prove": *ARTnews,* Summer 1978.

86   "I wanted to go home": Peter, p. 262.

CHAPTER 4: WE'RE GOING TO CHANGE ALL THIS

91   "I was familiar with almost every block": Zeckendorf, p. 37

91   "Well, what do you think of my properties": Ibid., p. 47

97   "Nelson, don't you think it's about time": Ibid., p. 97.

98   "I specified that the man was not to be": Ibid.

98   "When Zeckondorf asked": Pei at Rockefeller University, Feb. 2, 1995.

99   "Pei had never built anything": Zeckendorf, p. 98.

99   "Zeckendorf was already": Pei at Rockefeller University, Feb. 2, 1995.

99   "Pei was apprehensive about becoming": Zeckendorf, p. 98.

102   "The important thing": Pei address, Committee of One Hundred, Los Angeles, Feb. 25, 1995.

103   "This is what I *don't* want": Zeckendorf, p. 98.

104   "As effectively as the lone turret": Ibid., p. 99.

108   "Gone to Italy, Paris, London, Rome": *Neighborhoods,* June 1979.

112   "Architect I. M. Pei, regulated only superficially": *Interiors,* Mar. 1950.

116   "At seven o'clock he would call": *Manhattan, Inc.,* Dec. 1986.

117   "What the Pei firm has done so impressively": *Architecture Plus,* Mar. 1973.

117   "We would fly": Pei at Rockefeller University, Feb. 2, 1995.

117   "All the great cities of the world": *U.S. News & World Report,* Oct. 22, 1979.

CHAPTER 5: BROKEN PROMISES

124   "Denver, like so many other cities": Zeckendorf, p. 106.

124   "Even the fact that nothing vital": Ibid., p. 110.

127   "The early work of our firm": Diamonstein, 1983, p. 36.

131   "With my tongue but partly in my cheek": Zeckendorf, p. 107.

133   "We gave him a couple of dry martinis": Zeckendorf, p. 208.

134   "Was far from unfavorable": *Washington Post*, July 9, 1954.

135   "There were moments during these Washington years": Zeckondorf p. 2.

136   "I'm the guy who got the girl pregnant": Ibid., p. 224.

137   "He needed eight hours of sleep": Wiseman, p. 50.

139   "It was a competent and a pleasant design": Zeckendorf, p. 171.

139   "the faces at that table": Ibid., p. 189.

141   "Jim, you know we are not getting anywhere": Ibid., p. 175.

143   "I went to Gordon Bunshaft": Pei address, Harvard Graduate School of Design, Jan. 29, 1992.

145   "The slabs do": Pei address, YMHA, Nov. 29, 1983.

145   "At that time": Ibid.

149   "If you can raise the standards by even ten percent": *New York Times*, Mar. 14, 1965.

151   "I better—I owe you three million": Zeckendorf, p. 6.

151   "My God, I pay my shylocks more than that": Ibid.

152   "Now all action ceased": Ibid., p. 7.

153   "We did it on the backs of envelopes": *Washington Post*, May 17, 1983.

153   "I felt trapped in the role of looking": Wiseman, p. 69.

155   "On the one hand, feelings of sorrow": Interview with *Time* reporter, May 21, 1985.

157   "Instead of visiting cathedrals and palaces": *Washington Post*, May 14, 1978.

158   "I went and slept on the mesa": NCAR Archives, oral history, May 14, 1985.

159   "I had always looked over the shoulders": Wiseman, p. 73.

159   "I was floundering": NCAR Archives, oral history, May 14, 1985.

161   "I began to know how little": *Christian Science Monitor*, Mar. 16, 1978.

CHAPTER 6. THE KENNEDY BLESSING

165   "I have never had a job as easy": *New York Times*, May 23, 1971.

168   "We do not imitate": Kennedy Library Archives.

170   "The day Mrs. Kennedy came into my office": *Look*, May 16, 1967.

171   "Jackie and I interviewed a lot of architects": *Daily News* (New York), Nov. 19, 1982.

184   "Watching what he did": Walton address, National Arts Club, Jan. 28, 1981.

195   "Perhaps not since the pharaohs": *Women's Wear Daily,* Nov. 12, 1982.

CHAPTER 7. I. M. PEI & PARTNERS

198   "We have that chemistry": *Vanity Fair,* Aug. 1989.

204   "Pei is a person of complete honesty": *New York Post,* May 20, 1967.

204   "Well, I'm Chinese": *New York Times,* Mar. 14, 1965.

CHAPTER 8. WINDOWS OVER COPLEY SQUARE

207   "The story of the Hancock Tower": Campbell comments, Aspen Design Conference, Aspen, Colorado, 1987.

213   "Harry and I came to the": Pei interview with Chester Nagel, Sept. 18, 1985.

216   "It was, for a while": Cobb address, YMHA, New York City, Feb. 27, 1992.

219   "It was quite humiliating": Interview with *Sixty Minutes* correspondent Diane Sawyer, Feb. 22, 1987.

CHAPTER 9. THE MOST SENSITIVE SITE IN THE UNITED STATES

228   "I.M., one feels, is at least": *Architecture Plus,* Feb. 1973.

236   "Mr. Mellon felt": Walker, p. 35.

237   "If we don't use that land, someone's going to": *Time,* May 8, 1978.

245   "I was unnerved by it all": *People,* Feb. 13, 1978.

245   "If you're not able to": Diamonstein, 1980, p. 158.

246   "He can sit down and listen to": Diamonstein, 1983, p. 84.

246   "I get into a great inner turmoil": *Washington Post,* May 14, 1978.

246   "I sketched a trapezoid on the back": *National Geographic,* Nov. 1978.

CHAPTER 10. A BUILDING FOR THE AGES

255   "I turned to Pei and I said": National Gallery Archives, William Mann oral history.

255   "It caused a chaotic condition": Ibid.

256   "A little extra battlefield excitement": Ibid.

256   "Funny papers . . . they were so incomplete": Ibid.

256   "These meetings we would have": Ibid.

261   "The initial estimate was based on so many unknowns": Ibid.

262   "Ninety-five million dollars does seem": *Vogue*, June 1978.

264   "Contemporary buildings have": Diamonstein, 1980, p. 152.

265   "I was terribly disappointed": National Gallery Archives, I. M. Pei oral history.

267   "He looked and he looked": Ibid.

268   "Washington was so staid, especially then": Ibid.

269   "I.M., I think you've built yourself": *Washington Post*, May 14, 1978.

270   "Every morning as I came down to the Court": National Gallery Archives, Warren Burger oral history.

274   "As we have become impoverished": Johnson, p. 263.

CHAPTER 11. VINDICATION

283   "After the First World War": *Art in America*, July 1978.

CHAPTER 12. CHINA AGAIN

289   "I have two worlds": Pei address, Asia Society, New York, Sept. 24, 1991.

290   "Wine stewards tremble": *Washington Post*, May 14, 1978.

290   "all dark brown and stiff": William Walton Papers, Kennedy Library.

291   "When I was in college": Peter, p. 262.

305   "Chinese architecture is at a dead end, totally": *Interiors*, July 1980.

305   "Architecture has to come": *Daily Telegraph*, Aug. 1, 1989.

308   "in the end, the trees": *New York Times*, Jan. 23, 1983.

313   "The indoors and the outdoors": Diamonstein, 1980, p. 161.

318   "The Chinese bureaucrats were aghast": *House & Garden*, Apr. 1983.

319   "In emotional energy": *New York Times*, Oct. 25, 1982.

319   "You must see a Chinese garden": William Walton Papers, Kennedy Library.

320   "Tell the truth": Ibid.

320   "Old Chinese houses": *New Yorker*, May 30, 1994.

322   "I've seen this before": *Christian Science Monitor*, Apr. 29, 1985.

322   "A work of architecture is not": Pei address, to Asia Society, New York, Sept. 24, 1991.

323   "That to me is my greatest": Interview with *Sixty Minutes* correspondent Diane Sawyer, Feb. 22, 1987.

323   "Not at all": *AIA Journal*, May 1982.

CHAPTER 13. BAD FÊNG SHUI

327 "That is Chinese": *Daily Telegraph*, Apr. 1, 1989.

331 "I think [postmodernists are] missing": Pei address at MIT, Mar. 1, 1985.

331 "None was particularly memorable": Wiseman, p. 287.

331 "Western as any building": *New York Times*, July 2, 1983.

335 "How can I believe": *Daily Telegraph*, Apr. 1, 1989.

336 "The Hong Kong Chinese": Pei address, Committee of One Hundred, Los
    Angeles, Feb. 25, 1995.

336 "There is an ancient Chinese proverb": *Saturday Review*, Mar.–Apr. 1985.

338 "If an angle is pointing at you": *Wall Street Journal*, Aug. 9, 1988.

338 "Since, to many people": Letter to author, Feb. 11, 1994.

339 "It hurt me very deeply": Pei address, Asia Society, New York, Sept. 24, 1991.

340 "More than fifty years ago": *New York Times*, June 22, 1989.

341 "There was no organization": *New York Times*, June 22, 1991.

343 "How can Yo-Yo Ma": Ibid.

344 "A high school student": Ibid.

346 "To them—stability": Reuters, Mar. 31, 1994.

CHAPTER 14. A CERTAIN AGE

351 "Architecture really is the need": Diamonstein, 1980, p. 161.

351 "He leads them, subtly and marvelously": *People*, Feb. 13, 1978.

353 "This is a wonderful New Year's": *Dallas Morning News*, Aug. 6, 1989.

354 "The man has a good pair of ears": *Newsweek*, Sept. 25, 1989.

355 "Anyone who has seen": Pei address, YMHA, New York, Nov. 29, 1983.

362 "He came across as": *New York* magazine, May 21, 1990.

369 "not as a late modernist": *Architecture*, Feb. 1990.

370 "I no longer want to practice": Wiseman, p. 301.

374 "personal or philosophical reasons": *Architecture*, Feb. 1990.

374 "I passed by those enviable": Pei address, YMHA, New York, Nov. 29, 1983.

379 "When the committee from": *New Yorker*, Feb. 22, 1988.

380 "American music to me is like a tree": Ibid.

382 "When you think about": *Christian Science Monitor*, Mar. 16, 1978.

BIBLIOGRAPHY

BOOKS CONSULTED

Anderson, Martin. *The Federal Bulldozer*. Cambridge, Mass.: MIT Press, 1964.

Bernstein, Richard. *Fragile Glory*. New York: Alfred A. Knopf, 1990.

Berthoud, Roger. *The Life of Henry Moore*. New York: E. P. Dutton, 1987.

Blake, Peter. *No Place Like Utopia: Modern Architecture and the Company We Kept*. New York: Alfred A. Knopf, 1993.

Bordewich, Fergus. *Cathay: A Journey in Search of Old China*. New York: Prentice Hall, 1991.

Bray, Howard. *Pillars of the Post*. New York: W. W. Norton, 1980.

Bunting, Bainbridge. *Harvard: An Architectural History*. Cambridge, Mass.: Belknap Press, 1985.

Burton, Hal. *The City Fights Back*. New York: Citadel Press, 1954.

Cameron, Nigel. *Hong Kong*. Hong Kong: Oxford University Press, 1978.

Campbell, Robert, and Vanderwarker, Peter. *Cityscapes of Boston*. New York: Houghton Mifflin, 1992.

Chang, Julia. *Probing China's Soul*. San Francisco: Harper & Row, 1990.

Cheng, Nien. *Life and Death in Shanghai*. New York: Grove Press, 1986.

Coble, Parks. *Shanghai Capitalists and the Nationalist Government, 1927–1937*. Cambridge, Mass.: Harvard University Press, 1980.

Crow, Carl. *Foreign Devils in the Flowery Kingdom*. New York: Harper & Brothers, 1940.

Curtis, William. *Modern Architecture Since 1900*. Oxford: Phaidon Press, 1982.

Diamonstein, Barbaralee. *Inside New York's Art World*. New York: Rizzoli, 1979.

———. *American Architecture Now*. New York: Rizzoli, 1980.

———. *American Architecture Now II*. New York: Rizzoli, 1983.

Dillon, David. *Dallas Architecture 1936–1986*. Austin: Texas Monthly Press, 1985.

Fairbank, John K. *China Perceived*. New York: Alfred A. Knopf, 1974.

Fairbank, Wilma. *Chinese Architecture.* Cambridge, Mass.: MIT Press, 1984.

Faltermayer, Edmund. *Redoing America.* New York: Harper & Row, 1968.

Felsenthal, Carol. *Power, Privilege, and the Post.* New York: G. P. Putnam's Sons, 1993.

Finley, David Edward. *A Standard of Excellence.* Washington, D.C.: Smithsonian Institution Press, 1973.

Floyd, Margaret Henderson. *Architectural Education and Boston.* Boston: Boston Architectural Center, 1989.

Goldberger, Paul. *The Skyscraper.* New York: Alfred A. Knopf, 1982.

————. *On the Rise.* New York: Times Books, 1983.

Gutman, Robert. *Architectural Practice: A Critical View.* New York: Princeton Architectural Press, 1988.

Herdeg, Klaus. *The Decorated Diagram.* Cambridge, Mass.: MIT Press, 1983.

Hersh, Burton, *The Mellon Family.* New York: William Morrow, 1978.

Holleran, Michael. *The Sacred Skyline: Boston's Opposition to the Skyscraper, 1891–1928.* Cambridge, Mass.: MIT Center for Real Estate Development, 1987.

Irace, Fulvio. *Emerging Skylines: The New American Skyscrapers.* New York: Whitney Library of Design, 1990.

Jackson, Kenneth. *Crabgrass Frontier.* New York: Oxford University Press, 1985.

Jencks, Charles. *The Language of Post-Modern Architecture.* New York: Rizzoli, 1977.

Johnson, Philip. *Writings.* New York: Oxford University Press, 1979.

Keswick, Maggie. *The Chinese Garden: History, Art and Architecture.* New York: Rizzoli, 1978.

Koskoff, David. *The Mellons: The Chronicle of America's Richest Family.* New York: Crowell, 1978.

Kostof, Spiro. *America by Design.* New York: Oxford University Press, 1987.

Kristof, Nicholas D., and Sheryl WuDunn. *China Wakes.* New York: Times Books, 1994.

Levy, Matthys. *Why Buildings Fall Down: How Structures Fail.* New York: W. W. Norton, 1992.

Leys, Simon. *Chinese Shadows.* New York: Viking Press, 1977.

Lip, Evelyn. *Chinese Geomancy.* Singapore: Times Books International, 1979.

Mellon, Paul. *Reflections in a Silver Spoon.* New York: William Morrow, 1992.

Miller, Naomi. *Boston Architecture 1975–1990.* Munich: Prestel, 1990.

Moore, Charles. *Washington Past & Present.* New York: The Century Co., 1929.

Morris, Edwin T. *The Gardens of China: History, Art and Meanings.* New York: Scribner, 1983.

Morris, Jan. *Hong Kong.* New York: Random House, 1985.

Oles, Paul Stevenson. *Architectural Illustration: The Value Delineation Process.* New York: Van Nostrand Reinhold, 1979.

Pan, Lynn. *In Search of Old Shanghai.* Hong Kong: Joint Publishing Co., 1982.

———. *Sons of the Yellow Emperor.* London: Secker & Warburg, 1990.

Peter, John. *The Oral History of Modern Architecture.* New York: Harry N. Abrams, Inc., 1994.

Peyrefitte, Alain. *The Immobile Empire.* Translated by John Rothschild. New York: Alfred A. Knopf, 1992.

Plunz, Richard. *A History of Housing in New York City.* New York: Columbia University Press, 1990.

Purvis, Malcolm. *Tall Storeys.* Hong Kong: Palmer and Turner Ltd., 1985.

Rafferty, Kevin. *City on the Rocks.* New York: Viking, 1989.

Rambach, Pierre. *Gardens of Longevity in China and Japan.* New York: Rizzoli, 1987.

Remillard, François. *Montreal Architecture.* Montreal: Meridian Press, 1990.

Reps, John William. *The Making of Urban America.* Princeton, N.J.: Princeton University Press, 1965.

Russell, John. *Paris.* New York: Harry N. Abrams, Inc., 1983.

Rybczynski, Witold. *Looking Around.* New York: Viking, 1992.

Schell, Orville. *In the People's Republic.* New York: Random House, 1977.

———. *Discos and Democracy.* New York: Pantheon Books, 1988.

Seagrave, Sterling. *The Soong Dynasty.* New York: Harper & Row, 1985.

Searing, Helen. *Building the New Museum.* Princeton, N.J.: Princeton Architectural Press, 1986.

Sergeant, Harriet. *Shanghai.* New York: Crown, 1990.

Shachtman, Tom. *Skyscraper Dreams: The Great Real Estate Dynasties of New York.* Boston: Little, Brown, 1991.

Snow, Edgar. *Edgar Snow's China.* New York: Random House, 1981.

Spence, Jonathan D. *The Search for Modern China.* New York: W. W. Norton, 1990.

Terzani, Tiziano. *Behind the Forbidden Door.* New York: Henry Holt & Company, 1984.

Thomas, Christopher. *Architecture of the West Building of the National Gallery of Art.* Washington, D.C.: National Gallery, 1992.

Tucci, Douglas. *Built in Boston: City and Suburb, 1800–1950.* Boston: New York Graphic Society, 1978.

Tzonis, Alexander, and Lefaivre, Liane. *Architecture in Europe Since 1968.* New York: Rizzoli, 1992.

Walker, John. *Self-Portrait with Donors: Confessions of an Art Collector.* Boston: Little, Brown, 1969.

Wang, Y. C. *Chinese Intellectuals and the West, 1872–1949.* Chapel Hill: University of North Carolina Press, 1966.

Warner, Lucy. *The National Center for Atmospheric Research: An Architectural Masterpiece.* Boulder, Colo.: The National Center for Atmospheric Research, 1985.

Wei, Betty. *Old Shanghai.* New York: Oxford University Press, 1966.

White, Theodore. *Theodore White at Large.* New York: Pantheon Books, 1992.

Whitehill, Walter M. *Boston: A Topographical History.* Cambridge, Mass.: Belknap Press, 1968.

Williams, Stephanie. *Hong Kong Bank: The Building of Norman Foster's Masterpiece.* London: Jonathan Cape, 1989.

Wilson, James Q. *Urban Renewal: The Record and the Controversy.* Cambridge, Mass.: MIT Press, 1966.

Wiseman, Carter. *I. M. Pei: A Profile in American Architecture.* New York: Harry N. Abrams, Inc., 1990.

Wolf, Peter. *The Future of the City.* New York: Watson-Guptill, 1974.

Wolfe, Tom. *From Bauhaus to Our House.* New York: Farrar Straus Giroux, 1981.

Wu, Nelson. *Chinese and Indian Architecture.* New York: G. Braziller, 1963.

Yeh, Wen-hsin. *The Alienated Academy.* Cambridge, Mass.: Harvard University Press, 1990.

Zeckendorf, William. *Zeckendorf.* New York: Holt, Rinehart and Winston, 1970.

MAGAZINES AND JOURNALS CONSULTED

Abitare/American Artist/American City/AmericanHistory/American Institute of Architects Journal/Antiques/Apollo/Archis/Architect & Building News/Architects Journal/Architects Yearbook/Architectural Design/Architectural Digest/Architectural Forum/Architectural Record/Architectural Review/Architecture d'Aujourd'hui/Architecture Plus/Architecture & Urbanism/Art & Architecture/Art & Design/Art Bulletin/Art in America/Art Journal/ARTnews/Arts Magazine/Arts of Asia/Asian Architect and Contractor/Asian Building & Construction/Atlantic/Beijing Review/Blueprint/Boston Magazine/Building/Building Design/Building Design and Construction/Building in China/Burlington/Business

Week/Challenge/Chinese American Forum/Commentary/Commonweal/Condé Nast Traveler/Connaissance des Arts/Connoisseur/Country Life/Design/Designer's Journal/Development & Construction/Discover/D Magazine/Domus/Economist/Elle/Engineering News Record/Esquire/Flash Art/Forbes/Fortune/GA Document/Global Architecture/ Gourmet/ GSD News/GQ/Harper's/Harper's Bazaar/Harvard Architectural Review/Holiday/Horizon/ House & Garden/House & Home/ID/Industrial Design/Insight/Interior Design/Interiors/ Interview/Japan Architect/Journal of Garden History/Journal of Housing/L'Arca/L'Architettura/Library Journal/Life/Maclean's/Manhattan, Inc./McCall's/Metropolis/Montrealer/Museum/Museum News/Nation/National Geographic/National Review/New Republic/Newsweek/New York Review of Books/The New Yorker/Pencil Points/Progressive Architecture/Rolling Stone/Royal Institute of British Architects/Saturday Evening Post/ Saturday Night/Saturday Review/Skyline/Smithsonian/Southern Living/Sunset/Task/ Technology & Conservation/Texas Monthly/Time/Times Literary Supplement/Town & Country/Travel & Leisure/U.S. News & World Report/Vanity Fair/Vital Speeches/Vogue/ Western Architectural Engineer/Wilson Library Journal

NEWSPAPERS CONSULTED

Atlanta Constitution/Baltimore Sun/Boston Globe/Boston Herald Examiner/Chicago Tribune/China Press/Christian Science Monitor/Cleveland Plain Dealer/Dallas Morning News/Dallas Times Herald/Denver Post/Detroit News/Financial Times/Harvard Crimson/ Indianapolis Star/International Herald Tribune/Kansas City Times/London Daily Telegraph/London Times/Los Angeles Times/Manchester Guardian/Montreal Gazette/Montreal Star/New York Post/New York Times/Philadelphia Inquirer/Rocky Mountain News/San Francisco Chronicle/South China Morning Post/USA Today/Wall Street Journal/Washington Post/Washington Star/Washington Times

DISSERTATIONS CONSULTED

Cody, Jeff. "Henry K. Murphy: American Architect in China." Ph.D. dissertation, Cornell, 1989.

Nicholaeff, Doreve. "The Planning & Development of Copley Square." M. Arch. dissertation, MIT, 1979.

ARCHIVAL SOURCES

American Institute of Architects Library, Washington, D.C./Kennedy Library, Dorchester, Mass./Museum of Modern Art Archive, New York

City/National Center for Atmospheric Research Archive, Boulder,
Colo./National Gallery Archive, Washington, D.C./MIT Museum,
Cambridge, Mass./Rockefeller Archive Center, North Tarrytown, N.Y.

LECTURES AND SYMPOSIUMS

I. M. Pei, American Institute of Architects, Kansas City, June 6, 1979.

William Walton, National Arts Club, New York City, Jan. 28, 1981.

Wan-go H. C. Weng, Fragrant Hill Hotel, China, Sunday, Oct. 17, 1982.

I. M. Pei, YMHA, New York City, Nov. 29, 1983.

I. M. Pei, videotaped interview with Chester Nagel, Sept. 18, 1985.

I. M. Pei, MIT, Mar. 1, 1985.

I. M. Pei, interview with Lucy Warner, National Center for Atmospheric Research, May
14, 1985.

Aspen Design Conference, Aspen, Colorado, 1987.

I. M. Pei, Choate Rosemary Hall School, Spring 1988.

Didi Pei, Lincoln Center, New York City, April 1990.

I. M. Pei, Asia Society, New York City, Sept. 24, 1991.

I. M. Pei, Harvard Graduate School of Design, Cambridge, Mass., Jan. 29, 1992.

I. M. Pei and Michel Laclotte, National Gallery symposiom, Washington, D.C., Mar. 13,
1994.

Henry Cobb, YMHA, New York City, Feb. 27, 1992.

"Headquarters City: The New York of the Rockefellers and William Zeckendorf," symposium held at Rockefeller University, February 2, 1995.

PHOTO PERMISSIONS

AP/Wide World Photos: 88, 325 (bottom) ▲ Constance Breuer: 114 (top) ▲ Esto Photographics/Ezra Stoller: 107
(bottom) ▲ Sam Hurst: 279, 298 ▲ I. M. Pei & Partners: Robert Damorn/223; John Nye/326; Nathaniel Lieber-
man/357 (top) ▲ Kennedy Library; 162, 182 (top) ▲ Collections of the Library of Congress: 32, 38, 42 (top), 53,
52 (top and bottom), 60, 92, 107 (top), 122, 130 (bottom), 138 (top), 154, 172 (bottom), 199 ▲ Thorney Lieberman:
367 (bottom) ▲ Loeb Library at Harvard: 72, 85 (bottom) ▲ Magnum Photos: Marc Riboud/xiv, 15 (top); Inge
Morath/314 (bottom) ▲ David Martin: 288, 307 (top and bottom), 314 (top), 315, 325 (top) ▲ The MIT Museum: v,
62, 67 (top and bottom), 154 (middle), 183 (top), 206, 225 ▲ National Center for Atmospheric Research/National
Science Foundation: vii and 16 ▲ Holdings of the Gallery Archives, National Gallery of Art: ii–iii and 227; Yann
Weymouth/247, 251 (top and bottom), 254, 266 (top and middle), 271 (top and bottom) ▲ Pei Cobb & Freed: 182–
83 (bottom), 192 (top), 192–93 (bottom), 193 (top) ▲ Pei Cobb Freed & Partners: 8 (top and bottom), 9, 15 (bot-
tom), 85 (top), 106, 114 (bottom), 138 (bottom); George Cserna/154 (bottom), 172 (top), 183 (bottom): Diana H.
Walker/244, 266 (bottom); Shuichi Fujita/350; Richard Payne/357 (bottom); Paul Warchol/xi–xii and 366; Serge
Hambourg/367 (top) ▲ Tsuyuan Pei: 36 (top) ▲ Stuart Smith: 196 ▲ Dongsong Zhang: 42 (bottom), 333

INDEX